TRIBUNE 40

THE TRIBUNE

No. 1 FRIDAY, JANUARY 1st, 1937 PRICE 2d

IF DREAMS CAME TRUE *By Arthur Wragg*

Why Unity Is Vital—Stafford Cripps : While Mr. Brown Drones — Ellen Wilkinson : Parliament and Monarchy — "M.P." : Vanoc II.

Front page of the first issue of Tribune. And a cartoon from 28 May 1954, during the 'age of discipline' (see Section 4), when the Labour leadership and the Right wing saw the paper as a menace of some enormity.

AS OTHERS SEE US

TRIBUNE 40

The first forty years of a socialist newspaper

Edited by Douglas Hill

QUARTET BOOKS LONDON MELBOURNE NEW YORK

First published by Quartet Books Limited 1977
A member of the Namara Group
27 Goodge Street, London W1P 1FD

ISBN 0 7043 3124 1

Typeset by Bedford Typesetters Limited
**Printed in Great Britain by litho at The Anchor Press Ltd
and bound by Wm Brendon & Son Ltd
both of Tiptree, Essex**

CONTENTS

FOREWORD

Tribune still holds to its old-fashioned dogmas. That doesn't mean that we are opposed to new thinking, especially as many of our new thoughts have become official policy after something like a five-year time lag.

But the old dogmas are as good as ever. They include the following simple propositions.

That Socialism means nothing if it does not mean shaking capitalist society to its foundations.

That the values of capitalist society are profoundly evil and therefore must be profoundly changed.

That Socialism alone can ensure the enlargement of the freedom of the individual and his or her enjoyment of the beauty and all the best things of life.

That a Socialism which spurns or neglects to protect freedom of thought, speech and association is no Socialism at all.

That the British Labour Party can be made a most powerful instrument for achieving Socialism at home and peace abroad so long as perpetual remedial action is taken to prevent hardening of the arteries, softening of the brain, the domination of the young by the old or the domination of the heretics by the stuffy and the orthodox, the office-seekers and the power-maniacs.

Some of those who object to Tribune dislike one or other or all these propositions, even though they may not care to admit it.

[*Michael Foot*, 3 January 1958, on
the occasion of Tribune's 21st birthday]

In our forty years of existence, it is reality which Tribune has always examined. We have our heads proudly in the clouds when we preach socialist idealism, but we have our feet very firmly on the ground when we argue about how we will achieve the transition from our present society to the sort of democratic socialism we want to see.

Although I have been involved with the paper for only half its lifetime, the coherent thread which has run through our stand is that political arguments are not won by manoeuvring and secret coups, but by open and straightforward discussion. It is possible to suggest that this paper has sometimes got it wrong, but it is a tissue of falsehoods to suggest that we were not willing to say what we thought, and to say it at the tops of our voices.

A political paper lives or dies by the strength of its argument and its relevance to the circumstances of the day. Looking back over the forty years of our existence it is possible to claim that those who contributed to the paper were very much in tune with what was going on. They were drawn from many areas of the Labour movement and a wide range of occupations. They could all see how the existing order of our society was crippling the achievement of their ideals. They all explored the idea of a socialist order of society which would free them from the trammels of an acquisitive society that put greed and the achievement of wealth as its first priority.

There has never really been a 'formula' for Tribune, as there is for some other papers. It holds that the truths about socialism are self-evident, and believes that good arguments will drive out bad.

After the paper's fortieth birthday we intend to continue to apply the principles which have seen us through so far. There is nothing old-fashioned about them; they are as relevant today as they were on 1 January 1937. But that will not stop us from trying to make the paper better, even more interesting, even more of a credit to the Labour movement – whose inspiration is ours as well.

[*Richard Clements*, 7 January 1977, on
the occasion of Tribune's 40th birthday]

1 'THE SPIRIT OF ATTACK' (1937–9)

World depression and international fascism, unemployment at home and civil war in Spain – these elements loom largest out of all those which came together in 1937 to give form to a new socialist weekly. 'We are Tribunis Plebis, if you please,' wrote 'Tomfool' in Tribune's first ever poem, 1 January 1937:

> Come to forbid again, in times demented,
> War, Waste, and Want, Deception and Disease,
> That might, God save the mark, have been prevented . . .

Capital letters and all, 'Tomfool' – who was Olga Miller – managed an adequate trailer to everything that the paper would be forbidding in those visibly demented times. But, in a way, 'Tomfool's' lines do the new 'Tribune of the People' an injustice. It was not created solely to forbid, to speak out against, for that is merely reactive. Tribune's was an active voice from the start. Its first issue saw its first editor making explicit the paper's fundamental role, which remains no less fundamental in 1977. Tribune was created to *attack*. And the object of its attack?

> WHAT WE STAND FOR IN THE STRUGGLE FOR SOCIALISM
> We are part of a world system, the working of which is no longer compatible with either democracy or peace. If we want them we must

change the world system. We must change it swiftly, for if we wait, the initiative will be in the hands of those to whom neither democracy nor peace is an ideal charged with meaning.

The world system that is destroying hope in the world is capitalism. That it means the destruction of democracy Italy and Germany are there to show. That it means war, Manchuria and Abyssinia and Spain are there to bear their tragic witness.

It is capitalism that has caused the world depression. It is capitalism that has created the vast army of the unemployed. It is capitalism that has created the distressed areas. It is capitalism that is piling up vast armaments now for the war whose shadow bestrides all our lives. It is capitalism that divides our people into the two nations of rich and poor. Either we must defeat capitalism or we shall be destroyed by it.

The defeat of capitalism depends upon the unity of the working class. If its forces are divided, as in Italy and in Germany, it is defeated in detail. A united working class can take the offensive. It has the massed power out of which courage and hope are born. It is able to take the initiative from its opponents' hands. It is able to give direction to its effort. A united working class can go forward to a defined goal. It can move on the central positions. It has none of the doubts which, through hesitation and compromise, lead straight to defeat . . .

Our divisions have meant uncertainty, doubt, hesitation; these, in their turn, have bred irresolution. A so-called National Government has taken advantage of these divisions to move in the direction of Fascism. As the crisis deepens, it will take further advantage of them . . .

If we will the end of socialism, we must will the means to socialism. The first step to that end is a united working-class movement active in challenge and attack . . . The spirit of attack has been shown over and over again. It was shown in the councils of action in 1920. It was shown in the general strike of 1926. It was shown in the determination which defeated the Means Test scales two years ago. It was shown only the other day in the splendid solidarity which compelled official recognition of the hunger marchers. Our leaders must utilise this spirit. It puts the initiative in their hands. It is an irresistible spirit since it is informed by the will to victory . . .

[*The Editor*, *William Mellor*, 1 January 1937]

So Tribune set out on its mission to re-create Labour as a socialist party, a party that would in the short run try to have a positive effect on domestic and foreign policy – and in the long run would win electoral victory and take charge of policy, leading the country to what Stafford Cripps, in Tribune's first issue, called 'the sane ends of peace and plenty'.

But the likelihood of achieving these ends must have seemed more rhetorical than reasonable to many in the late 1930s. Though Labour's representation in Parliament had expanded somewhat in the general election of 1935, Baldwin had (in the Left's view) ensnared the Labour leadership into surrendering its birthright even more thoroughly than it had done under Ramsay MacDonald's 'gradualism' after 1931. It seemed that the only strong action taken by that leadership had been its attempts to quell any urgings from the Left – from, especially, that outspoken group who had formed themselves, during MacDonald's era, into the Socialist League. Cripps was its chairman, Mellor its (in Michael Foot's word) conscience, Aneurin Bevan – later – its driving force. Though the League, affiliated to the Labour Party, resisted all temptations to become a party within a party, Labour's executive looked upon it with nearly as much disfavour as it did upon those militants of the beyond-the-pale far Left – the Independent Labour Party (ILP), the Communist Party, the National Unemployed Workers' Movement. The League met defeat after defeat in its attempts, mainly at annual Labour conferences, to redirect its party's path. Yet it fought on, and fought also to unify – and so strengthen – the voices of the Labour Left.

Events in 1936 had intensified the process. At a disastrous Labour conference in Edinburgh the Labour Party – personified by men like Citrine, Dalton, Ernest Bevin and Greenwood – turned its back on the needs of republican Spain, which was facing Franco's Nazi-supplied battalions in the civil war begun that year. That conference, too, turned its face firmly towards the National Government's rearmament plans and other patently hard-core-capitalist intentions. The Left responded with unmitigated rage.

Out of that rage, the British Volunteers to the International Brigades marched to fight fascism in Spain. Out of that fertile rage, men like Victor Gollancz, John Strachey and Harold Laski created the Left Book Club, explicitly to concentrate the electrifying upsurge of radical passion that had been triggered. Out of that rage and that upsurge came a belief – inspired by the Popular Fronts of France and Spain – that all the groups and sects of the Left must put aside their traditionally mutual suspicions and join forces to fight the enemy that was at every gate. Nor was this belief – which at once became a campaign, indeed a crusade – merely to be named solidarity. The goal was Unity.

And out of that post-Edinburgh radical rage arose as well the new socialist weekly. Such luminaries of the Labour Left as Cripps, Bevan, Mellor, Laski, Ellen Wilkinson and George Strauss created it to be their mouthpiece, their megaphone, for this fiercely militant spirit of unified socialist attack. Tribune and the Unity campaign began life together on the same day.

UNITY – THE POWER WAY

. . . There can be no greater folly than that of perpetuating disunity in the ranks of the working class, when our opponents have already concentrated their power in a single political party under the aegis of the National Government. . .

When, as to-day, so many pressing dangers loom over the working class throughout the world, we must not waste our time and immobilise our energies in sterile discussions as to the merits and demerits of past events.

We must instead mobilise the very maximum of militant opposition to the National Government and all it stands for within our country on the basis of that unity for which, I am convinced, the workers are looking with expectancy. Time and events will not wait upon our doubts and hesitations . . .

To-day I ask you to write this resolution: 'I pledge to my fellow workers throughout the world my faith to strive unceasingly for unity as a step to power, by which power the workers shall control their lives in peace and plenty' . . .

[*Stafford Cripps*, 1 January 1937]

Many, of course, demurred: Sidney Webb entered Tribune's columns that January to warn of the fears that would be stirred within the Labour movement by this courting of communists and ILPers, although Harry Pollitt, a leading communist figure in the Unity campaign, gave assurances in Tribune on 22 January 1937 that the campaign was *not* 'directed against the Labour Party and its affiliated organizations'.

Needless to say, the Labour Right resisted. The press, including the *Daily Herald*, built up a Red scare – and then the Labour executive reached for its ultimate weapon: expulsion. In April 1937 the Socialist League was disaffiliated from the party, and promptly, sacrificially, dissolved itself to avoid becoming a splinter party. The campaign went on, but so did the executive's 'heresy hunting', as when William Mellor was refused party endorsement as a Labour candidate in September 1937. The outcome was probably inevitable. Labour's Bournemouth conference in October that year trounced all Unity's proposals, and sadly the campaign put itself to death.

It came to life again, however, a year later, when Mellor gave up the Tribune editorship and was succeeded by H. J. Hartshorn, a journalist from the *Sunday Mirror*. The new editor retained the overall format, but introduced numerous changes in detail of contents and appearance. And there were more far-reaching changes. For one, Tribune joined forces with the Left Book Club, giving Gollancz, Strachey and others a private preserve in the middle pages, where they advanced the causes of the club and expounded on socialist response to the fascist menace and Chamberlain's acquiescence.

For another, Tribune revived the call for Unity – though Cripps and others would probably never have agreed with the word 'revival' since they had never abandoned the conviction that only a united front could accomplish the Left's aims. By 1938 the general aims that Cripps had summed up as 'peace and plenty' had been gathered within one uncompromising determination: to bring down Chamberlain's National Government. Unity alone would do it; but this time Cripps and his supporters did not look to Unity with the other parties of the Left so much as to a parliamentary unity with all possible anti-Chamberlain forces.

By January 1939 the confrontation within the Labour Party came to crisis point. Cripps issued his memorandum to the party executive about the need for 'combined opposition'; it and the executive's reply were printed in Tribune on 20 January 1938. But the Labour Right answered more trenchantly than with debate – it acted just as it had in 1937. So in the following week's issue, 27 January, Tribune furiously editorialized: 'While Fascist shells and bombs were blasting a way for Franco's Moors into the suburbs of Barcelona, the Labour Party executive terminated Stafford Cripps's connection with the Labour Party. Stafford Cripps's crime is that he advocates unity with the progressive forces to overthrow Chamberlain . . .'

Expulsion or no, Cripps and Tribune fought their fight: 'UNITY MARCHES ON!' said the front page on 3 February. It marched then as a 'Petition Campaign', gathering thousands of signatures for a six-point petition calling upon 'the Parties of progress to act together and at once for the sake of peace and civilization' (10 February 1939). It marched still when Aneurin Bevan and George Strauss joined Cripps in expulsion, along with other campaigners for the petition. But its steps faltered when another Labour conference in the summer of 1939 left it, in Cripps's words, 'badly beaten'. As in 1937, the campaigners had little choice but to wind up their crusade. (Before long the coming of war would brutally over-ride old divisions and the expellees be readmitted to the fold.)

But some things had been salvaged from the petition débâcle. The strident grass-roots radicalism that had fed it remained intact; and Tribune remained its undaunted spokesman, even as it had been in 1937 after the crushing of the first Unity struggle. After all, the enemies, the crises, had not diminished in number or strength. Franco, Mussolini, Hitler – and Chamberlain: Popular Front or no, Tribune carried the fight to them all.

In 1937, Spain still took precedence. The National Government sat on its 'non-intervention' policy and clearly hoped the Republicans would go under quickly; Tribune raged. Editorials, news reports, background articles and, especially, eyewitness reports by visitors to the ravaged country filled Tribune's columns. One such report came from Clement Attlee:

SPAIN'S AGONY AND BRITAIN'S GUILT

. . . An enormous weight of munitions has been thrown into the scale on the side of General Franco. Heavy guns, up-to-date tanks and above all a huge reinforcement of the most modern and powerful aeroplanes have been sent to aid the Fascists.

The splendid fighting spirit of the Republicans was overwhelmed by sheer mass of metal. Observers have reported the intensity of the artillery bombardment, the massing of tanks and the employment on a single battle front of nearly two hundred aircraft operating against the infantry. The push is comparable in its intensity to those which were made in the great war under German direction.

In the face of this abundant evidence the British Government still professes ignorance as to these reinforcements of aggression. Actually we have been informed in the House of Commons that no case of the infraction of the non-intervention agreement has been brought before the Commission since 1936 . . .

The plain fact is that the British Government acquiesces in aggression while pretending still to support non-intervention . . .

[*Clement Attlee*, 25 March 1938]

Spain's agony grew worse, of course, until the day early in 1939 when Franco's triumph was complete, and when Chamberlain's government rushed in indecent haste to recognize his régime – a day called by Aneurin Bevan 'the blackest day in British history'. But blacker were coming.

Tribune had spoken out from the start against the dangers to world peace of Hitler's and Mussolini's ambitions, and of the overall spread of fascism. But in parallel it had also spoken out against the wrong – *suspiciously* wrong – response by Chamberlain and the government to this threat. William Mellor had voiced those suspicions in the first issue. Harold Laski voiced them again.

LABOUR AND THE ARMS VOTE

. . . It is of the essence of the Labour Party's case against the National Government that its foreign policy has been consistently vicious since it took office . . . Its rearmament programme is the expression of this policy. It contradicts the whole thesis of collective security; it is simply an adventure in power-politics of the old, bad kind. It assumes the worthlessness of the League. It fails to define the objectives of our foreign policy. It pays no regard to that 'indivisibility of peace' upon which the Labour Party has laid consistent emphasis since the close of the war . . .

The Labour Party's case is that Great Britain is not rearming for collective security. Its case is that we do not trust the purposes of this Government.

We say that its foreign policy has been defined wholly by its class-character, and that the only war in which it is willing to be involved is one which will serve the interests of the class it represents. We say that socialists can have no part in such a war, that it will be, in whatever guise it may represent itself, simply a war to preserve the authority of British capitalism in a world of competing capitalisms.

[*Harold J. Laski*, 30 July 1937]

Laski and Tribune regretted most of all the decision by the Labour Party's leaders to vote for the new defence estimates, or at least to do no more than abstain. Elsewhere in the paper the war preparations were briefly opposed because of a thread of pacifism in its attitudes, introduced mainly by Labour's revered elder statesmen, George Lansbury (who used the expression 'peace at any price' on 9 July 1937). But Lansbury came in for some attack within the Left for his views; the stronger consensus was that Chamberlain was – as in 1914 – rearming to use the flesh and blood of the workers to make the world safe for capitalism. And, in the process, the government anticipated easing the stagnation of industry with profitable expansion of arms manufacturing.

So, in place of Tribune's desire for strong collective-security pacts, especially with the Soviet Union, it got a government proposal for a £400 million arms loan, and more and more apparent connivance with Hitler's aims – especially those leading him eastwards. 'Will the Czechs Be the Next Victims?' asked a heading on 12 November 1937 – and two weeks later another heading cried out against 'CHAMBERLAIN'S CRIME – Betraying Democracy in the Name of Peace'. On 10 June 1938, Richard Crossman explained the problem of Sudetenland: 'The triumphant march of Fascism has made the Sudeten Germans believe that Hitler is invincible and that he can do what he likes without even risking war. They can't help admiring his power, and also they have been told pretty precisely what will happen to them if they don't admire it.'

It was clear to Tribune that Hitler *was* being allowed to do much as he liked in Europe: persecute Jews, set up slave camps, swallow Austria; all of which acts were vehemently exposed in the paper. And Tribune knew who to blame – especially when the object of its blame returned from Munich with the assurance of peace in our time, achieved through the betrayal of Czechoslovakia.

The outcry in Tribune went on for weeks. But a new note gradually began to creep in. If Chamberlain had, as it seemed, paved the way inescapably to war, then it was time to learn whether or not the nation was ready for that reality. Tribune's contributors looked at the military situation – and were dismayed.

The British Army remained underpaid, over-disciplined and class-ridden, protested many commentators, among them Frank Griffin on 17 September 1937. The Air Ministry was floundering in an 'unholy mess', wrote a correspondent on 29 April 1938: it had promised more than 3,000 planes for the preceding year and delivered only 864. More quickening moves towards conscription incurred Tribune's wrath; so did the government's vacillation over adequate air-raid precautions (ARP). George Strauss revealed some pertinent facts: '. . . Among the many other examples of this fantastic mismanagement . . . the most damning came from Hore-Belisha, Minister of War, himself . . . he admitted that, apart from the serious shortage of anti-aircraft guns, most of those which were available were deficient . . .' (11 November 1938).

Such facts emerged despite prior public demands by foresighted commentators – like J. B. S. Haldane in Tribune – that the nation learn the air-raid lessons of Guernica and Barcelona. Others at the same time demanded that some notice be taken of how, as arms spending soared, real wages fell, standards of living eroded, 'AND PROFITS SWELL IN A STREAM OF STEEL' (17 June 1938).

But even with the acceptance that Chamberlain's war seemed inevitable, Tribune never stopped insisting that there were better ways to approach it than by fattening capitalists and appeasing fascists, and never stopped reiterating the positive good that would come from a collective-security agreement with the Soviet Union. Even in the summer of 1939 the Left's demand for that pact remained as urgent as ever – until the news broke in August that Stalin had instead signed a pact with Hitler.

The shockwave from that action nearly overcame the Left's usual willingness to understand and accept Soviet motives in nearly all its policies. Tribune sought some cogent justification. '. . . The Soviet Government, seeing now beyond any possibility of doubt the game that Chamberlain and Daladier have been playing, responded by agreeing to the negotiations for the Soviet-German pact of non-aggression,' wrote the foreign affairs reporter on 25 August 1939. Russia had perceived the capitalist West's hope that the Nazis could be aimed eastwards against the communists; it had forgivably taken steps to protect itself.

Tribune had, of course, begun life no less pro-Soviet than the rest of the Left, convinced that socialism was being achieved in that country as a model for the world. Feature articles flowed out to laud the new social order in Russia. The American socialist Norman Thomas praised the Soviet Union for having 'achieved the basis of a socialist society in spite of immense difficulty' (4 June 1937). Other writers admired Russian achievements in industry, agriculture, the new social order; there was even a series by Barbara Betts, as Barbara Castle then was, on Russian women – 'WHERE WOMEN LIVE WITH NEW ASSURANCE' was the heading of the first piece (15 October 1936).

Yet the paper retained some objectivity. It may often have printed stirring extracts from Stalin's speeches, but a leader could also firmly state, on 18 February 1938: '. . . Many Socialists may complain of the severity of the Bolshevik dictatorship. Many Socialists may be horrified by the suppression of those in Soviet Russia who are critical of the régime. Nobody can deny that blunders have been made . . .' But – the 'but' is obvious – the piece went on to offer justification along the lines of the adage about omelettes and broken eggs. And the 'but' remained intact through all the heart-searching in 1938 over the implications of the Soviet purges and trials of that year. It seemed that the Left tried hard to understand, to condone, to excuse – because, as the common fascist enemy advanced, it was no time for socialists to turn and rend the nation in which all their hopes reposed. Those hopes, and that faith and optimism, showed most clearly on 10 June 1938 when a great American novelist expressed them for Tribune.

THEY WILL DEFEND THEIR FREEDOM

. . . Having watched the diplomacy of the Soviet Union from the beginning, I know that it is the one nation which has stood for world peace implemented by actions. Again and again they came into the council chambers of Europe with offers of real disarmament.

Their enemies sneered and said it was a bluff. But why did no one call the bluff? How simple for Britain, France and America to say, 'Of course, we are willing. Let us all proceed to disarm!'

They did not say it; and why? Because they are capitalist nations, and cannot survive without more raw materials and more foreign trade . . .

You will hear people talk about the coming war between Fascism and democracy. What I tell you is that this war has been going on for sixteen years.

It began when Mussolini sold out his comrades and destroyed the labour unions and co-operatives of Italy. It was continued ten years later when Hitler stole the label Socialism to fool the German people and destroyed their democratic Government.

It has been going on for nearly two years in Spain, for nearly a year in China: it has been won in Austria, and may be won in Czechoslovakia while I am writing.

Who is going to save democracy in this war?

Will it be the United States? We who have overthrown all the precedents of our diplomacy and denied the democratically-elected people's Government of Spain the right to buy arms for its own defences? We who have thus permitted a million cold-blooded murders in a year and eight months?

It appears that we now show signs of irritation against the gangsters of Japan; but is that because of real sympathy for democracy in China or is it because the Standard Oil Company needs the trade?

I say that in the struggle to save democracy there is to-day one nation and only one which can be counted on for whole-hearted and unstinted support – and that is the Union of Soviet Socialist Republics.

And again that is true, not because they are angels, but because they have a socialised economy, and mean to keep it . . .
[*Upton Sinclair*, 10 June 1938]

Beyond Tribune's unremitting international concentration on European fascism and Soviet communism, the paper managed a surprising breadth and regularity of world coverage. In Mellor's time there was a weekly 'Round the World' survey, emphasizing European developments (with much attention to the French Popular Front), but also gathering news and background in, for instance, Mexico, Algeria, Scandinavia, Palestine, Brazil, South Africa – anywhere that the goings-on should be of concern to the informed British Leftist. Plenty of pieces on America looked into trade unionism there as well as general political and social happenings; abundant reports and articles examined the Empire – politics in the 'white dominions', repressions in the West Indies and colonial Africa. Dominating these imperial considerations was the powderkeg that was the Indian sub-continent, seldom out of Tribune's columns for long. H. J. Hartshorn gave a 'Searchlight on the Empire' page to Krishna Menon, and Jawaharlal Nehru was a frequent contributor to the paper from its beginnings.

INDIA DEMANDS FULL INDEPENDENCE

. . . During my present visit to England I have again had the privilege of meeting old friends and new, and spoken about India to numerous gatherings. I found still a certain apathy and considerable ignorance, and inevitably the urgent problems of Spain and China and Central Europe absorbed attention. And yet I found a vital difference and a new and more realistic way of looking at the Indian problem.

Perhaps this was due to a realisation of the great strength of the Indian national movement to-day, perhaps to the gravity of the international situation and the apprehension that India might add to the danger of it when crisis came. Perhaps this very gravity, this sense of impending catastrophe, had forced people out of the old mental ruts and made them think afresh in terms of reality.

For the reality is this: that India wants, and is determined to achieve, full independence; that the problem of our appalling poverty clamours for solution, and that this will not be solved till the people of India have power in their hands to shape their political and economic destiny as they will and without interference from outside; that the organised strength of the Indian people has grown greatly in recent years and it is difficult for outside authority to check for long their march to freedom; that the international situation indirectly helps greatly the Indian national movement . . .

Labour, which is anti-Fascist, must equally be anti-Imperialist. It must stand for the ending of Empire. It must clearly declare for the independence of India and for the right of the people there to frame their own constitution through a Constituent Assembly, and it must be prepared to do everything in its power to bring this about . . .

[*Jawaharlal Nehru*, 22 July 1938]

Asia further drew Tribune's scrutiny through Japan's fascist/imperial aggressions, and through China's resistance to them in spite of the divisions and violences within China itself. The publication of Edgar Snow's *Red Star Over China* gave the paper a chance, on 15 October 1937, to excite its readers with the story of the birth of Mao's China.

RED CHINA LEADS THE FIGHT AGAINST THE INVADERS

An unknown land has been discovered. Its name is Soviet China. For many years the only news of this mysterious country to reach the western world came from the Chinese Nanking Government. It was, so we were told, a 'robber and bandit' state; its Government had been destroyed. Yet Moscow claims that Red China was a great state with eighty million inhabitants and a powerful army at its command. All was rumour and story. For no white man had ever crossed the borders into this land of mystery.

Now the first white man has returned from Soviet China. His name is Edgar Snow; he was out in the Far East as *Daily Herald* correspondent. Defying danger he managed to smuggle his way into this country, to live there, to meet its people, to talk with its leaders. On his adventures and experiences he has written one of the greatest books of our generation. It is the most remarkable story of our times . . .

The future of this Red Republic will be determined by the outcome of the present war. If Japan is beaten then Red Shensi will not remain isolated. The Red Star will rise all over the immense areas of China.

Chiang Kai-shek knows that full well. That is why he has time and again refused to organise Chinese resistance against Japan's imperialism. That is why he refused, until the very last minute, to accept the offer of the Reds to create one national united front.

Last, but not least, that is why the British Cabinet and Mr Chamberlain will not raise a finger to prevent Japan from conquering the North of China.

[*Julius Braunthal*, 15 October 1937]

But, in the final analysis, the 'informed British Leftist' mentioned before, who, one hopes, is the typical Tribune reader, was *British*. And just as no chance was lost (as in Braunthal's last paragraph) to relate European or Empire or worldwide events to failures and muddles in British politics, so all these concerns save that of the war itself could not crowd out of Tribune's columns the total commitment to the 'spirit of attack' on domestic fronts. Among these the most demanding of attention and energy were the ever-present crises of unemployment and poverty, and the paucity of Government measures against them. Ellen Wilkinson, who had led and inspired the Jarrow hunger marchers in 1936, set the tone in the paper's first issue:

DEPRESSION HAS HALF OF BRITAIN IN ITS HARSH GRIP

The trouble about the Special Areas is that they are considered 'special'. Premier and Ministers exude complacency about returning prosperity. Of course, and very regrettably, there are a few black spots, the distressed areas . . . and the impression is created that on our now healthy economic body there are just a few old sores left.

The public, given carefully selected statistics, doesn't realise that 'special' is a technical term and does not include all the distressed areas. Those marked 'special' are a selection which are placed under the special care of a Commissioner.

As Labour M.Ps point out weekly in the House, there are other areas with as high or higher rates of unemployment. Parts of Lancashire have a higher unemployment rate than Durham County.

As a matter of interest I worked out some statistics. Taking the average rate of unemployment in the 'Special Areas' as the criterion of 'distress', I added the areas with the same average.

The result is that nearly fifty per cent of the people in Great Britain live in areas which are scheduled as distressed, or have the same or higher average rate of unemployment. Is that a mere question of 'a few black spots'? Is this a problem that can be touched by charitable gifts, even of the Lord Nuffield size? . . .

Monotonously the Minister of Labour, Mr Ernest Brown, drones on about 'transference'. He has spent £250,000 on it in the last few months. This drains the life blood from the old industrial areas. New ones spawn round London. Comes the crash when the armament programme ends. Slough and Dagenham will be the Merthyrs and Jarrows of the 1940s.

Planned trading estates, cheap capital, free factories, any inducement to the capitalist graciously to take himself off to the special areas. Without some measure of compulsion, these schemes are expensive failures. The Ministry know it, but they sound well on Government newsreels, and don't inconvenience the Big Men any . . .

Compulsion in the planning of the economic life of a country, whole stretches of which have been sacrificed by capitalism, calls for detailed determination. It involves a completely new orientation of policy and the use of national authority in many forms. Nor can the areas of which I write wait for Socialism. They call aloud for action now.

Any government really alive to the appalling plight of masses of people – suffering from unemployment over long periods, from enforced malnutrition, from abominable housing conditions, from neglect, from despair – would move heaven and earth to bring immediate amelioration . . .

[*Ellen Wilkinson*, 1 January 1937]

Tribune never let up on elaborations and particularizations of that last paragraph – attacking government failure, exposing details of the people's plight – and, sometimes, their angry response.

STARVATION WAS NOT NEWS UNTIL WE MADE IT NEWS

. . . Snow lay thickly in Oxford Street on December 20. Churned to filthy slush by heavy traffic it did not dissuade us; hunger bites more deeply because of the cold. Lying in the road before onrushing traffic, with posters over our bodies proclaiming the demand for 'Work and Bread', we were warmed by the sympathy of thousands of shoppers who refused to assist the police to remove us . . .

Then – on December 22 – came our visit to the Ritz – for tea? – NO! – to expose our lack of food and the treatment received by us at the hands of the kind of people who can afford to frequent the Ritz, and who make no mistakes about *their* way to the Tea Lounge. The manager was perturbed – not at our empty bellies, which he could have filled as an example to Ernest Brown, but by the fact that I wore my hat inside the Grill Room.

'Workless Invade the Ritz', screamed the newspaper placards – while in the House of Commons, Ernest Brown was refusing to agree to the Labour suggestion that Winter Relief payments and Christmas grants should at once be made to the unemployed . . .

The next night was Christmas Eve. Tens of thousands of London's inhabitants thronged the railway stations – our demand for 'A Square Meal Now' stood in sharp contrast to their visions of turkey and

Christmas pudding – fare which we sincerely hoped awaited them at the end of their journey. We know that public sympathy is with our slogan rather than with that of the railway millionaires.

This sympathy was shown on Christmas Day, when a party of unemployed who visited the London home of Lord Rushcliffe, U.A.B. Chairman, only to find that he was out of town, had gifts of money showered on them by the inhabitants of neighbouring flats.

Penniless as they were, the demonstrators decided not to keep the money for their own personal use, but to spend it on printing new leaflets and posters to develop their campaign.

With the public our actions have brought results. Collections have been taken in some of the biggest factories, donations have been received from all quarters to aid our Movement in its campaign. Officials of the Unemployment Assistance Board, under pressure of public opinion, were compelled to meet our representatives . . .

Ernest Brown refused to meet us. We received his letter rejecting our request for a hearing on the morning of Friday, December 30. The same day we flew our banner from London's 204 feet high Monument. It proclaimed: 'For a Happy New Year the Unemployed Must Not Starve in 1939.'

Through the rain of New Year's Eve, down the Strand and towards Piccadilly we bore a coffin. Five hundred mourners marched behind to the beat of muffled drums and the music of the 'Dead March'. The coffin contained no corpse, but it dramatically reminded Britain that before winter ends unemployed men and women will be driven to the grave by the callous refusal of the authorities even to consider the plight of two million men and women. To crowds of West End revellers we brought home what the New Year means to the unemployed of Britain.

They learned other lessons that night – they saw the police draw their truncheons, watched the mounted 'cossacks' ride down hungry men and women, saw unemployed men dragged away to be thrown into cells, because they had dared to expose their poverty! . . .

[*Don Renton*, 6 January 1939]

But the 'poverty line' in the 1930s was not drawn as a border between the employed and the unemployed. Below it were thousands of men and women, in work, but drudging for a pittance and bare subsistence:

During the last four years the numbers of workers in employment have increased by 16.6 per cent. During the same period the Board of Trade index of production has increased by 38.3 per cent. Output per worker therefore since 1932 has increased by 18 per cent. Since that date real wages have improved by only one per cent, an increase which is rapidly being eaten up by the rapid rise in prices.

Who has gained the benefit of the increased production? Look at the figures of industrial profits and you will see the answer. Industrial profits since 1932 have increased by 52 per cent. Speed-up, rationalisation, new machinery have meant increased production. The ability of the profiteer to keep wages down to subsistence level has enabled him to reap all the benefits of increased output.

That is the meaning of capitalist prosperity. That is the reason for sweat-shop wages. Coal-owners and cotton kings, financiers and landlords have their United Front . . .

[*Michael Foot*, 21 May 1937]

By then, however, the trade unions were expanding membership and regaining vigour after the dispiriting days of setbacks, defeats and – some said – betrayals in the depression of the early 1930s. Even Patrick Gordon Walker wrote in Tribune of the new mood of 'militant unionism' (23 April 1937), which, he warned, ought to be channelled into political struggle via the Labour Party rather than into direct action. A week later William Mellor was surveying 'THESE DAYS OF STRUGGLE' as the unions fought for a fairer share of the temporary prosperity then enriching shareholders throughout Britain: the unions were on the move, and Tribune's spirit of attack moved with them every step.

'Judex', the industrial correspondent, who was sometimes Michael Foot and sometimes Barbara Castle, compiled weekly round-ups of union issues, claims, negotiations and activisms. In Hartshorn's time, John Hougan, the City correspondent, wrote a vitriolic series on the exploiting 'bosses' of several major industries. Crucial industrial actions put miners, busmen, railwaymen out on strike – not to mention shoe-factory workers and cinema staffs – and the paper reported background and developments in concentrated detail, showering equal venom on the Citrines and Ernest Bevins, whose anti-Left manoeuvrings undermined the struggles, and the industrialists and Government, whose responses extended regularly to police harassment and brutality against strikers.

Behind all this, Tribune kept its readers' eyes clearly fixed on the workers' goals: adequate wages, of course, more than just the restoration of the wage cuts of the early 1930s (and a *minimum* wage fixed above the poverty line) – but also such novelties as proper compensation for sickness or accident; *paid* holidays; and the 'revolutionary' proposal for a forty-hour week. These were the main proposals to improve the workers' conditions of life, and the paper spared no effort to expose just what those conditions were – not only for the unemployed or low-paid working *man*, but also for working women and the families of the workers. Medical investigations in the 1930s had thrown up disturbing facts about undernourished children, which Storm Jameson gathered together:

IF NEVILLE CHAMBERLAIN OWNED A DOG

. . . An overwhelming mass of evidence has been coming from medical officers and health workers all over the country to prove what every schoolteacher in the poorer areas already knew – that the children of the unemployed and of the lower-paid workers are half-starved, in the sense that the food they get is not nourishing enough.

'The children of the poor,' says one of these medical officers, 'suffer from a vast amount of anaemia, septic sores and rashes, eye inflammation and so on, the main cause of which is poor food. The well-nourished child does not suffer from these things.'

Any middle-class mother spends a week more *on milk alone* for one child than the total amount the wife of an unskilled worker or an unemployed man has left to spend on providing all the food for two children. Just think quietly about what this means – to the two underfed children.

Widespread malnutrition is a fact which no chatter about minimum standards can conceal, except from the wilfully blind, and from the spokesman of a Government which applies Means Tests to babies and hands their profits to armaments manufacturers on a plate.

Like the facts about malnutrition the facts about the slums are inescapable. Tyneside, the area known to me, does not contain the worst slums in England, I am told. If there are worse, I hope never to see them.

Here you can see not only 'normal' overcrowding (eight persons, two of them consumptive, living in three small rooms) but tenements with filthy and inefficient water-closets in the courtyard; families living in attics with rotten floors, cracked walls and bug-infested wallpaper and woodwork; single rooms housing families of eight and nine people.

Street after street in this area ought to be razed to the ground, and its rats and bugs burned with it. If Mr Chamberlain owns a dog he would not keep it in these rooms, which women break their backs and hearts trying to keep clean . . .

[*Storm Jameson*, 5 March 1937]

Dr Edith Summerskill enlarged the area of debate the following week, asserting that government gestures towards the nation's health – the school medical service, Lloyd George's health insurance, maternity and child-welfare provisions – were 'piecemeal' and suffering from the most 'serious gaps'. And she made one of the strongest early appeals in Tribune for the obvious solution – a 'comprehensive State-controlled system' for the national health (19 May 1939).

A call for the proper feeding of children naturally tied in with a call for their proper care generally – which mostly meant their schooling. An article on 29 January 1937 was headed 'CLASS AND CASTE IN OUR SCHOOLS', and amid the assault on privilege in education it managed neatly to outline that remedy which we now call the 'comprehensive system'. In 1939 Max Morris revealed other educational areas in need of remedy:

THEY ARE THE NATION'S FUTURE

. . . Perhaps the most significant thing in the child's life is the actual school building in which he is educated. Over five million children attend the public elementary schools; over four-fifths of these schools are out-of-date structures . . .

Our children are being brought up in ancient, gloomy structures, often worm-eaten, badly heated, difficult to clean, ill-lit and with none of the facilities that a modern school should have.

There are actually still in use 960 schools which the Board of Education put on a black list as far back as 1924 – fifteen years ago! . . .

At least two million children are being educated in batches of over forty, while well over one hundred thousand are in classes of over fifty. The Board of Education does not recognise a class as being 'overlarge' until it has more than fifty pupils.

[*Max Morris*, 10 March 1939]

Concern for the needs of children was matched by concern for the needs and rights of women – as workers or otherwise. In Tribune's first month of life, Joan Beauchamp produced an indictment of women workers' pay ('FOR TWELVE SHILLINGS EACH WEEK', 22 January 1937) and the concomitant appalling conditions, exploitative hours and the claw-back family means test. Later, Erika Boehm anticipated some of the modern equal-rights struggle when she asked rhetorically 'ARE WOMEN IN BRITAIN DENIED FREEDOM?' (19 March 1937).

The paper even bravely tackled the one subject, regarding women in society, on which opinions were and remain most traditionally emotional. 'Conscripted Mothers' is what Eleanor Hawarden called working-class women 'diseased and disabled because they have borne children more frequently than their bodies can endure' (26 February 1937) – thus placing Tribune's standpoint firmly on the side of Marie Stopes's then ongoing campaign for birth control. Nor was it just traditional male prejudice that 'conscripted' the women: government, the press and the experts were waving statistics about a declining birth rate and putting on heavy propaganda pressure to reverse it. An article by Gilbert Hall – 'THIS CRY FOR MORE BABIES' – acidly pointed out their motives:

> Capitalism cannot live on a declining or even a stationary population . . . The workers' reply must be to point out that what is sauce for the middle-class goose in the way of families is also sauce for the working-class gander; that it is an insult to suggest that the workers should begin increasing their families in the interest of the liberal, middle-class state, whilst there are still colossal unemployment and such blots as depressed areas . . .
>
> [23 April 1937]

In a similar vein, Tribune tackled, on women's behalf, the emotionally loaded problems in contemporary attitudes to marriage, divorce and even abortion – on which it demanded 'sweeping changes to the existing laws' on 22 July 1938.

Still, feminist readers then and now might have greeted with some irony the presence in the paper during these years of a chatty little column by Margaret O'Flaherty which began life as 'For the Labour Woman', later to be a 'Housewives' Notebook', devoted to shopping tips, 'cheap and tasty' recipes and general home hints and housewifery.

If this homeliness slightly undermined Tribune's campaigning for women's rights, absolutely nothing got in the way of its concern for overall *civil* rights, especially as the advent of war spawned a new authoritarianism among the nation's rulers. Ronald Kidd, secretary of the still brand-new National Council for Civil Liberties, saw 'DANGEROUS DAYS FOR LIBERTY IN GREAT BRITAIN':

> Within the last year or so, in many districts as widely separated as Edgware and Carlisle, the police have adopted the policy of ejecting

orderly hecklers from open-air meetings and in some cases arrests have been made for such heckling. I have no sympathy with anyone who wishes to create a breach of the peace at a public meeting, but heckling is one of the oldest features of English political life and it is highly improper for the police to be used, from a political motive, to suppress all Left-wing heckling . . . At anti-Fascist meetings, however, the Fascists are permitted by the police to create actual disorder and to break up the meeting, and in very few cases have the police taken action against Blackshirt disturbers . . .

[22 January 1937]

Oswald Mosley's activities came in, of course, for much contemptuous attention in Tribune, along with the unforgivable role played by the police in snuffing out any Leftist protests, as when the 'Notes on the News' column, in one of its regular tirades against British fascism, spoke of some photographs of Mosley marches which included the picture 'of a young girl prostrate on the pavement under police batons' (8 October 1937). But the battle of Cable Street had been won before Tribune's time, and more central among its civil-liberty fears were new government steps towards what Elwyn Jones, on 28 October 1938, called 'Censorship Over England', including the Incitement to Disaffection Act, the Official Secrets Act and the like. Then, on 1 September 1939, columnist John Hougan grew even more worried about the new 'public order' statute, the Emergency Power Act: 'The gains we have won in a century of democracy rest lightly in a dictator's hand. The National Government has the sole discretion to take away or leave alone the rights we have won . . .' (1 September 1939).

That, on the precise eve of war, summed up the ugly entirety of the social and political situation which Tribune had been created to fight and hopefully to overcome.

Aside from the rich abundance of articles carrying forward Tribune's spirit of attack on the fronts so far looked at (and a good few regretfully bypassed), the paper also provided a remarkable assortment of 'regular features' that did more than anything to solidify its character. The weekly columnists, there from the start, included Aneurin Bevan (as 'MP') on Parliament, 'Vanoc II' (Hayter Preston) with a general political commentary, 'Judex' on the unions. With them, for the lighter touch, was a series of pseudonymous humorous columnists.

And Hartshorn seems to have been even more a columnists' editor (even though he included a disclaimer in his first issue: 'The Editorial Board accepts no responsibility for the views expressed in any signed article' – 16 September 1938). 'Vanoc' remained in all his fierceness, joined by diplomatic correspondents 'Vigilante' and 'Perspicax', later both revealed to be K. Zilliacus, who by 1939 took to writing – unusually, for Tribune then – under his own name. With them John Hougan became a regular columnist on a wide industrial brief; Don Renton acquired a corner for a weekly comment; John Hird began an effective City column. Then Krishna Menon launched his 'Empire' page, Beatrice King contributed education reports, and there were also a weekly 'Workers' Guide' series (law and civil rights for the layman) and in mid-1939 a 'Guide for Conscripts' series (again an outline of rights). Add to all that the regular 'Notes on the News' feature, which Hartshorn turned into 'Your World in Brief' – capsule reports and comments on weekly happenings – plus an international news-and-comment survey, plus the contributions within the Left Book Club section – and it can be seen to have been a full and nourishing twenty-page read. Even so, there was more: regular and plentiful columns and articles on books, the arts and in those years even sport.

Tribune insisted from the outset, in its book-review section, that good writing of all sorts, poetry as well as pamphleteering, provided essential furnishing in any politically orientated mind. At the same time, Tribune reviewers shared a general distaste for the sort of aesthetically detached writing that kept purposefully remote from a world plunging into chaos. The paper's book coverage, then, fitted well into the mainstream of the 1930s marriage between literature and political awareness, and allowed a breadth of reviewing that went far beyond merely noticing new propagandas and tracts. In the two pages given to books by Mellor, guest reviewers like J. B. S. Haldane, Fenner Brockway, D. W. Brogan and G. D. H. Cole offered the benefit of their varied expertise, but the most regular books feature was Winifred Horrabin's weekly survey of new novels.

Book reviews shrank to one page only later in 1937; the paper then retained a weekly film review, but theatre reviews were rare, save for occasional notices of the new-born Unity Theatre, while other arts pieces like, say, a look at new records, never became regular features.

Sports commentaries did, very much so, at least in Mellor's

We've Noticed It, Too

" We are faced with the problem of unemployed people who are receiving more than the workers " (*Manchester Guardian*).

Three of Tribune's early regular cartoonists on three of its earliest preoccupations: 'Earthworm' (a Wigan miner) on official attitudes to the depression (24 June 1938); Challen on the agony of Spain (14 October 1938); 'Sax' on the Nazi aggressions (1 April 1938).

Tribune. Robin Bailey wrote on cricket or rugby depending on the season; there was a popular weekly column on boxing and less regular reports on athletics, tennis and other sports. Oddly, there was no coverage of the most important working-class sport till September 1937 – when a football column began. Some of its headings seem sadly anticipatory of those of 1976–7: 'HELP FOR THE POOR CLUBS', say, or 'England Must Have a Matchwinner at Centre-forward'.

Hartshorn's arrival led eventually to an expansion of the book section, especially when Roy Fenton became literary editor in early 1939 and brought to his two pages a good measure of breadth, style and infectious enthusiasm. His columns were also filled with reviewers whose names would appeal to literary nostalgiacs – among them Stephen Spender, A. L. Morton, Maurice Dobb, Edith Summerskill, Sylvia Townsend Warner, Louis MacNeice, Rex Warner, Anthony Hern, Pamela Hansford Johnson and even the Dean of Chichester.

For the other arts in Hartshorn's paper, Glyn Roberts reviewed films until his sudden death, at which Elizabeth Young took over and held that column. Edward Scroggie wrote irregularly on major art exhibitions, and a play or two – still mostly those at the Unity – might have squeezed into a few column inches. Under Hartshorn, sports coverage declined, and football nearly vanished. But, like Mellor, he made sure to give ample space to readers' letters, which continued and enlarged the arguments and dialogues sparked by the paper's articles.

Sometimes the letters generated their own sparks – as when, in that last edgy summer of peace in 1939, Hartshorn bravely asked readers for criticisms of Tribune, and got them. 'Biassed,' said one reader. 'No financial or monetary policy,' said another. 'Messy layout,' said (with some justification) a third. 'If it were not for Zilliacus and the local LP secretary, I'd put 5d towards the two-pence and get the *Daily Worker*,' said a fourth.

But probably he never did; nor did many others. The paper had thrived in its first three years, in readership if not prosperity, certainly in influence and reputation. Cripps commented on 3 February 1939, 'Tribune is now very much "on the map" and has achieved a larger circulation than any other political weekly in the country. Our paper has become a real factor in political life and is now established as the organ of a very definite and growing volume of public opinion.' And in an advertisement for itself on 28 April 1939, Tribune announced 'certified net sales' of 30,000 per week.

That came, though, not too long after a period when an appeal had had to be launched (in mid-1938) asking readers to get more readers, because sales figures were not rising fast enough to assure financial stability: the paper had needed to *double* its readership.

Yet with that prideful announcement of the 30,000, some stability had clearly been achieved. But inevitably there were to be renewed problems and upheavals of that sort to face – along with new changes in the paper, new targets for its attacks – in the second stage of Tribune's life that began with the declaration of war.

2 'FOR VICTORY AND SOCIALISM' (1939–45)

Through 1939 the contents list on Tribune's front page each week bore a slightly portentous heading – not 'Inside Tribune' but 'Inside History'. On 8 September of that year, the heading took on a direly expanded meaning, when below it Stafford Cripps and Aneurin Bevan sombrely addressed the readers to 'OUR DUTY':

> Out of the war, whatever else comes, will come an opportunity for the working class of the world to do something effective to save themselves from fresh tragedies and suffering. That opportunity they must seize and it is already time to start preparing for the moment when it arrives. War will accomplish less than nothing unless it marks the end for ever of Fascism and its aggressive brutality . . .
>
> [8 September 1939]

The war was only six months old when H. J. Hartshorn resigned and the editorship was assumed by Raymond Postgate, Left-wing author and journalist and, among other things, George Lansbury's son-in-law. Aneurin Bevan and George Strauss remained the mainstays of the editorial board, and assured readers that 'the purpose and aim of the Tribune will remain the same' (1 March 1940). It was a promise that was kept.

On the Ides of March, Postgate's 'new Tribune' emerged like butterfly from chrysalis. Suddenly the paper was a smallish, neat tabloid of twenty or twenty-four pages (when newsprint shortages allowed) at a price of sixpence. Visually it had adopted the general layout tendencies of the other prominent weeklies – longer articles spreading often over two or even three pages, judicious headings and much expanse of grey columns (a considerable change from Hartshorn's cluttered pages) with limited illustration. And those dense columns were given to a wealth of thoughtful comment, in-depth analysis, knowledgeable opinion written by a variety of experts and well-informed correspondents, commentators and critics.

And so it remained when Postgate left his editor's chair (the title of his round-up column on the week's significant events) in late 1941. Then Aneurin Bevan took charge, and early in 1942 produced his own editorial manifesto:

ABOUT OURSELVES

A Statement of Beliefs and Aims

Let us make a few things clear at the outset. The TRIBUNE is the organ of no political party and has no association nor understanding with any party. It was launched four years ago by a number of people who desired a weekly devoted to the promotion of understanding between and among those who, having 'Left' political views, wanted these translated into terms of appropriate action. To that general purpose we have been and we intend to remain, faithful . . .

We believe that the solution of many of our difficulties would be found if the people could be persuaded to take more control of the parties which are supposed to speak for them. It is not more parties we want but rather more democracy in the parties that already exist. Here we come to the centre of the position that the TRIBUNE takes up. We believe that it is only by the increasing participation of the people in the making of public policy and by the identification with, and fermenting of, all forms of political and cultural activities that mankind can win through the present struggle and realise a more natural, wholesome and stable world society. It was the fashion many years before the war – and it still is in some quarters – to speak of the failure of democratic forms of government and to undermine the self-confidence of the people by suggesting that there is something inherently incompatible between the enfranchisement of the people and intelligent and efficient government. It is ironical that these same cultivated and informed minds can think of nothing to put in its place but those principles of government under whose benign rule mankind spent thousands of years in brutish ignorance . . .

The time has come to insist upon the acceptance and application of a truth which a century and a half of experience has established with all the authority of science and of political philosophy. It is this – that mankind has progressed in all the arts and crafts, has achieved dignity and learning, the certainty of peace and the benediction of security, just to the extent that ordinary men and women won freedom and pushed their way into the central citadels of power.

That spate of the onrush of the ordinary people is still on. The past few years have shown that it is in those places where it ran too feebly, or was dammed up, that the poisons accumulated which now seek to infect the whole earth. The student of history now views a sufficient sweep of events over the past two centuries to perceive that two great forces were unleashed by the destruction of medieval Europe, the natural sciences and the emancipation of the common people . . .

This is the lesson that the TRIBUNE exists to preach and to insist upon the application . . .

Week by week the TRIBUNE will show how our propaganda reflects the profound distrust of our spokesmen in the democratic ideal. We shall expose every example of the failure to apply the principles of a dynamic democracy to the problems of war. We shall show how the inefficiency of British industry, the failure of our military intelligence, the flat-footedness of the Army command, the debility of our propaganda to enemy countries, and the short-comings of our grand strategy are due, in one form or another, to the fact that Britain is still controlled by those who think, either consciously or unconsciously, that ordinary men and women are there to be governed and not to govern.

The fact is, and we may as well face it, the people will have to take more charge of the war and this, of course, means the peace as well . . .

There remains one thing more to be said before we conclude this credo of the TRIBUNE. The decade that lies immediately ahead is bound to be the most fruitful in the history of mankind. In the course of it new conceptions of human society will be thought out and their application at least begun. We can see nothing in those who now guide us to lead us to hope that from them anything different can be expected than variants of the same ideas which have resulted in our present plight. Nor have we much more hope from the existing political parties. Even the parties of the 'Left' seem to be mentally muscle-bound and repeat old phrases with less and less conviction. It is from the unencumbered minds of ordinary people that vigorous ideas will emerge.

Already the problem is clarifying itself. Complex the society of the future is bound to be, as complex and subtle as is the mind of modern man. But one solution it will have found if it is to endure. It will reconcile the needs of an ordered economic life with the fullest effloresence of personal liberty. Without an ordered economic life the individual frustrates itself in a morass of fears and insecurities. Without personal liberty an ordered economic life is like a plant that never flowers. Here then is our problem. Let us press on and answer it.

[2 January 1942]

Under Bevan the pages of Tribune became even more sober and restrained in appearance, their tone even more firmly and maturely authoritative, their contributors even more noteworthy. Bevan's introductory statement, above, set the style; his Tribune maintained it, and also managed (as indeed had Postgate's) to escape, most of the time, being either predictable or dull.

Of course, it was not difficult to avoid dullness within the paper's and the nation's burning preoccupation, the progress of the war. Even in the first weeks and months of the 'phoney war', amid all the diplomatic juggling and military inactivity, much was happening – including the Soviet Union's smooth takeover of Estonia and the other Baltic nations, and its partitioning of Poland with the Nazis. Hartshorn's Tribune had hailed and tried to justify these annexations (as when a picture caption on 3 October 1939 asserted that 'Red Army men as they entered the former Russian territories of Poland were welcomed by peasants . . .'), and did so in terms hardly distinguishable from the *Daily Worker*. It was not quite the same, though, in December of that year when the Soviet Union shocked many supporters round the world with its invasion of Finland. Tribune claimed to understand, but not entirely to condone:

RUSSIA – AND FINLAND

. . . The suggestion that Russia enters Finland in the role of deliverer of the Finnish workers makes nonsense of Molotov's recent statement that Socialism could not be exported . . . If it be the defence of Russia's action that she makes war on Finland in order to confer the benefits of Socialism upon her, then the sooner Socialists dissociate themselves from the action the better. 'Socialism means war' is hardly a slogan which will endear Socialism to the workers . . .

We have spent years in teaching the workers to detest aggression. All that detestation is turned against Socialism when aggression and Socialism are identified . . .

Now the hunt is on and a wave of anti-Soviet propaganda is loosed on the world. Not only does the TRIBUNE refuse to join in this hunt, but we shall oppose it with all our strength.

We know that the spate of hate which is running against the Soviet Union is not on account of her attack on Finland. It is not because she is an aggressor that Russia is being attacked in certain quarters. It is because she is Socialist. We deplore her aggression, but we support her for her Socialism . . .

[*Statement by the Editorial Board and 'Vigilans'*, 8 December 1939]

The British press's 'orgy of red-baiting' was inevitable, as perhaps was the need for Tribune and a few other papers to remind the nation about who the real enemy was – especially when the war with that enemy had till then been little more than skirmishes at sea with prowling U-boats. But 'Vigilans', the foreign-affairs correspondent, warned on 5 January 1940: '. . . neither side appears anxious to take the initiative. Nevertheless Hitler may, for political reasons, find it necessary to try to deliver some decisive stroke . . .' It was properly prophetic, for in April Hitler struck at Norway, the English language acquired two new imported words – 'quisling' and 'blitzkrieg' – and soon afterwards the British nation acquired a new Prime Minister.

From then on all phoniness went out of the war. After Scandinavia it was Holland's turn, and Belgium's, under the treads of Hitler's panzers. Then the British Expeditionary Force was trapped, until the eleventh-hour remission that permitted the heroism of Dunkirk. 'One thing stands out above all others,' Bevan wrote on 7 June 1940. 'Our men were sent into action with too little equipment, insufficient mechanical aids like heavy tanks, and above all, were exposed to swarms of bombing planes against which the number of ours was pitifully small. We exposed flesh to steel, and it is no answer that it was the flesh of heroes.'

France soon fell, and Britain stood alone, an island fortress, with the war, nightly, on its doorstep.

THE PEOPLE OF THE TUBES

In nearly every London suburb between ten in the morning and, say, three in the afternoon, you will see scattered groups of children and women making their way to the entrance of the Underground stations. They purchase three-halfpenny tickets and descend by lift or escalator to the platforms. There they spread out old blankets and rugs, produce a few cushions and pillows. And wait. And they go on waiting throughout the day, sometimes working a rough sort of shift so that they take turns in going up and breathing the fresh September air. But this is not encouraged. It means taking a new ticket, and a breath of air at three-ha'pence a time is a luxury that these people at any rate can't afford.

For they are the advance guard of London's new underworld. They are staking their claims to a corner of the tube platform in readiness for the night that is to come. At about four o'clock in the afternoon the stream of women and children grows, and by five and six it has become a flood. By seven it is impossible to find sleeping – or even sitting – space in any tube in the London area, except in those rare stations that for technical reasons are unsafe.

These are the people of the tubes, driven underground into an atmosphere that rapidly becomes foetid, undergoing physical hardship and foregoing privacy in order to get away for a night from the menace of the Nazi bombers.

The movement started in the East End, soon after that area had had its first appalling visitation. It became clear then to the workers of the East End that, whatever Sir John Anderson might have to say for himself, deep shelters provided the only effective protection from the bombs that rained from the skies. And so these people from the East End, who have been slapped around by the representatives of wealth and privilege for generations, took things into their own hands. They invaded the tube stations, buying tickets which legally entitled them to entry to the platforms. They then illegally took possession. It is an old lesson of the working-class struggle that if enough people break the law together, and stand solidly together against possible action from the authorities, these authorities are powerless. And so it was.

The habit spread like the traditional wildfire. Within a day of tubes in the Elephant and Castle area being occupied in this manner, the station at Chalk Farm on the other side of London was similarly taken over in the biggest working-class demonstration London has seen. For that is what it is.

Ever since the war began progressive parties and societies have urged the Home Office to provide deep bomb-proof shelters in the thickly-populated parts of Britain, or, where deep shelters were technically impossible, to provide shelters like the half-sunken type known as the Haldane. The replies from the Home Office have varied in form from time to time, but the content has been more or less the same. First, they said, we don't like to think of large numbers of people being gathered together in a raid; we prefer the dispersal theory (which has, incidentally, been unkindly described as one of the more effective ways of seeing that the most people are killed in the shortest space of time). Secondly, they said, deep shelters would take too long to build (though they won't say how many could have been built by now if they had been started at the beginning of the war). Thirdly, they said, we hate to think of such a stalwart race as the British being driven underground like troglodytes just because enemy planes are overhead. And fourthly, they said, we think the brick-and-concrete surface shelters in the streets are admirably sufficient.

Well, the workers of London have passed the biggest vote of no-confidence in Sir John Anderson and his expert advisers at the Home Office that Britain has ever seen. For by their action in occupying the tubes they have given an overwhelming reply to the official attitude . . .

[*Anthony Hern*, 27 September 1940]

The concern for this ghastly arrival of the war into the lives and homes of so many ordinary British families was matched, in Tribune, with that undimmed, cheery strength of will and purpose which the whole nation shared, and on which we now look back so nostalgically. Tribune retained the lightness of touch that was the Postgate trademark (for example, miscellaneous gleanings from the wartime press became a weekly feature under the irreverent heading 'Blitz & Pieces') – and retained it even when the paper's own office went up in an incendiary bomb's flame, as Postgate described it:

TRIBUNE BECOMES PHOENIX

Like several thousand other Londoners, I came out of the Tube on Monday morning to go to my office in the usual way. I walked some way up the main street with ever-growing anxiety: surely it could not be . . . at any rate there would be something there . . . not US.

The scene was something like the old Victorian pictures of hell. Darkness at noon; a mist of smoke everywhere; huge curling hoses in tens and twenties lying across the street, sometimes twitching themselves like half-wakened snakes (there is tremendous strength in that water-pressure); high buildings smoking from their interiors, and suddenly from black windows almost gleefully a little dance of fire; firemen perched on fantastically high ladders, or operating engines, or coming out of the smoke suddenly, wiping their faces and looking at you with the stony expressions of extreme tiredness; women weeping, not from sorrow but from sore eyes . . .

The Artist, the Manager, and I went cautiously up our own street. (We ought to have been stopped). We could see only a little way, and hot, silent breaths came up at us from one side. We reached the door: the Manager opened it to see what was inside. Inside, there fell down a large object, unidentified, but blazing. The Manager withdrew his head with some speed. The Editor fell in a pool of water. The Artist made notes for what you will see on another page.

There was nothing there; and nothing to do.

But the TRIBUNE, like a phoenix, rises from its ashes and will continue to give the bird to Hitler and his allies here.

['*From the Editor's Chair*', 3 January 1941]

Somehow the paper came out without a break. But the destruction precipitated another urgent appeal for financial aid from the readers, and it looked for a while as if Tribune's rise from those ashes would turn out merely to be its death-throes. Yet the money flowed in – a few pounds here, a few shillings there – and facilitated the paper's move from the rubble of Milton House, Chiswell Street, London EC1, to new offices at 222 The Strand, from which now almost legendary address it was to flourish for more than two decades.

And even as the bombs fell and the flames rose, Tribune went in search of the other ghastlinesses that the war, and the Churchill coalition government, were perpetrating on the British people. Food shortages, rationing and queuing caused calumnies to be heaped on the new Ministry of Food; coal shortages chilled the country and led Tribune and Bevan to assault governmental 'lack of foresight and lack of imagination' for taking too many miners into the army (8 August 1941).

Worse still was the picture of wartime arms and munitions manufacturing, along with other examples of the untrammelled profit motive, exposed in a book entitled *Rats* (from Gollancz) which Tribune gleefully reviewed:

> . . . Huge profits made by armament firms, despite E.P.T., huge rake-offs by company promoters, capitalist rings placed in full control of key industries as the representatives of the State, and wielding its Authority, banks sucking tribute from the taxpayers for the privilege of counting money out of nothing, and at the same time ruining small businesses and harassing men who have left their businesses for the Army by imperative demands for the repayment of overdrafts; Building Societies making sure that if houses part-paid for on the instalment plan are bombed, the loss shall fall wholly on the householder, and not on them . . .
>
> [14 March 1941]

In other areas, muddle rather than greed drew the paper's condemnation. The task of evacuating urban children had been carried out with an undue share of blunders and lack of foresight, as Tom

Harrisson of Mass-Observation revealed in a special study, which showed that after the initial departure of the hundreds of thousands of children, the bulk of them were brought *back* to the cities during lulls in the bombing, then sent out again – 'unorganised and spontaneously for the most part' – when the blitz resumed. Harrisson wrote:

> This erratic tendency implies that people are not being kept adequately aware and *informed* of the probabilities. It shows that people are given too much scope for making up their own minds on inadequate data, leading to faulty action – faulty from the point of view of the war effort. Meanwhile, like a pathetic shuttlecock, to and fro, children go between town and country . . .
>
> [21 November 1941]

In Tribune's view, official ineptitude was damaging the nation's morale at least as much as Nazi bombs. And equally damaging was what the paper saw as steadily expanding encroachment on the people's civil liberties. Tribune raged against the ill-judged and panicky policy of 'interning' foreign residents, including thousands of outright *refugees* from Hitler (among them the long-time Tribune contributor Heinrich Fraenkel). The paper also cried out against what its legal expert saw as the erosion of press freedom by 'The Blue-Pencil Censor' (20 April 1940) – who used his weapons against Tribune on 28 June of that year, blanking out a page by the Military Correspondent.

The piece had called for an ultimatum to Franco to keep him out of the war. Postgate asserted his suspicion of political rather than military motives in the censorship, and in fact his suspicions were justified when the Press Censor, in the face of wide protest, admitted that his office had been wrong, that the piece 'did not contain matter which it was within the powers of the censorship to stop . . .' (5 July 1940).

The censors were rather more active, though, when their objects were further Left. The *Daily Worker* was suppressed – 'the suppression of *opinion*, nothing more', Postgate accused (24 January 1941).

Out of such official actions, clearly, came Aneurin Bevan's conviction, stated in his editorial credo already quoted, that 'Britain is still controlled by those who think . . . that ordinary men and women are there to be governed and not to govern' (2 January 1942). And little in the continuing prosecution of the war abroad served to alter Tribune's view of the nation's leaders. Defeat was following defeat: Tobruk fell, and so did Singapore and Crete; the dubious pact between Hitler and Stalin evaporated (shortly after Stafford Cripps had been sent to Moscow as Ambassador) and the Nazi armies were flung eastwards to thrust deep into the Soviet Union, to the distress of the Left and the visible delight of nearly everyone else.

Of all the attacks in Tribune's private war against the government in 1942 and 1943, probably the most notorious was a three-part series by the pseudonymous Thomas Rainsboro' (who was the leading Fleet Street journalist Frank Owen, whose identity remained a well-kept secret for some time). His slangy, glittering vituperation began by asking 'Why Churchill?' on 1 May 1942, continued the next week with 'Balkan Blunder' and concluded on 15 May with 'Churchill and Russia':

> . . . And will he act before 1943? Churchill has made up his mind to win this war. He is going to end the job that Marlborough was not allowed to end, the War of Succession. He is going to be the hero-victor of 1943. Nothing is to be allowed to interfere with that purpose and that project. Therefore no risks, until overwhelming strength is ours. It is not a dishonourable ambition. The question is: is it a reasonable proposition? If we could go on piling up arms and men till 1943 and then crack Hitler on the snout, it would be admirable. But what is Hitler going to be engaged on till 1943? War is not an addition sum but an equation in time. Have we time to afford Churchill's strategy?

And in case anyone thought that Rainsboro' spoke only for himself and not for Tribune, the editorial in that same issue, 15 May 1942, defended his critique of Churchill: '. . . How long can we afford a succession of oratorical successes accompanied by a series of military disasters? . . .'

Not for nothing, then, did Tribune's weekly heading above the paper's name on the front page change from the generalized 'Fresh and Fearless' of early 1941 to the more pointed 'For Victory and Socialism' later that year. Victory alone – Churchill's way, the Tory way, the profiteers' way – was not to be enough.

But by December 1941 Pearl Harbor had stung the United States out of isolationism, and the prospects were that Churchill's Britain would not be the sole architect of that victory. Tribune had long wondered what the United States's developing stance to the war would be: Harold Laski had pointed out on 9 August 1940 that British foreign and colonial policies over the years had not endeared this nation to the Americans: '. . . they remember 1919, and they ask for principles far more concrete than any they have so far been vouchsafed'. The 'lease-lending' of American warships brought 'a heartfelt sigh of relief' to Postgate (14 March 1941) and many Britons; but later that year Laski, again, was reminding the nation, first, that America was gearing up only slowly for industrial production on a war footing and, secondly, that 'Average America wants to help win this war for democratic Britain; it does not see sufficient signs that democratic Britain is, as a result of our war effort, coming into its own' (7 November 1941).

Even when the Americans went to war with Japan, British commentators worried whether they would prefer to restrict their fight to Asia and the Pacific. But of course Britain was not indifferent to the Asian war – not, as Tribune reiterated, so much in the spirit of fighting for freedom as in the anxiety to preserve imperialism. Over and over, for instance, Tribune demanded that 'India Must Be Given Her Freedom' (6 September 1940) as the first and most important indication that Britain would move away from exactly the same empire-building drive that had sent Hitler into Austria or the Japanese into Manchuria.

Freedom began to seem rather more likely a prospect in Europe as the war progressed towards its major turning points – the beginnings of the German retreat from the Soviet Union, the entry of the United States into the fight against Hitler and the Allied victory at El Alamein. In what seemed like no time, the Allies were forcing their way on to Sicily, the Red Army was thrusting west and Hitler went on the defensive. Except, of course, against the captive peoples of the occupied lands – notably the Jewish victims of the final solution, the details of which had begun to horrify Britain soon after Alamein:

> COUNTER-TERROR
>
> The British public has at last been made aware of the fact that the Jews of Occupied Europe are being systematically exterminated. As the grisly details seep through the demands for retribution grow. Horror is expressed on all sides. Indignation is rampant. Fiery words leave no doubt as to the fate that awaits Hitler's specialist corps of executioners.
>
> We would be more convinced of the sincerity of all this if it were

mixed with a little more sympathy for the Jews thus affected.

What is most important, in our opinion, is what shall be done for those Jews who are escaping the holocaust or those to whom such opportunity may be given. Will the United Nations aid and abet their escape? Will some effort be made to save the children? It is no use fulminating against the butcher unless something is done to help the victims to escape the butchery.

It is time we reminded ourselves that it is not only the Jews under Hitler who are suffering. Thousands of Hitler's Jewish victims are still wandering on the earth, searching for some place to live. We might also remind H.M. Government that we still have a few Jews locked up in internment camps, classed as 'enemy aliens and potentially dangerous'.

That is the supreme insult that has been added to all the injuries inflicted on the Jews . . .

['*What's Happening*', 18 December 1942]

That horror was especially sickening to all those who had always consistently abominated racism, as Tribune had in its many attacks on Nazi antisemitism and on the home-grown kind, from the Mosley marches of the 1930s to what Postgate now called wartime 'poisons of the mind' (11 October 1940). It was perhaps the most fundamental point, which the paper never forgot: neither democratic principles nor civilized values could be abandoned if meaning was to be retained in a war ostensibly fought on behalf of democracy and civilization.

The maintenance of 'civilized values' had in fact brought about some of the most striking changes that had appeared in the 'new Tribune' at the war's outset. Postgate thoroughly renovated and expanded the paper's books and arts coverage (abandoning sports along the way); but, more important, he had integrated it into the paper so that important books constantly provided the kernels of major feature articles. Also, he, and Bevan later, brought into Tribune's book columns some remarkable and major writers, whose cultural statements and subjects were, Tribune insisted, of as great importance to the readers as the words of major political figures like Cripps and Laski – even in a time of crisis, as Stephen Spender wrote: 'Poetry is an affirmation of that which is living in man's environment and a denial of that which is dead . . . The insistence of poetry that actuality is the language of the human spirit, which can be translated into universal terms of human experience, means that poetry can restore order to the symbols of men's minds, and, ultimately, this may mean that they can also restore order to the world of actuality' (11 September 1942).

Even Edith Sitwell herself appeared in Tribune, discoursing on poetry's ability 'to help reduce chaos to order, and to bring a light to the darkness' (16 October 1942).

Big literary guns, then, were rolled in to establish the indispensable importance of literature and the arts in a socialist paper and a socialist experience. Even at the height of the blitz or invasion scares or military defeats, the Tribune reader would have come across a thoughtful essay on Elizabethan poetry or the novels of Smollett. Or that reader might have found John Lehmann considering wartime poetry ('The pity of it is that Auden two years ago chose to turn American, and is not with us, experiencing here and now what we are experiencing, because I feel he might produce the poetry of this war we are all waiting for . . .' – 6 September 1940). Or J. B. Priestley offering some 'PLAIN WORDS ABOUT PLAYS' and how to write them ('A whole world of comedy and pathos, hope and fear, passion and resignation, suffering and courage, cries out to be represented and expressed, just as these scattered but innumerable audiences of hard-working folk cry out for the plays themselves' – 10 September 1943). Or E. M. Forster reflecting on the life of Edward Carpenter; or William Empson pronouncing on the teaching of the English language; or Arthur Koestler instructing a working-class reader on the reliability of book reviewers, of various heights of brow:

THE READER'S DILEMMA

. . . I believe I can guess what you feel. You start eagerly to read an article, let's say in the *New Statesman*; let's say by Raymond Mortimer or Stonier; after a few lines you stumble over an allusion which you don't understand – a reference to Proust, or Kafka, or Péguy – authors whom you have never read. But the writer of the article seems to assume that everybody has read or at least ought to have read, them; and so you begin to feel like a schoolboy who hasn't learnt his lesson, or, rather, like the uninvited guest at a party; left in the cold, humiliated, envious, resentful. And here we are at the crucial point: we are facing the wall, the tragic barrier which separates the progressive intelligentsia from the educated working class.

Let us not be hypocritical about it. The wall is there, and the more we try to explain it away, the harder we bump our heads against it. In the 'thirties Left intellectuals tried to masquerade as proletarians; it was a farce. They tried to write down 'to the masses'; it was a failure. They derided the highbrows; it was self-derision. It's no good trying to jump over the wall; our task is to abolish it. But that is a political, not a literary task. It is, I believe, the main and ultimate task of Socialism.

All this talk about highbrows and lowbrows is a smokescreen. The brutal facts are that your critic's parents were able to pay during an average of sixteen years so that he should read, browse, learn, soak in that spiritual nourishment for which you crave, at his leisure. You could only go to school for about nine years – and it was a different school and there was less leisure. This is what stands between you and him, between you and me. When we get tight, or sentimental, or rub shoulders at a meeting, the barrier seems to melt; but when we return each to our own routine it's there again. It's neither my fault nor yours; it does not help if I feel guilty towards you, nor you towards me. I share your feeling of frustration; I loathe the order which is its cause; but don't expect me for that reason to join in the popular game of highbrow-beating. Wipe out the highbrow, and you will soon march the goose-step. It is a Fascist diversion; our way is to attack the wall. As long as it stands, democracy is a sham.

And now to return to your question. Who told you that in order to enjoy reading you have to torture yourself with that type of sophisticated review? It seems to me an utterly false approach. Reversing the proverb, you force yourself to eat the grapes *because* they taste sour. My advice is, regard reading as a pleasure, and not as a task to be pursued with clenched teeth . . .

Read for pleasure, man, and don't bother about Péguy and *Finnegans Wake*! Go to the public library or the bookstall, browse, open a book at random, read a page, and you will see whether you want to read that book or not. Never force yourself to read a book – it is a wasted effort. That book is right for you which needs just the amount of concentration on your part to make you turn the radio off. Read fiction only if it excites you; all great works of fiction, even *Pilgrim's Progress*, are exciting reading for a certain type of reader at a certain period of his life. If the right book falls into your hands at the right time, you won't be able to put it down. At any other time it is wasted on you. And the same goes for essays, history, philosophy. If you don't feel that it has a direct bearing on your own personal interests, worries, problems – put it away . . .

And, mind you, I don't preach resignation. It is your right and duty to feel frustrated and resentful – but on a political plane. Watch carefully what you do with your resentment – it is the only historical asset of the poor; without it they would still live in serfdom. The others would like to deflect it into the wrong direction, against 'cleverness', culture, art; to make you spit on those values of which they deprive you. It is a subtle manoeuvre of diversion; the Nazis were not the first and not the last to succeed with it. Don't fall into the trap. Your opponent is not the highbrow, but the rich.

[28 April 1944]

And in all the issues of this war period the *regular* reviewers concerned themselves with important books of all conceivable sorts: books on war strategy or wartime domestic problems, about the Nazis, about the state of Europe or the condition of Britain, about the past or future of the Labour movement, about pressing social problems, not to mention a widely cast netful of novels, poetry, literary criticism and other contributions to the nation's bookshelves. These regulars were writers like Naomi Mitchison, Anthony Hern, Margaret Cole, Arthur Calder-Marshall, Andrew Hope, Henry Treece, Roland Gant, Alex Comfort, Olaf Stapledon, Stevie Smith, Paul Potts, Rayner Heppenstall and Tribune's long-serving and consistently readable reviewer of the new novels of the 1940s, Daniel George. But before he began his many years' occupancy of that role, it was briefly filled by the man whom many have called the pre-eminent literary journalist of our time – George Orwell.

Orwell began reviewing for Tribune in March 1940, irregularly, until late 1943 when Bevan brought him in to succeed John Atkins as the paper's literary editor. Then the flowering of Tribune as a literary as well as political weekly became complete. Through his articles and his later weekly column, 'As I Please', Orwell offered explicit images of the proper concerns of the literary person of the Left – which were far from being highbrow, bookish or remote. The column dealt with anything that drew Orwell's interest, curiosity or anger, which meant nearly everything, in as personal, arbitrary and outspoken a way as its heading hints.

Space regrettably does not permit adequate samples of the sharp-edged plain speaking of those columns, with which a quite separate anthology might be filled. In their time they outraged many readers – to Orwell's delight, since their angry letters gave him meat for more columns. But also, then as regrettably sometimes now, some of his correspondents aimed their outrage at the whole cultural area of the paper which Orwell dominated. In the first issue of 1945 Orwell replied to these attacks:

A NEW YEAR MESSAGE

. . . a more general defence, or at least explanation, of our literary policy is needed, because there are certain criticisms of an adverse kind that come up in varying forms over and over again. Our critics are divisible into two main schools. It would be manifestly impossible to satisfy both, and in practice, I should say, impossible to satisfy either.

The first school accuses us of being lowbrow, vulgar, ignorant, obsessed with politics, hostile to the arts, dominated by back-scratching cliques and anxious to prevent talented young writers from getting a hearing. The other school accuses us of being highbrow, arty, bourgeois, indifferent to politics and constantly wasting space on material that can be of no interest to a working man and of no direct use to the Socialist movement. Both points need meeting, because between them they express a difficulty that is inherent in running any paper that is not a pure propaganda sheet.

Against the first school, we point out that *Tribune* reaches a large, heterogeneous Left Wing audience and cannot be turned into a sort of trade paper for young poets, or a tilting-ground on which rival gangs of Surrealists, Apocalyptics and what-not can fight out their battles . . .

As to the charge that we are dominated by cliques (contributions sometimes arrive with a sarcastic enquiry as to whether 'someone outside the clique' may put a word in), a quick glance through our back numbers would easily disprove it. The number of our contributors is much larger than is usual in a paper of these dimensions, and many of them are people whose work has hardly appeared elsewhere.

The other school of critics presents a more serious difficulty. Any Socialist paper which has a literary section is attacked from time to time by the person who says, 'What is the use of all this literary stuff? Does it bring Socialism any nearer? If not, drop it. Surely our task should be to work for Socialism and not waste our time on bourgeois literature?' There are various quick answers to this person (he is easily quelled, for instance, by pointing out that Marx wrote some excellent criticism on Shakespeare), but nevertheless he has a case. Here it is, put in an extreme form by a correspondent in last week's issue:

> 'May I ask if the Book Reviews in your paper contribute largely (if at all) to its upkeep? If not, why is so much precious space taken up each week with descriptions of books which (I guess) few of your readers buy?
>
> 'As a Socialist, my aim in life is to destroy Toryism.
>
> 'For this purpose I require all the ammunition I can get, and I look to *Tribune* as the main source of supply.
>
> 'You may reply that some of the books would be useful for that purpose, but I think it would be a very small percentage, and in any

case I have neither the money to buy nor the time to read them.'

This correspondent, by the way, like many others who write in the same vein, is under the misconception that in order to read books you have to buy them. Actually you could read most of the books mentioned in *Tribune* without ever buying a book from one year's end to the other. What else are libraries for – not merely Boots, Smith's, etc., but the public libraries at which anyone who numbers a householder among his acquaintances can get three tickets without any charge whatever? But our correspondent also assumes (a) that a Socialist needs no recreations, and (b) that books are of no use to the Socialist movement unless they consist of direct propaganda. It is this viewpoint that we tacitly challenge when, for instance, we use up a whole column on a poem, or print a popularisation of some little-known dead writer, or give a good review to a book written by a Conservative.

Even the most unpolitical book, even an outright reactionary book, can be of use to the Socialist movement if it provides reliable information or forces people to think. But we also assume that books are not to be regarded simply as propaganda, that literature exists in its own right – as a form of recreation, to put it no higher – and that a large number of our readers are interested in it. This involves, unavoidably, a slight divergence between the political and the literary sections of the paper. Obviously we cannot print contributions that grossly violate *Tribune*'s policy. Even in the name of free speech a Socialist paper cannot, for instance, throw open its columns to anti-semitic propaganda. But it is only in this negative sense that any pressure is put upon contributors to the literary end of the paper. Looking through the list of our contributors, I find among them Catholics, Communists, Trotskyists, Anarchists, Pacifists, Left-Wing Conservatives, and Labour Party supporters of all colours. All of them knew, of course, what kind of paper they were writing for and what topics were best left alone, but I think it is true to say that none of them has ever been asked to modify what he had written on the ground that it was 'not policy'.

This is particularly important in the case of book reviews, in which it is often difficult for the reviewer to avoid indicating his own opinion. To my knowledge, some periodicals coerce their reviewers into following the political line of the paper, even when they have to falsify their own opinions to do so. *Tribune* has never done this. We hold that the reviewer's job is to say what he thinks of the book he is dealing with, and not what we think our readers ought to think. And if, as a result, unorthodox opinions are expressed from time to time – even, on occasion, opinions that contradict some editorial statement at the other end of the paper – we believe that our readers are tough enough to stand a certain amount of diversity. We hold that the most perverse human being is more interesting than the most orthodox gramophone record. And though, in this section of the paper, our main aim is to talk about books as books, we believe that anyone who upholds the freedom of the intellect, in this age of lies and regimentation, is not serving the cause of Socialism so badly either.

[5 January 1945]

Some of the antipathy to Tribune's literary pages was probably occasioned by the extraordinary influx into them of the real literary thing – not just reviews but considerable short fiction and poetry. Stories had, of course, often been featured in previous years, and the willingness to print them had extended to a short-story competition that had swamped Orwell's desk in May 1944. But in the same New Year piece in which he defended his literary policy, Orwell regretfully announced that the printing of stories had to be abandoned as a consequence of that chronic ailment of Tribune through all its forty years – a lack of space sufficient to print all the good things that were there to be printed.

Poems, however, went on appearing. After Postgate's time Tribune's literary pages became what they still are in 1977, a place where good new or younger poets could have as strong a chance (or perhaps stronger) of seeing print than established ones, and thereby of reaching a far larger audience than in their usual stamping ground of the hard-up 'little magazines'. Nor were these poets required to adhere to any strong line of what a poem in a socialist paper should be. Many were naturally about the war, including one of Orwell's own infrequent excursions into verse, 'Memories of the Blitz':

. . . The blimp has a patch on its nose,
The railings have gone to the smelter;
Only the ghost and the cat
Sleep in the Anderson shelter . . .

[21 January 1944]

Out of the same impetus, after Aneurin Bevan had invited poets to submit their work in his 'new Tribune' of 2 January 1942, came frequent appearances by writers like Roy Fuller, Patric Dickinson, Laurie Lee or William Empson. In other issues the weekly poem might well have been unabashedly socialist, like Paul Potts's 'Because of Silone':

. . . And men in Fontamara heard
The pulse beats of history hammering out your news
That the working class is now the word made flesh
And that Christ hung up on Calvary
  Is man on main street, Stalingrad.

[31 December 1943]

But it might just as well have been the delicate imageries of Kathleen Raine's 'Seed' –

. . . Now the lilies open, and the rose
Released by summer from the harmless graves
That, centuries deep, are in the air we breathe
And in our earth, and in our daily bread . . .

[5 February 1943]

– which seems a world away from both war and socialist politics. Yet it is not a world or even a step away from *all* the values that socialists strive, hopefully, to preserve, and that Orwell and his contributors exhibited in Tribune.

Sadly, Bevan's Tribune had room for only token nods to the other arts, such as Winifred Horrabin's 'Shows' (film and theatre) column – weekly until the worsening paper shortage forced its sacrifice along with some other features. Otherwise, writing about music or art exhibitions or records occurred very rarely and very briefly – except for the unflagging (in Postgate's time) survey of 'war radio' by Fred Harold. But that was not so much a review as a collection of snippets from what foreign broadcasters had to say about the progress of the war.

Even so, there was no shortage in Tribune of comments on domestic broadcasting – though, again, not as reviews but as socio-political notes, mostly derogatory. Indeed, Postgate seemed to have a vendetta against the BBC, for its 'reactionary' and 'public school' attitudes, but also for its bumbling or ill-judged efforts at censorship and news management. Postgate's ire rose, for instance, over 'The refusal to allow Sir Hugh Roberton and the Orpheus Choir to broadcast . . . due to a BBC ban, officially imposed, because Sir Hugh holds pacifist views and refused to renege them. This is peculiarly disgraceful and stupid . . .' (6 December 1940). And it rose more often and more fully on general principles, as when Postgate attacked the BBC for providing not a *news* service but 'a *commentary* on the news, telling us what we are to think, with some items of news embedded in it' (28 February 1941).

Other attacks on the BBC were in many cases only indirectly concerned with the effects of the war on the corporation or its audience. So it was with many Tribune considerations of British life in the 1940s. The war never receded entirely into the background, but some contributors on domestic subjects were more anxious to deal with, first, the carry-over of old pre-war obstacles to true democratic and socialist progress, and, secondly, programmes for sweeping reforms that would overcome the obstacles and bring into being a brave new world at the war's end. Such programmes were even being broadly outlined when the war itself had scarcely begun – as when Postgate ran a 'Where Are We Going?' symposium in mid-1940, in which Harold Laski anticipated 'UNFETTERING BRITISH DEMOCRACY' by freeing unions' bargaining methods, reforming education, nationalizing 'pivotal' industries and more (26 July 1940).

The metamorphosis of the sorry past into the hopeful post-war future preoccupied writers on specific subjects like housing, city planning and the environment generally, especially with the opportunities for replanning that were to come in rebuilding the blitzed areas. So, on 4 February 1944, Foster Dickinson could call for 'Homes, Not Shelters'. But the chances of a fresh start after the war opened up in front of commentators on that all-pervasive problem of poverty – including Margaret Cole in a no-punches-pulled series in June–July 1940 on 'THE TWO NATIONS IN BRITAIN' which itself dealt with housing ('the rich have houses, the poor have "housing" ') and also with income inequality, food and health and educational class differences.

Margaret Cole returned to that subject often in Tribune's columns, notably in book reviews, where she was at her acerbic best on the public schools and educational reform in general: 'Pre-war British education, with its snobbish segregation of classes, its ludicrous under-valuation of technical skill, and its absolute lack of interest in the vast majority of the nation as soon as it reached the age of fourteen, came very near to losing us the war; and our rulers know that this must not happen again' (29 August 1941).

In similar attacking vein was Jennie Lee – in the 'As I Please' column which she took over from Orwell when he left the paper in early 1945: 'It is only when the price ticket is removed from the school gate that really democratic schooling can flourish. Until then some parents are in the impossible position of having to put up with their children being trained to react either as serfs or snobs' (9 March 1945).

By then, that milestone in British education, the so-called 'Butler Education Act' of 1944, had been fought over and finally passed. But Tribune's K. Holland saw it as no more than 'PIE IN THE SKY' as long as it proposed to increase the number of children in schools without at the same time making concrete proposals for increasing the numbers of teachers and adequate school buildings.

But if, from the viewpoint of the 1940s, there was one special area where reform was desperately needed, it was in the general state of industry and the working man. The arrival of the 'national unity' of war had not wiped away any of the scars of the 1920s and 1930s. Austen Albu felt that Britain's workers had become 'deeply cynical about the powers of those who control our economic life' (27 November 1942). As the war stormed on, workers' grievances and disenchantment mounted with the launching by the coalition Cabinet of anti-strike and anti-union legislation in 1944. Labour's leaders connived in it, Aneurin Bevan fought it with all his strength – and was again nearly expelled from the party as a result.

Yet by then the hopes for future change were beginning to resemble real prospects, for the Allied advance across Europe was accelerating, and even the most die-hard pessimists admitted, after D-Day 1944, that victory was in sight. So post-war domestic planning gained even further space in Tribune. If there was an individual article in the paper during the 1940s that gave the clearest hint of peace-time changes to come, it was not really Arthur Smith on 'Who Holds Up Land Planning?' (2 June 1944) or Bevan's 'Fascism for the Coal Mines' (26 January 1945), but an earlier piece, from 1942, on an independent report that launched a thousand battles. It embodied the revolutionary principle of the state's *overall* responsibility for the welfare of its citizens; and Bevan's exuberant appraisal of it was one of the first reverberant rallyings to the attack on behalf of that principle that would shake the nation for the rest of the 1940s, and shakes it still:

BEVERIDGE MANIFESTO

In a general sense the decision to allow a report on social conditions to appear at this time was the work of a guilty national conscience. No return to the conditions of the past were thought possible. The Left were demanding the pledge of a new world. The Right (in the days of military inactivity) realised the perils of withstanding concession. No doubt they believed that a goodly array of burnished platitudes would stay the avalanche of public opinion until they were stronger for the fight and until their conscience had relapsed into its old accustomed inertia. Nothing else can explain the political lunacy (from their own point of view) of Mr Churchill and his friends which has tolerated the publication of Sir William's findings. For the mouse has been in labour and has brought forth a mountain.

Sir William Beveridge is a social evangelist of the old Liberal school. He is an honoured member of the Reform Club, and the horizon of his political aspirations is, therefore, not boundless. He specifically disavows many of the tenets of revolutionary Socialism. But he has a good heart and a clear, well-stocked head, and he has discharged his task with Liberal fervour and even a trace of Liberal innocence.

What kind of world would the honest Liberal like to establish? He would like to make a truce between private enterprise and State ownership. He would like the two to work in harness together, but, above all, he would like, by resolute action, to appease the most obvious pains and to succour the most grievous casualties which capitalism produces. From this dangerous angle Sir William has approached his task. He would like to establish a tolerable minimum standard of security for every citizen, for the injured worker, for the widow, for the aged, for the unemployed, for the sick and for the growing child.

This is a commendable ambition, and the desire to achieve it is certainly not confined to those who have dabbled or delved into Socialism. But the merit and novelty of Sir William is that he has set down with the authority of a statistician and on Government notepaper the conditions which must be satisfied if this modest ambition is to be achieved. Here it is in black and white – a plain description of man's necessities, how much (or how little) he must have in his pocket if fear and want and hunger are to be lifted from his cares and if the grandiloquent phrases of the Atlantic Charter are to be translated into fact. In short, Sir William has described the conditions in which the tears might be taken out of capitalism. We should not be surprised, therefore, if all unconsciously by so doing he threatens capitalism itself.

Sir William states plainly that human claims must come first. The miner choked by silicosis, the worker who loses a finger in his machine, the old man and his wife who have done their lifetime of service, the widow who has lost her husband, the husband whose job has become momentarily redundant, the child whose parents cannot give him the best, none of these and none of the others who have suf-

From the wartime Tribune, one of Jack Chen's drawings to accompany Anthony Hern's article on 'The People of the Tubes' (27 September 1940); 'Probo's' view of Britain's attitude to the Second Front (7 August 1943) and the government's stance on the Beveridge Report (19 February 1943); and Mullally's ironic footnote to VE Day (11 May 1945).

"We're visiting friends in Hampstead—underground!"

"The Second Front is desirable, old boy—but hardly urgent"

THE GOVERNMENT TAKES A "BALANCED" VIEW

fered the disabilities of our society in the past must suffer in the future. It is an outrage that men should be the victims of these harrowing fears. To keep their bodies healthy, to ease their minds, to release their souls – these are the first claims on the State. The claim of property must come second. . .

It will still be a battle, but we must thank Sir William for a weapon. And if it be asked how it happens that a reformer so sedate has been able to fashion a weapon so sharp, and how a Government so timid should have presented materials for its fashioning, we must answer in the famous words of Karl Marx, 'that war is the locomotive of history'.

[*Editorial*, 4 December 1942]

Three years later, that 'locomotive of history' ran out of track. But Tribune joined the celebrations after VE Day, May 1945, almost perfunctorily – looking past them at the Herculean tasks ahead. Hitler was gone, but the real enemies remained, entrenched as ever. And Tribune went without pause into the attack on them, for victory and socialism, as the build-up to a general election began a third and most momentous stage of its existence.

3 FACING THE FUTURE (1945–51)

Britain went to the polls in July 1945 and shocked the world by turning out the war leader whose near-mythical stature had seemed to assure, to most prophets, an irresistible Tory victory. Explanations abounded for this turnaround, but at the time Labour felt exultant rather than analytical, and Tribune exulted with the party, especially with the host of new MPs. 'Already our people had started off robustly by the spontaneous singing of the Red Flag,' wrote Jennie Lee about the new Parliament in her 'As I Please' column, adding fondly, 'Soon they would know that this was not "done" . . .' (10 August 1945).

In the same issue a Tribune editorial offered assurances: 'It will be the function of "Tribune" to sustain the Labour Government against the enemies of Socialism . . . Its duty each week will be to interpret the Labour Government to the people and the people to the Labour Government' (10 August 1945).

A few months later, the paper had added to these undertakings a more practical note of qualification, in an editorial whose heading invested new political meaning in a New Year's cliché:

> OUT WITH THE OLD, IN WITH THE NEW
> Here in Britain, the return of a Labour Government with a clear working majority gives us a superb opportunity. It could not have happened at a more opportune time. These early post-war years are beset

with dangers and difficulties, but it is precisely at such times and in such conditions that the people ask for leadership that is bold and new, programmes that are at once iconoclastic and constructive . . .

Tribune is proud of Britain's Labour Government, and will do everything in its power to sustain it in these tasks. We will do this because we are devoted to the socialist ideal. But, because we are an independent socialist journal, and not an organ of diplomacy, we give notice – if any is needed – that we are not prepared to tell lies in the service of any Government, even a Labour Government. We will continue to offer, at all times, socialist analysis and comment. This means that, from time to time, we may give offence to Ministers and Government departments, for it is the way of all governments to prefer praise to adverse criticism. But this we promise: that when our views do not march in step with the Government's policies, the divergence will not be rooted in caprice or niggling disagreement. We may not always be correct in our political advocacy; the doctrine of infallibility belongs, with the Inquisition, to an earlier era. But we will demand at all times that our arguments be proved or disproved by their relevance or lack of relevance to Socialism's fundamental principles. We will reject any other standard of judgment . . .

For the most part, we shall keep our eyes on the British Government, for it will be over this Government's actions that we can exercise the greater measure of control. But *Tribune* is a journal of international socialism. This means that it must be interested in the foreign policies of all nations, that it must judge these policies in the light of its international socialist faith, and that it must cross swords with all who seek to endow any Government, here or abroad, with a semi-religious immunity to criticism . . .

[28 December 1945]

In the same end-of-the-year issue, Jack Wilkes, the long-serving Parliamentary Correspondent (who was, in fact, George Strauss), weighed up the new government and concluded that in its first months it had proved to be 'second rate' – sorting too slowly through the coalition leftovers, groping too confusedly towards new policies and planning, progressing too hesitantly towards socialism. Yet Wilkes and most others still wanted to give the benefit of the doubt, knowing that the government faced a dauntingly immense task as it set out to reshape Britain at a time of post-war hardship, shortages and crisis which called for inordinate effort merely to keep up with events.

The party's manifesto had borne the title *Let Us Face the Future*, and that theme was taken up again by J. P. W. Mallalieu in a closely argued series published by Tribune through late 1946 and early 1947 under the overall title of 'Did Labour Face the Future?' The consensus generally seemed to be that it had – that, in spite of towering problems and needs remaining to be tackled, huge forward steps had been taken in those fifteen months. The paper's weekly informational-cum-editorial roundup of 'What's Happening' encapsulated what had been accomplished in a few breathless paragraphs which hint at a picture of new parliamentarians flogging themselves to exhaustion to sweep away generations of misrule:

THINGS DONE

People are odd. We have just lived through a revolution and because there was no riot, no death, no terror – and no romance – in it, we have passed it by. Instead, the limelight is on the Royal crush in Leicester Square, and on the daily grumbles which our free and disinterested mammoth Press helps us to remember. Perhaps it's the fault of the Labour Party. It has not produced a recorder or current historian to do for us in peace what Churchill did during the war. But it is not quite so simple: people tire far more quickly of glorious and finest hours than of grumbling about queues and shortages and prices.

But in case anybody is interested, it is worth recording that the first session of the Labour Government's Parliament which ended on Wednesday did more revolutionary things to this country than the first three years after the 1917 Revolution did for Russia.

It has passed more acts of social reform and national advancement in this one year than most Conservative and Liberal Parliaments have passed in a quarter of a century. The 84 major and minor acts that are now the law of the land include Family Allowances, the National Insurance Bill, the National Health Scheme, the Nationalising of the Bank and of Coal, the Civil Aviation Bill and a vast range of industrial control measures that have saved this country from the chaos now visiting the decontrolled United States.

Extraordinarily little is known about this revolution of ours and the wars of economic intervention we have to face from inside the country and from outside and very few people abroad are aware of the real meaning of the transformation that this Parliament has wrought. The Government Information Agencies have failed badly in this and it is hardly surprising; the Central Office of Information does not appear to have heard of any changes that have occurred since Labour took office. It seems far more concerned with plugging the line abroad that everything is just sweet continuity . . .

['*What's Happening*', 8 November 1946]

From a survey of steps taken to a statement (aimed for the 1947 Labour Conference) of those urgently outstanding was a natural progress for the Left. The statement came in a widely influential pamphlet – *Keep Left* – not explicitly Tribune's but obviously Tribunesque by its signatories, who included Foot, Mikardo, Crossman, Mallalieu, Donald Bruce, Benn Levy and other Left-wing MPs (not to mention George Wigg and Woodrow Wyatt!). Jennie Lee summarized its main proposals, regarding manpower shortages and economic planning especially, asserting also that 'The Labour Movement is getting ready to do what it has done so often in the past – to lead its leaders' (9 May 1947).

Some of the pamphlet's other proposals were recalled much later by Ian Mikardo, in his new, breezy but keen-edged Tribune column ('Another Man's Poison'), who pointed out how many of *Keep Left*'s proposals had become policy – among them, more 'urgency' in forward planning, some particularized profits taxes, a Ministry of Economic Affairs, and so on (17 December 1948).

The Left was never averse to praising the government when praise was due. The great nationalizations produced a rich seam of rejoicing throughout those years, from the initial acquisition of the Bank of England – although Ivor Moresby's look at 'The New Lady of Threadneedle Street' saw it as mostly a 'symbolic act' (12 October 1945). Attlee's government also reached out quickly for civil aviation, electricity and gas, and eventually the railways. But more deeply satisfying than any of these was the nationalization of coal. 'The Pits Are Ours', glowed a 'What's Happening' editorial on 1 February 1946, after the Bill's second reading, and echoed the unselfconscious pride of that heading with another, later, when the Bill became law: 'The Mines Are Ours' (24 May 1946).

Behind this socialist pride lay the same grim picture of obstacle and hardship that faced the new government everywhere – and that cropped up especially between Labour and that other crucial nationalization on which so much forward planning depended, steel. The paper outlined some of the vociferous public opposition in the Tory press ('WOOLLINESS ON STEEL', 3 May 1946) and the more backstairs opposition organized by big business ('THE STEEL CONSPIRACY', 9 August 1946). Then 'THE STEEL MYSTERY' (23 August 1946) began to wonder – was Attlee backing away from the fight? Certainly the problems were manifold: 'The bigshots of the steel industry have roundly refused to co-operate with the Government in the essential re-organization and modernization of the industry as long as the re-organization schemes were linked up with preparations for nationalization'. But, Tribune warned time and again, the Left would stomach no 'INDECISION ON STEEL' (20 September 1946), and certainly not a 'RETREAT FROM STEEL' (8 August 1947).

So the battle, and the hesitancies, dragged on. And other battles became entangled in the fight over steel – including the continual ire in Tribune over the government's failures in public relations, keeping the people informed about Labour's purposes and principles which *Keep Left* had pronounced upon. Still, there was some excuse – not the least in the unremitting hate-Labour campaign in the Tory-dominated media, who were almost daily (in the words of a Jon Kimche article on 4 April 1947) 'Preparing for Attlee's Funeral'. The factionalism and news-management of the national press, to which we are still victim in the 1970s, brought in 1946 a respected journalist to a state of high dudgeon in Tribune's columns:

WHO CONTROLS THE PRESS?

The Royal Commission that is to inquire into the Press will, I trust, cover the widest possible ground. Unless it does, many of my doubts about the freedom of my profession will not be dissipated.

I should like to share Beverley Baxter's belief, expressed to the Commons, that every London editor would behave as the man in charge of the *Daily Express* did once – threaten an advertiser with a 25-year ban if he did not withdraw a threat to cease advertising in its columns for two years unless there were a change in its editorial policy.

If I did share that belief it would give me greater confidence in the liberty of my profession than I now possess. It would make me less likely to believe, for instance, what I was told after I had attended a Bertram Mills circus lunch, for the *Daily Express*, some years ago that, because Mills was a big advertiser, my article had been submitted to the management for approval . . .

Then will someone authoritatively deny the rumours that, in certain newspaper quarters, there was inside-the-office talk of a deal with Hitler? Who will tell us the source of the money with which newspapers were purchased? Did any of it come from industrial speculation? If so – I do not say it did – the fact might reasonably cause a prejudice in favour of Big Business.

What, too, is the extent of 'petticoat government' that is often whispered about – most slanderously, I am sure – in at least one important newspaper building? Surely it is not true, as they often say, that 'the boss's wife must see a proof'.

Then, in how many Socialist towns are all the local newspapers controlled by anti-Socialists and in how many Tory towns, if any, is the entire Press anti-Tory? If it is true in any one town, how can it be true that we live under a democratic system? . . .

Then, how often are newspaper peerages given as a reward for eulogies of the Government of the day? Is it true that they are always conferred so that their owners can improve the debates in the Lords by contributing that wise political judgment seen in the leading articles they pay other people to write?

Is it true, too, that leading articles written in London are sent over the Creed machines to chain-store editors in provincial towns who are no longer allowed to have a printed opinion of their own unless some millionaire in far-away London gives his O.K.?

If the answers to these questions, and to many others I could suggest, prove to the country that its Press is really free and uncontrolled, the sittings of the Royal Commission will allay many of the suspicions I hear whispered. They will, indeed, hearten me as to the future.

For a tied-house system in journalism, if it exists, means that millions could be wrongly informed, wrongly guided, and made to become fearful when they should be stalwart, and panicky when they should be calm.

[*Hannen Swaffer*, 15 November 1946]

Labour was visibly ringed round by an 'unholy alliance' (Michael Foot's phrase, 12 August 1949) of enemies. Among them, standing especially four-square in the way of the Steel Bill, was an obstructionist House of Lords – which had in 1947 also bared its elderly teeth over the nationalization of transport and the docks. Steel and other crucial legislation was delayed while Labour cleared away this and other dead wood left over from days of pre-democratic privilege. 'The Real Issue in the Fight with the Lords' was simply that '. . . Labour demands the right in its fourth year of office to possess the same immunity from decisive intervention by the House of Lords which every Tory Government in this century has in practice possessed' (Editorial, 17 September 1948).

The Parliament Bill finally became law, and the way was cleared for the public ownership of steel in 1950–51 (in time to become a Tory priority for *de*nationalization – but that is anticipating).

In other areas where Labour faced the future, Tribune proved less impatient or dissatisfied. In late 1945, Ivor Moresby sympathized with the problems of Attlee's new Minister of Housing, Aneurin Bevan, while other writers were kind about plans for dealing with questions of town planning, rents, landlords and land ownership itself. Two years later Jennie Lee remembered that 'We Promised Them Houses' and found that, 'To date, more progress has been made in housing than in any other major Government commitment' (23 May 1947). Her article *in toto* hinted at many of the complications and stumbling-blocks (shortage of materials especially), but again, achievement was manifest and recognized. Earlier the poet and author Emanuel Litvinoff had recognized it too, writing about East London's clearance of slums and remembering just what it was that needed clearing:

HOMES IN THE SKY

Side by side in a small street off Bethnal Green Road twin tenements faced across six yards of cobbles and paving stones to a square factory building whose small windows were covered in wire mesh. These tall forbidding buildings were the dominant features of a street of cramped artisan dwellings. There was little to distinguish the tenements from the factory except that the former were over-populous and their windows drably curtained and dimly gas-lit at night. Each consisted of ten apartments, erected like a structure of orange boxes placed one on top of the other, and each apartment of two small rooms and a narrow scullery. Between them they gave shelter to a population of 100 to 120 men, women and children. A cobbler and his family of five lived and worked in one of the ground floor flats, a furrier with a wife and three children carried on business next door to him, and two widows of the 1914–18 war supported large families by home dressmaking in upper apartments of the same tenement.

The lives of these inhabitants were exposed by day and night to the public ear in a pathetic, inescapable medley of sound. The rooms were soundboxes uninsulated against the neighbours and the street. A child cried with toothache monotonously, like the noise of water running down a drain, and people were kept awake until it fell asleep through exhaustion. The voices of men and women talking or quarrelling in bed penetrated the walls and ceilings of neighbouring flats. On the attic floor, six flights up the narrow stairs, there lived a woman who got drunk every Saturday night and wept maudlin tears until long after midnight. Down in the small stone passage the amorous scuffling of courting couples was audible to the top of the building. Machines trundled: men and women laughed and quarrelled: children played and battled: people were born and died in this public atmosphere. Circumstances forced on them a kind of reluctant community.

The sixty dwellers of each tenement shared the amenities provided by a tiny yard about 15 feet square filled by three w.c.'s and a large wooden dustbin. Every morning a procession of people carried night-soil buckets down to the yard to be emptied into the W.C.'s, of which no more than two seemed to be in working order at the same time. There would also be a procession carrying refuse to the wooden bin which was entirely inadequate for the purpose so that half-way through the week rubbish was piled all over the yard. The water supply could be cut off from the upper flats simply by running the taps on the ground floor. More than twenty young children used the yard, the narrow stone passage and the street outside as a playground. Epidemics, when they came, spread amongst them like disease among rabbits . . .

[*Emanuel Litvinoff*, 18 October 1946]

Articles like this enhanced Tribune's continuing concern with the plight of the poor: as Ivor Moresby's heading on 12 April 1946 expressed it, 'The Rich Still Sit On Our Backs'. Barbara Castle followed a similar theme when considering the previous government's late vote-catcher of family allowances in which she saw the built-in catch of the 'clawback', which she called 'FAMILY DISALLOWANCES':

One of the most hard hit groups is the widows getting 10s. a week contributory pension. These women have been struggling to bring up a family on 5s. each for the first two children and 3s. each for the rest. To them the extra 5s. would have been a boon but they find that, since the payment of Family Allowances, they get nothing extra for the second child and only 2s. a week more for the rest of the family. If they go to the Assistance Board to have these benefits supplemented (and in 1944 nearly 34,000 widows applied for supplementation), they are once again deprived of the extra help that Family Allowances are intended to give because the Board will take these payments into account . . .

[30 August 1946]

So went the pattern of Tribune's response to Labour's government in those years. Jewels there were in the new crown, but only the most blinkered apologist could fail to note that they were fewer than had been hoped, often smaller and sometimes in rather poor settings.

Except for one – the one that was the personal achievement and triumph of Aneurin Bevan. Hugh Ferguson blew the trumpets for it:

A PEOPLE'S MEDICAL SERVICE

Two years ago, when the National Government's White Paper on a National Health Service appeared, *Tribune* welcomed it as a great advance, in spite of the various compromises it proposed. Now a Labour

Minister of Health has submitted his own National Health Service Bill to Parliament to give the service its final shape and throw it open to the public in 1948. If it is implemented in the spirit in which it is drawn up, it should make Britain's public health service a model for the world.

While the Tory Press does its worst to draw public attention to the grievances of the doctors, the ordinary citizen has hardly had time to consider what the new Bill will mean to *him*. He has been used to insurance stamps and means tests, to endless queues, on the one hand, and Harley Street on the other, to a multiplicity of services which worked in isolation from each other and among which it was difficult for him to find his way. Above all, he has been used to the idea that the best medical service is only available to those who can pay for it.

Now he is faced with a completely new situation. Medical care and ability to pay will no longer be connected. Every man, woman and child in the country will be entitled to a complete medical service, without charge. Each person will retain the right to choose his own doctor from among those practising in the neighbourhood, but that doctor will in future work from a health centre, with diagnostic aids and auxiliary staff at his disposal so that he can devote his full time to his patients. He will be a member of a medical team instead of practising alone and competing with his colleagues for patients.

Through the health centre, the citizen will have access to the services he needs, from nursing and domestic assistance at home to medical appliances and in-patient treatment in the hospital. In short, medical care will become a public responsibility, which implies that it must be of an equally high standard for the rich and the poor, for towns-people and for those living in the country, that medical resources must be fairly distributed, planned in accordance with need and paid out of public funds. These principles have long been part of the Labour Party's programme . . .

In some other respects it is less far-reaching than the Labour Party's National Plan for Health. While it enrages some of the diehards of the B.M.A. who are mainly concerned with medical 'private enterprise', it may disappoint some of the Labour Party's friends who hoped that a full-time salaried service and complete separation between public and private practice would stand at the beginning of the Labour Party's health plan . . .

[29 March 1946]

This new legislation, following what Tribune had called 'A People's Bill' establishing the National Insurance provisions

(1 February 1946), went through despite entrenched opposition from the BMA, the press and their vested-interest allies – even though Bevan's opponents ('THE SILLY MUTINEERS' – 29 November 1946) tried to keep up a guerrilla action after the battle was won. They were still deep in their last ditch in 1948, which 'What's Happening' astringently called 'Their Kampf' (6 February 1948). But their *kampf* led to their Waterloo, and in early 1949 in a Tribune interview Bevan could announce that the NHS was operative and that, 'Well over 90 per cent of the population, probably nearer 95 per cent, are taking part in the scheme; 90 per cent of the dentists, and roughly the same proportion of doctors' (14 January 1949). In that success, it could be said, Labour had not only faced the future but had gone far towards *creating* it – that is, creating the society we live in in the 1970s.

With Bevan's and George Strauss's departure from the paper to the government in 1945, Tribune had had to face a new future of its own. Michael Foot, Jennie Lee and Patricia Strauss had gone on to the board in those heady days of post-electoral change; and the editorship had gone to Jon Kimche and Evelyn Anderson. In late 1946 a 'new Tribune' was announced, but it was new mainly in terms of page numbers (some paper restrictions had been lifted) and a new-look front page, which lasted only three weeks under an avalanche of readers' criticism. Still, the paper was making itself new over those years, not only because of new editors but because of new problems and battles and obligations. When the paper reached its tenth birthday in 1947, the editor and some leading 'old hands' greeted the occasion with some nostalgic notes on that first decade. Bevan and Strauss naturally chose the birthday to remind Tribune readers about the new government's need for all the friends it could get; Victor Gollancz joined the celebration to recall the spirit that had created Tribune, but also to mourn its (he felt) absence from the new socialist government: 'The plain fact is that, while our Government has many fine, and one or two magnificent achievements to its credit, it has shown an almost complete absence of the one thing which above all was wanted in the most desperate crisis that humanity has ever faced – I am thinking about the post-war, not the war, crisis – namely, moral leadership . . .' (31 January 1947).

But of all the articles in that anniversary issue, that by George

Orwell offers some of the most tasty titbits about the paper's past (and Orwell's) and how it developed:

AS I PLEASED

. . . I did not learn of the existence of *Tribune* till some time in 1939. It had started in 1937, but of the thirty months that intervened before the outbreak of war I spent five in hospital and thirteen abroad. What first drew my attention to it, I believe, was a none too friendly review of a novel of mine. During the period 1939–42 I produced three or four books and reprints, and I think it is true that I never had what is called a 'good' review in *Tribune* until after I became a member of the staff. (The two events were unconnected, needless to say.) Somewhat later, in the cold winter of 1939, I started writing for *Tribune*, though at first, curiously enough, without seeing it regularly or getting a clear idea of what kind of paper it was.

Raymond Postgate, who was then editor, had asked me to do the novel reviews from time to time. I was not paid (until recently it was unusual for contributors to left-wing papers to be paid), and I only saw the paper on the somewhat rare occasions when I went up to London and visited Postgate in a bare and dusty office near London Wall. *Tribune* (until a good deal later everyone called it 'the' *Tribune*) was at that time in difficulties. It was still a threepenny paper aimed primarily at the industrial workers and following more or less the Popular Front line which had been associated with the Left Book Club and the Socialist League. With the outbreak of war its circulation had taken a severe knock, because the Communists and near-Communists who had been among its warmest supporters now refused to help in distributing it . . .

Early in 1940 there was a large meeting in a public hall, the purpose of which was to discuss both the future of *Tribune* and the policy of the left wing of the Labour Party. As is usual on such occasions nothing very definite was said, and what I chiefly remember is a political tip which I received from an inside source. The Norway campaign was ending in disaster, and I had walked to the hall past gloomy posters. Two M.P.s, whom I will not name, had just arrived from the House.

'What chance is there,' I asked them, 'of this business getting rid of Chamberlain?'

'Not a hope,' they both said. 'He's solid.'

I don't remember dates, but I think it can only have been a week or two before Chamberlain was out of the Premiership.

After that *Tribune* passed out of my consciousness for nearly two years. I was very busy trying to earn a living and write a book amid the bombs and the general disorganisation, and any spare time I had was taken up by the Home Guard which was still an amateur force and demanded an immense amount of work from its members. When I became aware of *Tribune* again I was working in the Eastern Service of the B.B.C. It was now an almost completely different paper. It had a different make-up, cost sixpence, was orientated chiefly towards foreign policy, and was rapidly acquiring a new public which mostly belonged, I should say, to the out-at-elbow middle class. Its prestige among the B.B.C. personnel was very striking. In the libraries where commentators went to prime themselves it was one of the most sought-after periodicals, not only because it was largely written by people who knew something at first hand about Europe, but because it was then the only paper of any standing which criticised the Government. Perhaps 'criticised' is an over-mild word. Sir Stafford Cripps had gone into the Government, and the fiery personality of Aneurin Bevan gave the paper its tone . . .

During this period I occasionally wrote articles for *Tribune*, but only at long intervals, because I had little time or energy. However, towards the end of 1943 I decided to give up my job in the B.B.C., and I was asked to take over the literary editorship of *Tribune*, in place of John Atkins, who was expecting call-up. I went on being literary editor, as well as writing the 'As I Please' column, until the beginning of 1945. It was interesting, but it is not a period that I look back on with pride. The fact is that I am no good at editing. I hate planning ahead, and I have a psychical or even physical inability to answer letters. My most essential memory of that time is of pulling out a drawer here and a drawer there, finding it in each case to be stuffed with letters and manuscripts which ought to have been dealt with weeks earlier, and hurriedly shutting it up again. Also, I have a fatal tendency to accept manuscripts which I know very well are too bad to be printed. It is questionable whether anyone who has had long experience as a freelance journalist ought to become an editor. It is too like taking a convict out of his cell and making him governor of the prison. Still, it was 'all experience', as they say, and I have friendly memories of my cramped little office looking out on a back yard, and the three of us who shared it huddling in the corner as the doodle-bugs came zooming over, and the peaceful click-click of the typewriters starting up again as soon as the bomb had crashed . . .

For six months during the summer of 1946 I gave up being a writer in *Tribune* and became merely a reader, and no doubt from time to time I shall do the same again; but I hope that my association with it may long continue, and I hope that in 1957 I shall be writing another anniversary article. I do not even hope that by that time *Tribune* will have slaughtered all its rivals. It takes all sorts to make a world, and if one could work these things out one might discover that even the ———serves a useful purpose. Nor is *Tribune* itself perfect, as I should know, having seen it from the inside. But I do think that it is the only existing weekly paper that makes a genuine effort to be both progressive and humane – that is, to combine a radical Socialist policy with a respect for freedom of speech and a civilised attitude towards literature and the arts: and I think that its relative popularity, and even its survival in its present form for five years or more, is a hopeful symptom.

[31 January 1947]

'Orientated chiefly towards foreign policy,' said Orwell. So the paper had been, understandably, during the war; so it very much remained after the peace, perhaps also understandably, given Jon Kimche's strong international awareness. And so it largely continued when Kimche relinquished his share of the editorship to Michael Foot in 1948 (Evelyn Anderson remaining co-editor). Foot launched himself into the driving seat with a sweeping introductory editorial – blatantly headed 'Declaration of War':

'The Editors of Tribune wish their readers a Happy New Year, and beg to inform them that Tribune will spend the next twelve months fighting for Socialism, lambasting the Tories, exposing humbug, discrediting frauds, and generally upholding *together* the claims of the community and the right of heresy in the fields of art, science, literature and politics . . .' (2 January 1948).

Foot's 'heretical' Tribune shouted battle-cries, crusaded and laid about it fearlessly, sometimes to the distress of friends as well as enemies. Soon enough, in fact, the new editor picked a delicious fight with a doughty old battler who had been a sometime ally, and who left the young editor with a few honourable bruises:

THE WAY AHEAD

Bernard Shaw stopped thinking about fifteen years ago. He can still write like an angel, but how fortunate it would have been for his reputation if all those praises of Mussolini, those protests to *The Times* about income-tax, and all the rest of the gibberish he has poured forth in the past decade could be forgotten. He writes an article for the *Daily Herald* as if all the great convulsions of recent times had never happened. Many years ago he hit on the paradox that Stalin in Russia had adopted his own ideas of Fabianism. He hasn't been able to think of anything new since. The upheavals involved in collectivisation, forced labour, diplomatic secrecy and bureaucratic tyranny – all these are mere trivialities. Was he not always opposed to notions of parliamentary democracy? Very well, then. Stalin's methods only prove how right was Shaw. The same great man who had nothing sensible to say on the greatest war in history has nothing to offer now but the same fulsome flattery for Sovietism which he once lavished on Italian Fascism. Meanwhile, under the old man's nose, more houses – and better houses – are being built for poor people in the blitzed cities of Britain than in Moscow, and little English children are growing up taller and stronger than any generation before . . .

[*Michael Foot*, 21 May 1948]

Shaw, naturally, replied in kind to this 'unprovoked attack' the next week. 'It may be, as he says, that I ceased to think fifteen years ago; but as I was then at least thirty years ahead of my time, he has still fifteen years to catch up with me.' And he went on: 'I maintain that our Parliamentary Party System is not only utterly undemocratic, but far too slow for Socialism . . .' (28 May 1948).

Foot promptly went for him again, with a ringing defence of the advances made by socialism within parliamentary democracy, and castigated the sage for the joking tone of his reply. Shaw came back:

The careers of Mussolini and Hitler were produced solely by the disgust and disillusion of the proletariat with party parliaments, which, as I pointed out again and again, took thirty years to do the work of a week and ended in thirty years' work having to be done in thirty days by sheer bloodshed. Ask any Irishman. I am an Irishman.

The difficulty about governing Englishmen, as Cromwell discovered, is their incorrigible quarrelsomeness. Mr Foot is quarrelling with me out of sheer pugnacity. It broke up all the Socialist Societies except the Fabian Society, where I had no end of trouble holding the Fabians together. That is why I had to say that the chief obstacles to Socialism were the Socialists . . .

And now I am quite ready to shake hands with Mr Foot, and beg him to stop hitting me in the face for no earthly reason. At 92 I have no time left for such games.

[11 June 1948]

Foot did stop hitting him – but he never desisted from hitting, hard and often, anyone else whom he felt needed it. As his Tribune was 'pugnacious' politically, so it was unconventional, unpredictable, in other areas – notably its literary and arts coverage. After all, Orwell was still literary editor when Foot joined the paper; and in his day readers might one week have Sean O'Casey's Irish communism illuminating an essay on Gorky or Yeats or Irish theatre, then another week have Robert Graves ruminating on Milton, Edith Sitwell dissecting the meaning of *Hamlet* or Feliks Topolski proffering the idea of extended state support for the arts.

Other cultural issues coming in for their share of attention were both familiar and new: the BBC, as always, and the monopolistic tendencies of the J. Arthur Rank Organization (on which Michael Foot had often a few words to say to the young head of the Board of Trade, Harold Wilson), and later the Festival of Britain on the South Bank which led to the further projection of the National Theatre idea. On that, Tribune's new theatre reviewer, Richard Findlater, worried about '. . . the cramped space available and the dangers of isolation in a wilderness of office barracks' (5 October 1951).

In the course of those years the books and arts pages introduced many new contributors, not the least T. R. Fyvel, who in 1948 faced the unenviable task of following Orwell in the literary editorship. He managed it with ease and style, which were also generally the hallmark of his pages, along with quality of reviewers. Any note of frequent contributors in the late 1940s might upset the other notables left out – but, risking that, present among reviewers were Julian Symons, Roy Fuller, Richard Hoggart, C. V. Wedgwood, Stevie Smith, Jack Lindsay, Peter Vansittart, William Empson (occasionally), Naomi Lewis, Oswell Blakeston (a regular still, today), David Wright, Edmund Crispin, Frederic Mullally (who also reviewed films, awhile), Robert Muller, Jon Manchip White, John Berger . . .

Coverage of the other arts expanded after the war: joining the usual film and theatre reviews were columns on music, radio, art exhibitions, even ballet (which last came to be written by Audrey Williamson, who returned to Tribune in 1975 as television reviewer). Sport still did not earn a regular corner, in spite of J. P. W. Mallalieu's frequent interruption of an article on Parliament to write in praise of cricket or to extol Huddersfield Town FC at the expense of the Foot-favoured Plymouth Argyle. Orwell, though, watchful as ever of the future, warned about the spawning of 'international ill-will', not good relations, by international sports competitions (14 December 1945); and no one who has seen World Cup matches or Olympic Games could disagree.

Poetry kept its place in Tribune, even if that place was mostly fillable holes at the feet of columns. Again offence to the overlooked must be risked by a nostalgic note of names attached to many Tribune poems of this period – Roy Fuller, George Barker, Vernon Watkins, Alan Ross, Kathleen Raine, David Wright, Alex Comfort, D. J. Enright, Charles Causley, Patric Dickinson, Sydney Tremayne, Gavin Ewart, Vernon Scannell. Not to mention C. Day Lewis once, even John Betjeman once, and astonishingly a translation from Lorca by that noisy Right-winger, Roy Campbell.

The range was as wide as ever, so by no means all or even most poems were explicitly 'political'. One that was, though, deserves quoting if only to lighten the mood – a parody by that occasional versifier, full-time playwright and Labour MP Benn Levy:

TO THE HONOURABLE MEMBER FOR WHERESIT

If you can temper reason with your hunches
And back the latter and then hedge your bet,
If you can fight your foes but pull your punches
For fear that they may be your allies yet,
If you can pledge yourself in accents moral
But leave a loop-hole for a later day,
Disown ambition but accept the laurel
After ensuring that it come your way,
If you can wriggle from the vows you uttered,
Made to placate the simple and the pure,
If you can sense which side your bread is buttered
When even the tomorrow is obscure,
If you can seem to move when you are halted
And spread the notion mighty things are brewing,
If you can shed with sentiments exalted
A smoke-screen over what you are not doing,
If you can show that national salvation
Depends on action now, not merely soon,
But follow with the hallowed declaration
'The present moment is not opportune,'
If you can lay your cards upon the table
But play your hands from out another pack,
If from the general forensic Babel
You can recruit your own compliant claque,
If you can dream of autocratic glory
But to democracy obeisance make,
If you can bowdlerize your country's story
To justify the course you seek to take,
If you can calculate the nicest minute

At which to cry your evangelic mission,
Yours is the earth and everything that's in it,
And, furthermore, you'll be a politician.

[26 December 1947]

Continuity within change was the character of Tribune's review pages under T. R. Fyvel and his successor, Bruce Bain – a regular contributor of many pseudonyms who had earlier tackled the task of reviewing Orwell's *1984*: '. . . George Orwell is a prophet of the larger pessimism, one of the most perceptive moralists of our time, and his brilliant tract should provoke us all to take our heads out of the sand and look into his crystal . . .' (17 June 1949).

By then, of course, Orwell was severely ill in hospital – and his death in early 1950 was only one of many mournful changes that impinged on the general continuity, in the 1940s, of Tribune and of British socialism. It was a period for obituaries of many major figures whose writings had appeared in the paper's columns since 1937: H. G. Wells in 1946; Ellen Wilkinson in early 1947 (Jennie Lee wrote movingly of 'her gift of courage, of laughter and generosity of spirit, as well as the outward shell of her activities' – 14 February 1947); Sidney Webb later that year; Orwell in early 1950; Harold Laski in the spring of that year ('His mission in life,' wrote Ian Mikardo on 31 March 1950, 'was to translate the religion of the universal brotherhood of man into the language of political economy'). Old and familiar enemies also fell in those years – Baldwin in late 1947, for instance, or Ernest Bevin in 1951.

Michael Foot's note on Bevin was as gracious as could be expected, given the amount of venom expended in his direction by the paper during his rule as Foreign Secretary. For, as said earlier, in spite of domestic 'pugnacity' and cultural breadth, foreign policy – Bevin's – seemed above all else to be the area of the Attlee government's policies and progress that worried the paper most from the first day of the Labour victory.

'We are the victims of a coalition on foreign affairs none the less real because it is as yet unratified, a coalition which exacts its sacrifice now of Socialism abroad but which will almost certainly in time exact its sacrifice of Socialism at home,' wrote Lyall Wilkes, MP, in an article entitled 'ISSUE EVERY LABOUR MP MUST FACE' (1

November 1946). But those who did face it, Michael Foot soon pointed out, were branded as 'rebels' or worse. A 'break with the past' was called for in foreign policy as in other policies – even if, Foot added, that call were to be 'in some small measure . . . due to Communist influence within our ranks' (22 November 1946).

That communist influence, for what it was worth, produced, during those years, many a 'red scare' in the media and many an unedifying internecine wrangle within Labour. Orwell and Konni Zilliacus clashed in Tribune's letter columns in early 1947 over what Orwell (in another paper) had termed the 'underground' communist undermining of Labour policies. More of the same emerged with the furore over the so-called 'Nenni letter' – or telegram – in the spring of 1948. About twenty Labour MPs ('simpletons who did not know what they were supporting', Tribune editorialized on 23 April 1948) signed the message to the Italian socialist leader who had joined forces with communism in Italy's elections. Tribune felt the message itself was 'an act of sabotage'; but it did not feel that such a description fitted its own unceasing and often virulent attacks on Ernest Bevin for his failures, in its view, to respond positively to the events in a very eventful era.

At first the European condition revolved mainly around reconstruction, demobilization, occupation and, ultimately, the beneficence-with-strings that was American 'Marshall Aid'. In the course of all this, Tribune can be seen moving steadily into an almost ferocious anti-Soviet (anti-Stalinist) position – and, by virtue of that progress, into a perhaps over-compensatingly pro-American stance. The view of the Soviet Union can be seen when Arthur Koestler entered the columns of Kimche's Tribune to warn against

APPEASEMENT OF SUSPICION

A new spectre haunts the world: the appeasement of suspicion. In 1938 we were appeasing the German mania of grandeur: today we are appeasing the Russian mania of persecution . . .

During the war pressure was brought upon the press and radio in this country not to utter any criticism which might upset our Soviet ally's delicate temper. Books critical of the Stalin regime were withdrawn from publishers' lists; any mention of the facts that Russia has a one-party system and is a dictatorship were suppressed . . . But as it passed through the filter of Soviet censorship and through the controlled channels of the Tass Agency, the Soviet press and radio, the gentle cooing of the Western voices became transformed into the barking of mad imperialist dogs.

There were two reasons why the common man in the U.S.S.R. had to be vaccinated with the serum of distrust against foreign influences. The first is external, the second internal . . .

The Western powers had supported the armies of the counter-revolution during the civil war; they persecuted Communists; they waited hopefully for the collapse of the Soviet regime and tried in various ways to speed it up; their reactionary press and politicians spread shameless lies about conditions in Russia . . .

The Western countries had, of course, as sound reasons to be suspicious of Russia as was the case the other way round. Up to the middle 'thirties the avowed aim of the Communist International was the violent overthrow of their regimes . . .

However, by the middle 'thirties the persecution-maniacs in the West who still lived on the Red Scare had by that time become a dwindling, reactionary minority. The majority was convinced that despite the difference in social and political structure, the Soviets and the West can do business with each other and find a stable *modus vivendi.*

Thus the original shock was gradually lived down in the West, while it was artificially fanned and preserved by the centralised propaganda apparatus of the Soviets. Why? We now come to the second, internal cause for this attitude.

The transformation of Soviet Eurasia from a backward agrarian to a modern industrial country was a gigantic task which required gigantic sacrifices imposed upon the population . . . In consequence of this, the five-year plans, instead of lifting had to lower the living standard of the masses . . .

But it would have been too much to expect the masses to understand the paradox that the workers and peasants in a socialist country were worse off in food, clothing and housing than the workers and peasants under the capitalist yoke . . .

The Soviet Government has achieved, for the first time in history, a complete State monopoly not only over the production and distribution of goods, but also over the production and distribution of ideas, opinions and emotions. World peace can only become a reality if suspicions are abolished. Suspicions can only be abolished if the Soviet Government can be induced to turn the master-switch of their propaganda factory.

[5 April 1946]

Michael Foot's editorship took the anti-Soviet stance even further, especially after the shock and disgust felt in the West upon Stalin's takeover of Czechoslovakia ('Murder in Prague', front page, 27 February 1948) which was followed rapidly by the crisis over Berlin and the months of the American airlift. In his 'The Way Ahead' article of 21 May 1948, which contained in part the attack on Shaw, Foot had a word for American capitalism – 'powerful and arrogant' and destructive, yet mitigated by 'new forces' since Roosevelt's New Deal 'which are not called Socialism but which still have the chance to win the day and to preserve and expand freedom'. Not so the Soviets: 'The Stalinite answer, to put the matter crudely, is that . . . freedom should be suppressed or that it should not be kindled in places where it did not exist before.' Stalin's dictatorship, he wrote later, was no more than 'A Revolution Betrayed' (5 November 1948).

Not many of Tribune's readers would have disagreed. But some worried about the over-reaction implicit in this violent anti-Stalinism, and wrote to say so.

KEEP LEFT

Week after week, I have read in *Tribune* condemnations of Russia, but hardly a word about the United States. With most of these condemnations I agree, but are we to believe that the American capitalists have become so good-hearted? Is it democracy or capitalism they are so worried about?

When we Social Democrats condemn the Communists it is because they abolish political democracy, but when the American capitalists condemn them it is because the Communists do away with private ownership. Why don't the Americans worry about democracy in Franco Spain, or in Greece, where we installed a king who put up with Metaxas' dictatorship for so long, or in their own Southern States?

In May 1947, a pamphlet was published called *Keep Left*, which Michael Foot and Ian Mikardo took part in writing. This pamphlet warned of the dangers of tying up ourselves with a reactionary American *bloc*, which was trying to establish forward bases against Russia in Greece, Turkey, Japan and the Middle East. It warned of the fallacy of collective security against Communism . . .

That policy was right then, and such a policy is still right today. Communism will not be beaten just by force . . .

You can only beat Communism by opposing it with democratic Socialism and not with reaction. What are we Social Democrats afraid of? . . .

[*Ezra Nathan*, *Manchester*, 5 November 1948]

The editors replied to Nathan, revealingly:

Tribune holds as firmly as ever to the view that a vigorous democratic Socialism is the only sure answer to Communism. We have never ceased to preach that doctrine, nor have we failed to state our criticisms of British or American policy in Greece, Palestine, Germany, Spain or elsewhere.

On the other hand, the major threat to democratic Socialism and the major danger of war in Europe arises from Soviet policy and not from American policy. It is not the Americans who have imposed a blockade on Berlin. It is not the Americans who have used conspiratorial methods in an effort to destroy democratic Socialist parties in one country after another. It is not the Americans who have blocked effective action through one United Nations agency after another. On the contrary, since *Keep Left* was published, the American Government has launched the Marshall Plan, which offers a sane method whereby Western Europe may be reconstructed as a Third Force in the world. We are resolved to build that Third Force, but since the Russians have vowed to destroy it, we must defend ourselves. – Eds, *Tribune*.

[5 November 1948]

Whatever coloration we put on this view, it seems to remain clear that Tribune felt the United States to be the world's hope for democracy, as the 'betrayal' and aggressive power-bloc-building of the Soviet Union became manifest. Those implacable Leftist enemies today of 'American imperialism' might wonder now at such a position: but in the revulsion against Stalinism of the late 1940s we might see at least comprehensible cause. Yet Tribune had not assumed an entirely slavish, rose-coloured spectacles adoration of things American. Tribune, and Michael Foot, were passionate above all about democracy – British-style parliamentary democracy, socialist democracy. Eastern Europe had lost its chances for it; in the real world of the 1940s, the West had to defend it by every practicable means, and the United States had the means. Such was the judicious message within Tribune's welcome to the pact that created NATO – which 'serves only strictly defensive purposes' by giving pause to potential Soviet aggression ('What's Happening', 18 March 1949).

It might be mentioned that Tribune had not been so blithely hopeful of international pacts some years before at the birth of the United Nations, when it commented on the general 'scepticism' about that organization's practicability – 'It is, indeed, widely, if not universally, recognised that no international organisation can succeed unless the Great Powers . . . are prepared to act in common' – adding that world events 'should make us more chary than ever of entrusting our salvation to the exclusive care of the most powerful' (Editorial, 11 January 1946). That chariness had apparently faded a good deal by the time NATO was created.

This time, though, it was not a Mr Nathan of Manchester who objected, but a Tribune director. Ian Mikardo resigned from the board because of his disagreement with the paper's stance on foreign policy, especially on NATO and the Soviets. He remained as columnist, and explained himself by recalling the message of the *Keep Left* pamphlet – the need to create a healthy 'third force' between the United States and the Soviet Union rather than to take sides:

> It's true that the Russians have been bloody-minded, to put it at its lowest, since before the end of the war. It doesn't matter for my present purpose how far their awkward-squad stuff has been justified . . . What does matter is what ought to have been our reaction to the attitude of the Russians. And on that it's always seemed to me that many people, including the Foreign Office and the editors of Tribune, abandoned much too quickly all hope of the arbitrament of reason and accepted much too quickly the inevitability of a Third World War . . .
>
> [20 May 1949]

Michael Foot replied, and his position was never clearer.

SOCIALISTS AND THE ATLANTIC PACT

First, we must retort at once that no responsible leader in Britain or the United States has accepted the inevitability of war. All of them, we are sure – and this goes for Mr Attlee, Mr Bevin, Mr Acheson or President Truman – desire peace as passionately as Ian Mikardo or anyone else. Equally, the British, American and Russian peoples want peace, and the British and American peoples, because of their democratic institutions, almost certainly have the power to ensure that their Governments shall never embark on open aggression or the crime of a preventive war. The same power in the same degree is not possessed by the Russian people, and the Soviet leaders cannot be placed in the same category as the other national statesmen. No one imagines that they, like the Nazi leaders, would desire war as an end in itself. But the Soviet leaders did directly precipitate world war by their pact with the

Nazis in 1939. They believe as a matter of theory that the end of establishing Soviet Communism wherever they can justifies any means for its attainment. They believe also as a matter of theory in secrecy, censorship, dictatorship and the ruthless annihilation of the rights of individuals; all these beliefs help to release them from the restraints on the exercise of power which operate in a democratic society, however imperfect that society may be.

This distinction is the first which makes invalid Ian Mikardo's idea that we should look upon the United States and the Soviet Union in the same light. But there are others of a similar nature. The United States does not operate in every country where it can a fifth column dedicated to the service of United States foreign policy. It certainly seeks to influence, persuade, and encourage peoples and persons in other countries to follow policies which it approves. But there is all the difference in the world between this attitude and the methods adopted by the Soviet Government to shatter the societies of other countries, whether it be the Germany of Weimar, the India of Nehru or the France of the Third Force . . .

Turning to the immediate European situation, the distinction between the diplomatic aims and methods of the two major Powers is equally emphatic. Whatever follies have been committed by American policy in Europe since 1945 (and they are manifold), the major purpose *and the major result* has been to provide aid without which recovery from the war would have been infinitely more arduous. The major purpose of Soviet policy has been the complete subjection of as many countries as possible to the Soviet will . . .

These broad distinctions – and many more could be cited – made it inevitable that Britain should develop closer ties with the United States than with the Soviet Union. The choice was not the result of some sinister plot or some betrayal of Socialism contrived by Ernest Bevin. It was the inexorable consequence of the combined Soviet challenge to the British Commonwealth, American capitalism and democratic Socialism. Stalin lumped all three together as the enemy, reserving only a special venom for the Socialists, whom he regarded as his most formidable ideological enemies . . .

[20 May 1949]

The anti-Stalinist position, he seems to be saying, makes for strange bedfellows.

But it need not be assumed that Tribune rested easy in that bed with American capitalism. The paper watched with distaste and horror the rise to power and infamy of Senator McCarthy ('He has already done more damage to America's reputation abroad than

Moscow radio could do in a year' – 'What's Happening', 7 April 1950). The paper even presented Alistair Cooke being thoughtful on the trial of Alger Hiss:

> What is there in this trial, more than any other, that reflects an inevitable personal tragedy which the court cannot appease or resolve? It is, I think, the fact which constantly emerges through this dishevelled stockpile of memory that the main characters were idealists at a time when the nature of loyalty – to the state, to one's beliefs, to one's family and fellow men – was undergoing one of those historic and permanent changes . . .
>
> [22 July 1949]

Further, some of Tribune's regard for the United States was tempered by an undiminishing concern for that nation's possession of the ultimate weapon, which had left a 'SHADOW OVER THE PEACE' (17 August 1945) after its original, double use on human beings. Orwell was prophetic about the bomb, also not too long after the peace in Asia: ' . . . every development in military technique has favoured the State as against the individual, and the industrialised country as against the backward one. There are fewer and fewer foci of power . . .' (19 October 1945). Years later, the H-bomb had made post-Hiroshima fears seem Lilliputian, and in Tribune Alex Comfort belied his name with thoughts on 'The Psychopathology of the Bomb' – the breeding of fear, anxiety, guilt and paranoia out of Cold War demonologies plus nuclear capabilities (17 March 1950).

And yet, also in Tribune in the same year, Woodrow Wyatt could muse a little about the *uses* of nuclear weaponry, within a theme later to be summed up in the catchword 'deterrent':

> The only answer to the constant undermining attempted by Russia and her agents is courage and a determination to resist. If Finland could stand up to the Russians and ward them off so can Britain and Western Europe. When the Russians see that the West are prepared to suffer everything, including the devastation of some of their major cities, rather than give in to the onslaught of world Communism, then they will not try to impose their will by force.
>
> To some it seems very shocking that the use of the atom bomb to check Russian aggression should be advocated. To me it seems more shocking that any weapon which could save Western civilisation from annihilation should be put into cold storage . . .
>
> [4 August 1950]

Strange bedfellows, again. Yet perhaps Wyatt's view was not wholly representative: a few years on, it will be seen, Tribune would be in the forefront of the ban-the-bomb campaign.

Another unlikely (to our eyes now) bedfellow for Tribune in those years, along with American capitalism and nuclear deterrents, emerged from some brand-new and long-range thinking about the future of Europe. Of course, in terms of specific events, within the paper's 'orientation towards foreign policy', its European coverage could hardly be faulted. Its columns bulged with examinations of the occupation and partition of Germany; the electoral and constitutional ups and downs of France; and all the terrible tales of starving, ill and oppressed refugees wandering among the ruins left by war. Much attention was especially reserved for those areas where the old world's (and Britain's) leftovers still boiled and fermented, among them prominently Greece – on which Francis Noel-Baker summed up the 'war of extermination', between government forces and communist guerrillas, which had been going on since 1940 (30 May 1947).

Even more articles summed up the progress of socialism in Europe, often written for Tribune by the peripatetic international secretary of the Labour Party, Denis Healey. But, too, there was Ignazio Silone on socialist divisions in Italy (before the Nenni crisis); or Jonathan Grant on the rise of another kind of socialism in Yugoslavia as Tito began to go his own way. So Tribune's European awareness was maintained; and then it was extended further, as the 1940s came to a close, and that long-range thinking mentioned above began to develop.

Many Left-wing foreign-policy considerations (as the *Keep Left* pamphlet, and plentiful allusions in Tribune editorials) had been approving the idea of a European 'third force' in the world. Later, much foreign-policy consideration, not only on the Left, began to expand that notion into a vision of unity. It first bore the slightly bathetic name (like the famous telegraph company) of 'Western Union'. By 1949, though, it came to be specified as 'European Union'. By whatever name, it seemed, Tribune liked the idea.

Still, the paper's view was not a wholehearted commitment: Tribune followed a narrow and perhaps idealistic line, but did so fairly consistently. It noted the problems – of the relations with the Commonwealth, of unity with non-socialist governments that lacked the advantages of controlled and planned economies: '. . . the surest way to kill the whole ideal is to announce that the nations must federate to make Europe safe for capitalism', said an editorial on 10 September 1948. But in the same article the advantages were listed:

> One purpose is to enable Western Europe to free itself from exceptional American aid. Another purpose is to assist Europe in increasing its own production. A third purpose is to prevent the infiltration and increase in the strength of Communism. A fourth purpose is to enable a coherent defence system to be built up in Western Europe . . .

The paper's approach seemed to be to give European unity every consideration and benefit of the doubt, but also carefully to watch the fine print. Tribune's principal Europe-watcher, Evelyn Anderson, put it succinctly:

> The main contention of the Labour Party Statement on European Unity is that, for moral as well as practical political and economic reasons, we must give top priority to the maintenance of full employment and social justice. Every step towards closer European cooperation should be judged first and foremost in the light of this overriding need. If full European unity can only be brought about by sacrificing the permanent achievement of full employment, such complete union is not only not worth having but it would also defeat its own ultimate objectives of economic independence and political inviolability . . .
>
> [16 June 1950]

So, for all the paper's qualified interest in the idea of European unity, within that statement exist seeds enough of Tribune's later – and certainly more wholehearted – objections, when the unity idea had been partially realized in the shape of the Common Market.

Readers will have noticed, within the discussion of the European idea, Tribune's emphatic concern with the Commonwealth – within which, implicitly, lies the fact of Labour's mightiest contribution to the tempests of change round the world in the late 1940s: the shedding of an Empire. Few subjects claimed more column inches in the paper than the turmoils and upheavals in the colonies or ex-colonies, and their neighbours. It is impossible to do justice to all these outpourings, especially to the detailed and continuous attention paid to the central jewel of British imperialism, India, and its road to independencc. That was an achievement worth celebrating:

> INDIA INDEPENDENCE BILL
> Two minutes in last Friday's Parliament made history. The speaker called on the Prime Minister; Attlee nodded his head; the Clerk of the House read the title and preamble of the 'India Independence Bill'.
> In fact, the first phase of the abdication of George VI, as Emperor of India – an abdication scheduled to be completed within 42 days – had begun; it was introduced into Parliament with casual nonchalance, as if Members were approving a new gasworks for Manchester.
> The Bill, an extraordinary document of 20 clauses, unusually lucid, transfers all power to the two Dominions of India and Pakistan, with populations of 220 million and 80 million respectively, and to 630 Indian States with a total population of about 100 million.
> The Government has attached considerable importance to every aspect of the Bill – including its title. There was indeed a slight hitch over its forthrightness. To speed the Bill through Parliament in the limited time available, the approval of the leaders of the Opposition was sought before its publication.
> Only Mr Churchill objected; he wanted the word 'Independence' removed from the title of the Bill. The other Conservative Party leaders did not relish this particular last-ditch . . .
> ['*What's Happening*', 11 July 1947]

As we know, racial and religious violence, famine and a multitude of other evils followed on the partition and independence of India. But at least Britain had not grudgingly given that freedom after another colonial war, like so many that were fought elsewhere, or threatened to be fought.

Britain, indeed, fought a few of her own, in other areas. In Malaya, where Fenner Brockway saw the wave of 'terrorism' in 1948 as in large part 'the responsibility of communists', but also stressed: 'Nevertheless, Britain is again playing right into the hands of the Communists and Russia by the methods it is adopting to crush the terrorists . . .' (1 October 1948). In Cyprus, 'entering a period of anarchy and terrorism', as a Correspondent wrote on 31 December 1948. Most of all, and to Tribune most reprehensibly, in Palestine.

With all the emotional overtones of post-holocaust Jewish needs, countered by prevalent antisemitism among British army officers in Palestine – which Tribune reported and deplored, and which worsened as Stern gang terrorism escalated – it is no surprise that this small piece of Empire took up about as much space, especially in Kimche's Tribune, as the rest of the ex-colonies together. Added to it all was an early perception of the central piece in the problem, summed up in the heading of a Nigel Davenport article in 1945, 'Oil and Power Politics'. But among all the words expended in Tribune on the Middle East turmoil, there was one particular theme in the late 1940s which never lost its central position – that the mess was all directly due to wrongheaded decisions by Ernest Bevin.

WHY DO THEY DIE IN PALESTINE?

What's the use of mincing words or resorting to polite formula when the British Government has embarked on a course which may not only recoil on its own head but even more so upon the great hopes of the British Labour Movement and its high aspirations . . . the Labour Government – our Labour Government – has set out on a road along which the milestones will be the graves of innocent British soldiers and of embittered, fanatical Jews, passionately believing in the justice of their terrorism . . .

We can choose to continue along this road of terror, and of counter-terror which strikes as much at the innocent as does the terror itself. There will be no moral roadhouse where one can conveniently pull up half-way, once this starts. Murder will breed murder; reprisal will invite reprisal – already the symptoms are evident. The terrorists threaten reprisals for the executions. The Government shows its fear by its hole-and-corner method of execution. British troops, themselves, begin to threaten reprisals against the Jewish population. The Arabs hardly enter into this any more: in fact, they are quietly watching what has become a British-Jewish war. Where will this end, but in a sea of bitterness and hate and without advantage either to Britain or the Jews?

The alternative to this two-fold terror is for the Government to put aside its pretence that it bears no responsibility for the present situation. It gave the most extravagant and categorical undertakings to the Jews and it has broken them with cynical disregard for consequences . . .

We hold no brief for these terrorists. They have made the conditions of their people infinitely worse in Palestine than they need have been; they are endangering the security of Jewish communities throughout the world by their threats to expand their activities to other countries – and they have been the cause of continuous British loss of life in Palestine. But, in reply, can the Government produce nothing better than another bout of words in New York – accompanied by bombs, hangings, curfews and reprisals in Jerusalem? . . .

[*Editorial*, 25 April 1947]

'Terrorism' by many names, and military operations against it, became commonplace in many imperial nations' colonial holdings, as when (to Tribune's outrage) the Dutch put troops into Indonesia and the French, later, into Indo-China. Elsewhere, early warnings appeared of potential violences to flower later, as in Kenya, where Dinah Stock protested when Africans could see 'even their elementary needs set aside in favour of white settlers' (13 September 1946). Rather more distant early warnings were heeded by Tribune in Southern Rhodesia, as it then was: '. . . complete segregation is resented as bitter humiliation' ('What's Happening', 7 March 1947).

So it had long been resented in South Africa, as many Tribune writers made clear, among them a non-white writer, B. M. Kies, bitter on the occasion of a royal visit: '. . . to us it seems not a little strange that, in order to recover from the strains of six years of war against Nazism, your King and Queen should choose to visit the very country where there exists not only a *Herrenvolk* rooted in its idea of its divinely-given racial superiority and mission to rule, but also a system of government comparable in its essentials to that of Nazi Germany . . .' (14 March 1947).

And yet, to return to the original point, whatever left-over colonialism and outright error existed still in the Foreign Office and colonial administrations, Labour *had* performed superbly towards what Churchill called 'scuttling' the old imperial dominations. Rita Hinden, Tribune's long-serving correspondent on the colonies, summed it all up:

LABOUR'S GREATEST ACHIEVEMENT

The necessary, but barren, anti-imperialism of the past has now been merged into a great constructive vision, and there are many – not only in our own country – who believe that what has already been accomplished towards realising this aim, particularly in India, Pakistan and Ceylon, will be proclaimed by history as the crowning achievement of the 1945 Labour Government . . .

In some ways the change has been spectacular. Six territories – one a sub-continent – within the Empire have ceased altogether to be dependent. India is now an independent sovereign republic which has preferred to remain linked with the Commonwealth; Pakistan and Ceylon are Dominions equal in status with Canada and Australia; Burma has chosen to leave the Commonwealth altogether. Newfoundland has abandoned her position as a bankrupt dependant, and federated with Canada; Malta has secured the internal self-government for which her own National Assembly asked. The remainder of the Empire has not yet achieved sovereignty, but the West Indies are on the path towards federation from which it is only a step towards Dominion status if they will it – the spade work has already been done. The West African Colonies now have African *majorities* on their Legislative Councils and are on the threshold of further changes which will bring them to the very verge of self-government. In East and Central Africa, African representatives sit on every Legislative Council, and their number is being constantly increased . . .

One does not have to be a mere irresponsible dreamer to prophesy that another five years of a Labour Government might well see the birth of three or four more independent nations who may then choose to remain within the Commonwealth as the Asian Dominions have done. The small Anglo-Saxon *Commonwealth* of 1945 has already been extended to include some four hundred millions of Asians; by 1955 it will probably have added a further thirty million or so of fully-fledged Negro citizens – and the *Empire* will have been correspondingly diminished . . .

There are many abuses remaining, and many intractable problems still hardly tackled. We have made scant progress in solving the dilemma of the mixed society, where different races live side by side (as in East Africa and Malaya) and refuse to intermingle with each other. Illiteracy is still a bad blot on the record; agricultural methods are in many places still hopelessly backward, and industrialisation has hardly begun. The soil is still being washed or blown away over huge tracts of Africa and malnutrition in many areas remains a scourge. Yet the foundations of a better life have been laid. If they continue to be built upon with the energy of these last years, the future promises well for the sixty million people in the British dependencies . . .

[17 February 1950]

At the same time, though, that new ruler of the waves, the United States of America, seemed determined to construct itself a new imperialism, especially in Asia. And for all its pro-Americanism in other contexts, Tribune saw the dangers clearly when Americans fought the Huks in the Philippine jungles in 1946, to set up what S. R. Ratnam called 'America's New Banana Republic' (19 July 1946). Even more deplorable to Tribune was the American espousal of Chiang Kai-shek in China – another story told at considerable length in the paper up to Jonathan Grant's innocently headed article after Mao's victory: 'Are China's Communists Different?' (29 April 1949).

The world soon began to have some of the answer to that question – as it had further sign of the hegemonic nature of America's crusade against communism. In 1950 the North Koreans marched south – and Tribune was fervent with its praise for the American intervention – 'the correct and inevitable course' – and with its denunciation of 'Communist aggression' (30 June 1950). More anti-communist proclamations followed, noting the dangers of appeasement, excusing America's acting *before* the Security Council authorization, but also warning that the 'inefficiency and corruption' of the South Korean government would have to be overcome to justify the West's support (7 July 1950).

Some worry crept in, though, mainly over whether the America that supported Chiang really understood the Asian situation. And some dissent emerged as well. When Michael Foot reasserted again his belief in 'the principle of collective defence against wanton aggression' (28 July 1950), Sydney Silverman painted a bleaker picture of the future of Asia as long as American power was propping up the falsehood of Formosa and keeping Mao beyond the pale:

> What is to be our attitude to the revolution which is sweeping Asia? Colonialism is dead. The passion for national liberation and national independence is fused in revolutionary fervour with the passion for social justice . . . For them as for us the real issue will ultimately be between democratic and totalitarian Socialism. Do we really want to see the great democratic nations always and everywhere siding with their enemies and making them believe that everybody is against them but the Communists? . . .
>
> [28 July 1950]

Many lessons were to be learned from the Korean war – about the nature of Asian and 'third-world' needs and old post-colonial hatreds; about the strengths and weaknesses of the UN; about the true nature of America's world-leadership intentions; about Soviet ambitions, and the potentially heated areas of the Cold War. And hard lessons, too, had to be learned about Britain's declining influence in the world, and the limitations on her role in power politics because of her increasingly shaky internal and economic condition.

As the 1940s gave way to the 1950s, Britain was heading for economic rocks. The problems of post-war reconstruction, even with socialist planning and American aid, had been daunting enough. On top of that, for years, came balance-of-payments deficits, dollar deficiencies, rationing and shortages, declining exports as traditional markets consistently turned elsewhere. Some signs of recovery may have gleamed through the clouds in 1947 and 1948, but even so, no publicly visible corner had been turned – as stressed by Donald Bruce, then Tribune's regular economic correspondent:

BRITAIN'S WAY TO RECOVERY

To-day Britain is devoting no less than 20 per cent of her national income to building up capital resources at home . . .

In total, approximately two-thirds of our physical capital losses have been made good since the end of the war. About £5,500 million's worth of capital works have been accomplished. This amazing achievement is reflected all over Britain. New factories and plants are going up in the industrial districts, many of them in the old 'distressed' areas. Enlargements and improvements to existing installations are being effected to the limit of available resources. Great efforts are being made to catch up on arrears of maintenance to the railway system, to modernise the mines, to extend the capacity of generating stations, to increase oil refinery capacity and to mechanise agriculture. And simultaneously, capital works of a less directly productive nature, vital as they are to the welfare of the nation as a whole, are being pressed forward – work on houses, hospitals, schools and other public buildings.

The strain on our national resources is tremendous. We are using all the steel and timber available. More factory and commercial building could only be accomplished at the expense of schools, hospitals and housing.

But this problem – having too much to do and not enough to do it with – throws a considerable burden on the individual citizen as well as on the country's economic structure. For the last three years, the British people have had to send abroad more and more of the goods they could well do with at home in return for less and less food and raw materials. That this is due to a continuous rise in prices in the Western Hemisphere, over which we have no control, does not make it any the less uncomfortable. Add to this the further strain of a capital programme which takes a five per cent larger slice out of the national income than pre-war, and the position becomes positively Spartan . . .

What are the alternatives? The capital programme could be reduced. A greater proportion of production could thus be diverted directly to the home market or exchanged for imports destined for the shop counters. A significant increase in living standards would be made possible.

On the face of it, the idea is attractive. It would also be suicidal. The increase could be only temporary. For, in the meantime, our productive capacity would slowly but progressively deteriorate, as compared with the Western Hemisphere. Our goods would become less competitive, both in price and quantity, and we should be able to buy fewer vital primary products with them. The brief 'binge' would therefore be followed by something more serious than the customary 'hangover'. *It would mean the certainty of Britain's decline . . .*

[31 December 1948]

Prophetic words, for there would come a time when such a 'binge' would allow the British people never to have had it so good, to their ultimate and probably permanent cost. Meanwhile the remedies – devaluation, tougher taxation, wage restraint, continuing austerity – eroded the Labour government's popularity. As usual, the media's tame experts fanned public displeasure with what C. A. R. Crosland called 'The Mumbo-Jumbo of the Orthodox Economists' (6 January 1950). But Cripps's Budgets retained emphasis on socialist planning, full employment and preservation of the social services, and won Tribune's guarded praise.

Then illness forced his resignation, Hugh Gaitskell became Chancellor, and Korea launched Attlee's government on the disastrous road to costly rearmament. Now inflation truly became the enemy as taxes and prices ballooned; and Labour's response was what Tribune called 'a timid and squalidly inadequate financial policy' (20 April 1951).

Before then Labour had fought a general election, in 1950, on the realization or steps towards it of its 1945 undertakings. But Labour barely scraped through into a 'near stalemate' position in Parliament. Another election was inevitable before long, and Tribune felt that the impoverishment of the government's economic and political response to crisis, the too-ready abandonment of socialism, would wreck its chances. In the process, as it turned out, the specific nature of that response and that turning away destroyed what hopes remained for unity within the party. Aneurin Bevan resigned, magnificently.

WHAT THEY REALLY SAID

Aneurin Bevan's speech . . .

. . . It is now perfectly clear to any one who examines the matter objectively that the lurchings of the American economy, the extravagant and unpredictable behaviour of the production machine, the failure on the part of the American Government to inject the arms programme into the economy slowly enough, have already caused a vast inflation of prices all over the world, have disturbed the economy of the Western world to such an extent that if it goes on more damage will be done by this unrestrained behaviour than by the behaviour of the nation the arms are intended to restrain . . .

I say therefore with the full solemnity of the seriousness of what I am saying, that the £4,700 million arms programme is already dead. It cannot be achieved without irreparable damage to the economy of Great Britain and the world, and that therefore the arms programme contained in the Chancellor of the Exchequer's Budget is already invalidated and the figures based on the arms programme ought to be revised . . .

The demands made upon the world's precious raw materials will be such that the civilian economy of the Western world outside America will be undermined. We shall have mass unemployment. We have already got in Great Britain under-employment. Already there is short-time working in many important parts of industry and before the middle of the year, unless something serious can be done, we shall have unemployment in many of our important industrial centres . . .

The fact is that the Western world has embarked upon a campaign of arms production upon a scale, so quickly, and of such an extent that the foundations of political liberty and Parliamentary democracy will not be able to sustain the shock. This is a very grave matter indeed. I have always said both in the House of Commons and in speeches in the country – and I think my ex-colleagues in the Government will at least give me credit for this – that the defence programme must always be consistent with the maintenance of the standard of life of the British people and the maintenance of the social services, and that as soon as it became clear we had engaged upon an arms programme inconsistent with those considerations, I could no longer remain a member of the Government . . .

[4 May 1951]

And he was echoed and supplemented by his fellow resigners, Harold Wilson ('It is not a matter of teeth and spectacles . . . if the financial programme of rearmament runs beyond the physical resources which can be made available, then rearmament itself becomes the first casualty, the basis of our economy is disrupted and the standard of living, including the social services of our people, is endangered') and John Freeman ('I do not believe it can be right for us . . . to follow a policy which is calculated to rob us of our vitality as a

"It must be nearly three weeks now since it happened, and still no sign of Jenkins settling down."

"By God, Gertrude—I see it all! No milk, nationalised sugar, then they'll tell us to put lemon in our tea like the dirty Russians."

Both Mullally (10 August 1945) and Ronald Searle (23 September 1949) enjoyed mocking Tory outrage over the post-war Labour victory, while Horner (18 February 1949) added his comment on one of the finest achievements of the new government.

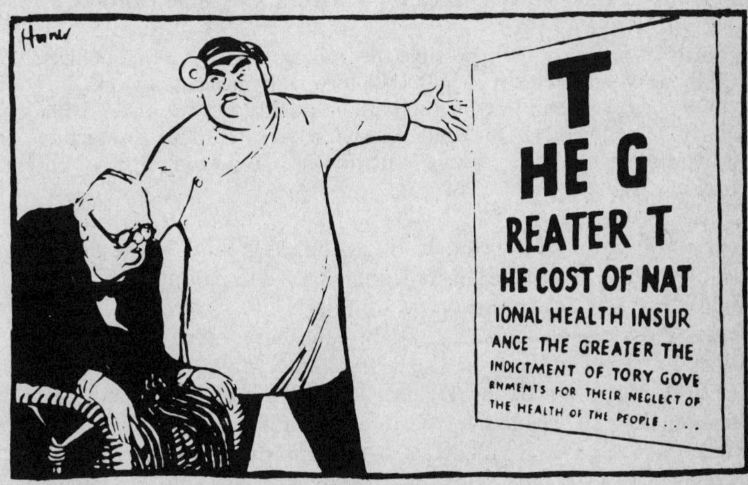

NONE SO BLIND . .

nation, to cause a great degree of avoidable hardship among our people and to deprive us of much of our influence for peace' – 4 May 1951).

Few Tribune readers will need reminding of the storms, calumnies and near-libels that broke round their heads – principally the assertion that they did their deed out of manic personal ambition (if so, Ian Mikardo scoffed, 'they went a cockeyed way about it' – 18 May 1951). In any case, the party was split, and the Tories were making hay with it and with the state of the economy in the run-up to the fateful election.

Meanwhile Tribune's own fighting strength had been diminished by the state of its economy. It had chosen to deal with its crisis by a sad decision on which it tried to put the best possible face – by calling it 'A New Venture in Publishing':

> From next week forward Tribune will seek to provide a new and somewhat different service for its readers . . . The first proposal in the new Tribune scheme is . . . to put on the market a series of topical pamphlets at the low price of 6d. each. The pamphlets will contain between 20,000 and 30,000 words and will be published every month . . .
> [15 September 1950]

But this apparently positive, brave and valuable new venture could not for long hide the harsh reality, buried in the same editorial:

> Partly in order to make possible the publication of these pamphlets, Tribune will henceforth be published fortnightly instead of weekly . . . Of course, we would prefer to continue publication weekly . . . But there is a difficulty. During the past few years costs of production have been going up steeply. Circulation has been going up too, but not as fast as we would wish . . .

Fortnightly or not, Tribune fought on, as boldly as the new red ink of the paper's name on its front page. The pamphlets – all too long, regrettably, for the scope of this book – were potent, provocative, food-for-socialist-thought and argument at its best. Michael Foot's assault on the Tory 'guilty men', *Still At Large*; Geoffrey Bing's study of Ulster, *John Bull's Other Ireland*; Roy Jenkins's closely argued look at income distribution, *Fair Shares for the Rich*; and above all, in 1951, the famous analysis of a socialist response to crisis, *One Way Only*, by Bevan, Wilson and Freeman, and its fighting follow-up, *Going Our Way* – such publications thoroughly made up for Tribune's halved presence on the news-stands.

As it turned out, though, not enough were going their way, or Labour's. The 1951 election put the Tories into power and Labour, disrupted still with blame-laying and mutual recrimination, into the wilderness. It would be many years before those wounds in the Labour movement could be allowed to close and heal, even into the livid scars that remain still, twenty-five years on.

4 PREACHING HERESY (1951–8)

Nothing of import, save economic necessity, need be read into the probably unnoticed change in Tribune's self-descriptive front-page banner – from 'Socialist – Fortnightly – Fearless' to, in early 1952, 'Socialist – Fortnightly – Sixpence'. The paper visibly remained fearless during the 1950s, even though Labour supporters might well look back on those years as the age of discipline.

But soon that heading needed changing again: Tribune became a weekly once more, when rising sales allowed, and did so with an unusual flourish – by reducing its price ('Down Goes the Cost of Living!', 8 August 1952) to 4d.

Author and journalist Laurence Thompson previewed the new Tribune with some cheeky digs at the Labour movement's inadequate support for socialist papers:

> Is it that the movement would rather slumber than think? It always has been so. With a cautious eye on that succession of active controversialists who have been MPs for *Forward* (North), I would say that no Socialist paper in this country has ever become, in Hamilton Fyfe's phrase, 'a good property' . . . What is wrong with us? Is it the journalists, or the readers? The place is alive with good Socialist journalists, so that the editor of the *Sunday Express* wrings his hands and laments in public. Do we become, when we write in our own papers, so narrow

and sectarian that we cannot hold the reader's interest? . . . But when I come to the readers, I am speechless. Eleven million people vote Labour. Ten and a half million are co-operators, eight million belong to trade unions, six million to the Labour Party. What did you say your circulation was again?

[22 August 1952]

Editorials of the time similarly sought to dig spurs into the slumbering movement. One week before the new weekly's advent, the front page asked for readers' help in one of its clear summaries of the glooms and dooms of the world it lived in:

Supreme above all other questions is the issue of world peace. Somehow an escape must be found from the desperate anxieties of the cold war which now casts its shadow across the lives of ourselves and our children. Somehow we must strive to turn the energies of the nations away from the mad dreams of military conquest to the only war which Socialists wish to prosecute – the war against poverty and ignorance, against disease and hunger, to enlarge the empire of the human mind . . .

And meantime here in Britain we are faced with a tremendous challenge. Our economic situation is much more perilous than most of our people recognise. Within a few years our very livelihood may be at stake. Great changes in our national life must be undertaken, great sacrifices must be borne, if we are to build a new country and a new Commonwealth of security and freedom. None can believe that the inspiration to accomplish this work can come from our present rulers. It is urgent that the whole Labour movement should be rallied for the battle to get the Tories out.

These are some of the causes in which the new Tribune will fight. But, as in the past, we cannot believe that the true solution of our problems will come from orthodox and official opinion. It will often be necessary to preach heresy, and to risk the arguments which follow. That is one of the functions we shall strive to perform. That is why we ask for your help.

[*Editorial*, 19 September 1952]

On 26 September 1952, the recipient of this hoped-for support reached the news-stands – 'Alive and Kicking', as its first leader asserted, and also wholly reborn in size and appearance. In some ways it was a reversion to the Mellor–Hartshorn days: a large-format paper, sparkling with pictures, cartoons, bouncy black headlines and a fair number of advertisements, even if that sparkle had to be contained within only eight pages. Gone was the red ink of the paper's front-page name; gone, too, was the aura of sober deliberation that had characterized those weighty, authoritative, reflective pieces which filled the 1940s Tribune. The renewed Tribune was a *newspaper* again, visually – and in other ways, as during the 1950s 'behind-the-news' reportage earned at least as much space as opinion and comment.

But even the comment had reverted – back to the old 'rowdy' style, lashing spiritedly out in every direction, storming, scoffing, lecturing, hectoring, sending up and tearing down enemies of all hues. With these changes went a crucial change of editor. Michael Foot had moved on to other things (though he remained on the editorial board with Jennie Lee, J. P. W. Mallalieu and, once again, briefly, Ian Mikardo). Robert J. Edwards brought the 'new Tribune' into being.

The paper's boisterous new start carried over into a series of splendidly tub-thumping public meetings which extended its message and its broad-spectrum attacking image. But that image was beginning, or continuing, to disturb the many who held different views of the role of Labour newspapers (and of Labour). The party had begun earlier, as was seen, to polarize – the 'Bevanite' Left, the 'official' (increasingly 'Gaitskellite') Right; 1952 saw this process accelerate. And, useless though it may be to pin blame, two elements in the process seem clear.

First, Tribune in late 1952 was hell-bent on being a gadfly again, eschewing moderation or reservation in its aggressive 'preaching of heresy'. And in turn – though that turn was often the first turn – the Right wing and the Labour leadership were hell-bent on quelling any attempt to question, criticize or dissent from the official party line.

Inevitably this clash, this polarization, came to be symbolized by the two rival groups' consistent demands: from the Bevanites, a demand for adherence to 'our Socialist purpose' (Bevan's words, 26 September 1952); from the leadership, a demand for unity and loyalty in all circumstances. Let it be said that it was not the Bevanites or Tribune who found socialism and Labour unity incompatible.

Nor did the paper find argument, debate and controversy incompatible with loyalty: it was not the Bevanites, either, who wished to *silence* their opponents in the conflict. When Arthur Deakin, leading Right-wing *bête noire* of the Left, spoke of the Left's disruptive power-seeking (the term was more usually a Tory distortion to belittle the Bevanite case) Tribune offered him room in its columns to explain himself. He accepted, and slashed away at the idea of a dissident 'pressure group' within the Labour Party – one of the first uses of the term 'Tribune Group' (12 March 1952).

The paper countered 'Brother Arfur's' attack: 'Altogether, the most deadly potential enemy of the Labour Party at this stage in its history is intolerance. Everyone knows that varying views prevail . . . Such differences can be resolved by open debate. They can never be resolved by mechanical disciplines' (Editorial, 21 March 1952).

And this insistence on the need for free discussion and unhindered debate never relaxed in the months and years to come. To aid it, Robert Edwards's new Tribune opened its columns to assorted opponents in a series called 'The Case Against Us' – where, for one, Denis Healey dismissed the paper's policies: 'Since April 1951 Tribune has betrayed the responsibilities it once shouldered so courageously' (10 October 1952). Perhaps significantly, Hugh Gaitskell – who had already aroused the Left's fury with his assertion that 'one in six' of constituency party delegates at 1952's stormy Labour conference 'appear to be Communist or Communist-inspired' (quoted 10 October 1952) – chose another forum from which to attack Tribune. In the Tory *Spectator* Gaitskell spoke menacingly of some sort of 'restraint' needed for the Left-wing papers, 'some new arrangement'. Reporting this, Michael Foot asked grimly, 'Are you proposing some interference with our freedom?' (24 October 1952).

The answer was fairly swift in coming. The Parliamentary Labour Party issued a stern resolution demanding 'the immediate abandonment of all group organisations within the Party other than those officially recognised' (quoted 31 October 1952). More broadly important, the party issued a directive against members making 'personal attacks' on each other, which led Ian Mikardo to some blistering ironies:

> I rejoice that we are not going to have any more personal attacks by members of the Parliamentary Labour Party on other members of the Parliamentary Labour Party.
>
> Never again, O my exuberant heart, will I be referred to as one of 'a little band of splenetic furies' (1). I rejoice.
>
> Never again will there be talk of 'parlour revolutionaries and other mischief-makers' (2). That's a great step forward.

No more, not ever more, will those who write about Nye Bevan include me in the list of 'sycophantic friends about him' (3). Let us praise this day for evermore . . . For never again will even the more eminent amongst us refer to some of his comrades as 'extreme Left-wingers . . . some with outlooks soured and warped by disappointment of personal ambitions, some highbrows educated beyond their capacity' (4).

. . . I rejoice at this new upsurge of self-restraint, even though it will undoubtedly rob us of many lambent pearls of English literature. We shall, for instance, have to sigh in vain for any more like 'an uneasy coalition of well-meaning emotionalists, frustrates, crackpots and fellow-travellers, making Fred Karno's Army look like the Brigade of Guards' (5).

But it ensures that we don't ever again hear some sizeable fraction of the constituency party delegates to the Party Conference (who include many Labour M.P.s) as appearing 'to be Communist or Communist-inspired', or the proceedings of that Conference characterised as 'mob rule by a group of frustrated journalists' (6). So let us all raise up our voices on high and give thanks . . .

['*Ian Mikardo's Straight Talk*', 31 October 1952]

Mikardo's quotations were from Labour MPs George Brown, Herbert Morrison, Maurice Webb, Sir Hartley Shawcross, Stanley Evans and Hugh Gaitskell.

Naturally Tribune would not be muzzled, though in *its* view it paid all due obedience to these requirements, in the paper and at its continuingly successful public meetings. Then came the time when Tribune had harsh words to say about Tory capitalizing on the 'Deakinite' outbursts against 'the political wing of the Labour movement' (16 January 1953). The Labour National Executive struck, with a resolution of censure. Tribune struck back: '. . . if the label of "personal attacks" is to be fixed on to examples of legitimate criticism, freedom of discussion within the Labour movement would be undermined and eventually destroyed. We shall continue to print the truth as we see it. Nobody will stop us' (6 February 1953).

More and worse followed. Tribune accused Sir Lincoln Evans of aiding and abetting the Tory 'denationalization' of steel; Evans issued a writ. Rumour had it that the TUC, under Deakin's thumb, contemplated withdrawing their donations to the Labour Party generally, some of which obviously went to support Bevanite candidates, and instead funding only 'candidates whom they regard as worthy' (6 November 1953). Ian Mikardo's column drew more censorious executive fire, and again Tribune flared back 'In Defence of Free Speech' (4 December 1953). The 'no personal attacks' edict meant more threats from the Parliamentary Labour Party throughout 1954 – but when Deakin flayed striking dockers with the old 'communist plot' smear tactics, Tribune could not remain silent:

> . . . He showed (1) that he did not know what the strike was about and (2) that he had little interest in finding out. He was quite content to dismiss the whole business as a Communist plot.
>
> Such an attitude on the part of the most powerful trade union leader in the country can do infinite harm to the trade union movement . . .
>
> [22 October 1954]

Down came the wrath of the NEC, who 'took the view that the article constituted an unwarranted, irresponsible and scurrilous attack on the leadership of the Transport and General Workers' Union at a crucial time', according to the letter to Tribune from the Labour Party secretary, Morgan Phillips (12 November 1954). Back came the counter-wrath of Tribune, white-hot and wholly unrepentant, putting once again

> THE CASE FOR FREEDOM
>
> . . . we flatly repudiate the suggestion that the article was scurrilous or that it constituted a personal attack on Mr Arthur Deakin, the individual concerned. The whole article was a criticism of Mr Deakin in his public capacity as a trade union leader. We concentrated on his own public statements and the consequences which we considered they implied.
>
> If the whole article is to be construed as a personal attack and therefore an offence against the injunction that members of the Labour movement should not make such attacks on one another, this injunction becomes a rule forbidding all debate in which a name is employed as a label to identify sponsors of a particular argument . . .
>
> After reflection we say that the terms of condemnation which the N.E.C. applies to the *Tribune* article could aptly be applied to Mr Deakin's own speech. It might have been described by some people as being an unwarranted, irresponsible speech made at a crucial time in the progress of the dock dispute and a speech which might easily have impeded an honourable and orderly settlement of the dispute . . .
>
> Altogether, the right to criticise or attack the leadership of a trade union forms part of the established right of free speech possessed by every citizen of this country . . . Trade union leaders are not a special

breed of humanity always to be shielded from the rough breezes of democracy, rare birds to be protected by special game laws. They are there partly to be shot at – like all other elected persons who must run the risks of public life if they aspire to hold the prizes and the power . . .

It has never occurred to us to demand that members of the Labour Party should be called upon to reconcile their attacks on Michael Foot, J. P. W. Mallalieu, Jennie Lee or, indeed, Aneurin Bevan with their membership of the Party. The last-named of these four has been attacked persistently and sometimes, in our view, viciously . . .

The N.E.C. asks us in its letter to state our intentions for the future. That can be done briefly. We reaffirm our belief in the purposes of the Socialist movement as Robert Blatchford stated them. We reaffirm our belief that the Labour Party is the instrument which can build a new society in Britain and best lead the nations towards a genuine peace. In striving to serve the Party and those causes, we shall continue to print the truth as we see it. We trust that others will do the same . . .

[*Michael Foot, Jennie Lee and J. P. W. Mallalieu*, 12 November 1954]

And just to fan the flames, Francis Williams wrote to support the paper, backhandedly: '. . . I write now to express my complete and wholehearted support for you in your present dispute with the Executive . . . I have often been in the position of regarding *Tribune* as a menace to true Socialist policy. But the attempt of the Executive to shut you up seems to me a much more dangerous menace . . .' (19 November 1954).

All these internecine conflicts – which did not by any means come to an end in 1954, though they diminished a little with Bevan's election as party treasurer in 1956 – may have revolved around basic issues such as how much socialism (if any) in Labour policy, the nature of free comment, and perhaps also the undoubted personal acrimony between Bevanites and their Deakinite/Gaitskellite opponents. But radiating from these 'hub' principles were arguments to do with specific items of policy, which particularized the polarization of Labour. Many, even most, of these arose from foreign policy and international affairs.

Almost the first party-dividing question in the early 1950s concerned the rearming of Germany, which Tribune feared and opposed, as did many on the Left. But the Labour Right fell in with America and the Tories, insisting that an armed Germany could valuably aid the strengthening of the western alliance against the Soviet 'menace'.

Lord Stansgate, for Tribune, voiced the Left's fears of 'THE DANGER FROM GERMANY':

> The German army will be the most powerful in Europe. The German people will be behind it so long as it serves the national aim. What is that aim? To recover in some way their lost lands.
>
> German rearmament must therefore create new tension . . . Are we quite sure that we can keep a rearmed Germany on our side? We remember 1939 . . .
>
> [8 August 1952]

The Tribunites fought the idea in Parliament, but – tied up as it was with Big Power talks – to no avail. Not even when the paper bluntly put the question 'What Makes Germans Different?' (Percy Redcar, 16 July 1954), suggesting that the seeds of Nazism were only in suspension, awaiting a chance to sprout again. (Some readers, like Michael Kidron on 30 July 1954, found more than a hint of racism in such statements.) In any case, the West Germans did not get unity but did get tanks and guns; and when a new Hitler did not arise the next day, concerned individuals turned their attention away from refighting old battles.

There was, after all, no shortage of new ones. The United States began its Eisenhower era, with McCarthyism in full flower (fertilized by the support of Vice-President Nixon) – with John Foster Dulles pulling the puppet strings of Syngman Rhee, General Franco, Chiang Kai-shek *et al.*, his idea of talismans against the demonic spread of communism – with all its wealth and military might spreading repression, corruption and a clear neo-imperialism round the world behind a mask of 'defending freedom'. The Soviet Union loomed, a sullen and near-paranoid giant, behind its Warsaw Pact buffers, reaching out to obstruct and threaten and provoke. All nations shivered in the clutch of the Cold War, except some – mostly, inevitably, someone's colonies or ex-colonies – who liked it hot. And it was hard to recall the time when, decades before, Russia had seemed the white hope of socialist idealism – or the time when, more recently, Tribune had acclaimed American world leadership as the ultimate safeguard of democracy.

Those days were gone. Now it was 'U.S. ELECTION BRINGS PERIL OF A SLUMP':

> . . . little faith can be placed in General Eisenhower's capacity to resist the demands of the Republican Right wing.

> That pious hope has been killed by the conduct of the General himself during the election campaign. He made no effort to tame the indecencies of McCarthyism . . .
>
> [*Editorial*, 7 November 1952]

Britain's 'dollar dependency' irked the Left all the more, given this disenchantment with American policy – and Harold Wilson echoed his pamphlet *In Place of Dollars* with some strong advice to Chancellor R. A. Butler, on a visit to Washington:

> You should know, if anyone does, that your Government has been riding on a record American boom, and that Britain is now so utterly dependent on the U.S. economy that another 'lurch', even a very slight recession, could halve our dollar earnings almost overnight and plunge us into another crisis.
>
> The danger we see is that if you talk in Washington as you have been doing in London it will encourage the Americans in insisting on yet another of the disastrous policies they sometimes force on us. And with your dependence on American aid – don't forget it was a Tory Government that asked for aid – will you be in a position to resist them? . . .
>
> [6 March 1953]

But beyond crass American intervention in the British economy – largely what Wilson and Tribune saw as the nation being 'pushed into an unfair share of the total burden of Atlantic rearmament' – the Left most feared the blinkered, fixated anti-communist crusading in world councils, a major threat to peace. With headlines like 'Save Us from the Generals' (11 June 1954) or 'Washington War Party' (18 June 1954) Tribune exposed the American hankering after a showdown with communism, and the influence of the military in the Eisenhower–Nixon administration. At the same time, the paper had no illusions about Soviet intentions – not even when that nation entered a momentous new era:

> NOW LET'S BURY THE STALIN MYTH
>
> Stalin, the man, is dead. What about Stalin, the myth? It is as well that the myth should be buried in the same coffin . . .
>
> Of course, the achievements of the Stalin era were monumental in scale. Under his guidance the Soviet Union was collectivised and a largely peasant people were made literate.
>
> Thanks to these achievements, the Russian armies which were broken by the Germans in the first world war repelled and destroyed

them in the second. Since then Communist power has been extended to the China seas and to the centre of Europe.

Who, in the face of these colossal events, will dare to question Stalin's greatness? How superhuman must be the mind which presided over these world-shattering developments?

At first glance these question appear to make only one answer possible. But there are other scenes in the drama which should not be forgotten . . .

The Nazi-Soviet Pact and the frightened sycophancy towards Hitler which Stalin displayed in the two subsequent years still stand out as probably the most grievous and colossal blunder of the century . . .

The same blindness afflicted him after 1945. He was busy clamping his power on the satellite states which had been allotted to his sphere of influence, busy despatching Marshal Zhukov to obscurity for fear that he should challenge his own prestige, busy no doubt on many indispensable tasks, but amazingly unaware of the greatest event of the post-war epoch.

China was preparing to shake the world on a scale not known since the Russian Revolution of 1917. But Stalin still believed in the star of Chiang Kai-shek! As little perhaps as the planners in Washington did the great revolutionary leader understand that the operations of revolution were still engulfing the world . . .

The old society is collapsing over large stretches of the planet. Vast masses of people in Asia, Africa, the Middle East and elsewhere are not content to submit to the old poverty and the old imperialism. They are shaking these burdens off their backs and nothing will stop them.

It is at least arguable that these commotions might be more intense and widespread if it had not been for the stolid, brutal determination of Stalinism to fit every social and national uprising into the same harsh, fixed pattern. It should at least be evident that the attempt to denounce and destroy each such rising as a Kremlin plot is the one way to construct the world Communist conspiracy which is so much feared.

As for Russia itself, the question remains open whether Stalin's dictatorship has been sufficient to destroy the constructive momentum of the Revolution which gave him the real sinews of Soviet strength . . .

But it may be that Socialist regeneration in Russia itself is just another of the world developments which the infallible Stalin could not foresee.

[*Michael Foot*, 13 March 1953]

But the new Kremlin leader, Malenkov, offered small hope for an easing of tension, especially when Soviet tanks rolled through the streets of East Berlin in June 1953, to crush striking, demonstrating workers in an ominous foretaste of satellite suppressions to come. And though the tension was potent enough in Europe, elsewhere in the world the Western 'defenders of freedom' were already in armed conflict against communism – especially in Asia, where Mao's China added that imposing extra threat. As we all know, the American leaders could never see any solution other than obsessional sabre-rattling, viewing the opposing power blocs as 'gods and devils' (Aneurin Bevan, 17 July 1953) with the devils even more spiky of horns and tail if they happened to be Oriental. So nothing had been learned in Korea, where truce talks dragged on and bogged down, summarized by James Cameron in a review of a book by that pillar of the American free press, I. F. Stone:

THERE HAD TO BE A KOREA

By now the pattern of defeated hopes and outraged sense in Korea is just about complete. One stage only separates us from the final irony, which will be the resumption of full-scale war on *none* of the original principles, the liberation of Korea from the Koreans.

The grotesque farce of the truce talks have set a level of cynical hypocrisy outstanding even by the standards of contemporary international doubletalk. The scandalous behaviour of Syngman Rhee is matched by the very nearly incredible lunacy on Koje Island. Only one advantage results: this repellent business has now reached a point where it is possible to protest without, as has been customary hitherto, being denounced as an idealist, a Communist, or an imbecile . . .

This emergence of skeletons from the Korean cupboard is not a merry sight. The fact that it must be observed with the greatest satisfaction by Peking and Moscow scarcely improves it. In the middle of the skeletons, now, arrives a clattering parade of bones, 348 pages long, that might otherwise have escaped attention . . .

Not all of it is Hidden History. There has been no serious mystery, at least, about the peculiar role of Mr John Foster Dulles, and the actual circumstances of the war's beginning have been disturbing and puzzling people for long enough. Even Mr Stone's elaborate researches have been unable to determine the answer to the real 64-dollar question: whether on June 25th, 1950, North Korea did indeed attack without provocation or whether, as seems hard to deny, the attack was encouraged politically by the bellicose Syngman Rhee and provoked militarily by three feints across the border. The U.N. Commission on the spot – it is worth recalling now – has not even yet committed itself . . .

But eventually, eleven months ago, the truce talks began – the macabre tangle of casuistry that from that day to this has provided no evidence whatsoever of any goodwill on either side. Of the Communist motives, good or bad, we are in the customary ignorance. Of the American negotiators it can at least be said that they gave the impression of taking every precaution against peace breaking out inadvertently. The talks were, and have been, conducted in a cultivated climate of disruptive news-leaks and unhelpful propaganda, with high-explosive prodding as required . . .

Mr Stone's book will pretty surely be accused of muck-raking, a challenge which, if I were Mr Stone, I would be inclined to accept, on the principle that any situation full enough of muck can do with a little raking. His conclusions are his own affair. They are, rightly or wrongly, summed up for him by General Van Fleet himself, talking to a Filipino delegation in June of this year:

'Korea has been a blessing. There had to be a Korea either here or some place in the world.'

Herewith it is proposed that this phrase belonging as it does with the other historic documents of free men, be engraved in a fair script over the peace-portico of Panmunjom: There had to be a Korea. The past tense will translate well. In Korean, there is practically no other.

[*James Cameron*, 13 June 1952]

So, too, not far away, there had to be an Indo-China.

For over six years, France has been fighting a war in Indo-China. It has cost her 200,000 casualties and over £1,000 million. One of the richest areas in Asia has been laid waste. Money and materials that would have solved France's desperate economic crisis have drained away into the mud-fields and rice-paddies of this rain-sodden peninsula.

Why is France fighting this war? This is the question that thousands of Frenchmen, who have seen their brothers, sons and friends leave by the troopships to Indo-China, never to return, have been asking for years. A succession of Right-wing governments have given them high-sounding answers: to save the Far East from Communism, to revive the glories of the French Empire, and so on . . .

[*Paul Johnson*, 2 October 1953]

The Indo-China war was then the prototype of a fading imperial power reaping as it had sowed. Britain too faced this bitter harvest all over the world. In Malaya, where a regular Tribune writer, Bob Millar, told of 40,000 troops fighting a 'police action' to protect the £12 million rubber and tin profits made by British companies the previous year (13 November 1953), and where a new Tribune writer,

Ian Aitken, decried Britain's 'barbarous and stupid' policy of repression and reprisal (14 May 1954). In Singapore, later, where Lee Kuan Yew emerged within a violent far-Left struggle for independence. And, beyond Asia, in British Guiana, where Britain sent the traditional gunboats when Cheddi Jagan threw his Marxist People's Progressive Party against the exploiting might of 'King Sugar'.

Anti-colonialist struggles brewed as well in the Honduras, in Malta, especially throughout Africa. That continent had already seen the macabre rising of the Mau Mau, at its worst in the earlier 1950s. 'Mr Lyttelton's Big Mistake' (3 October 1952) occurred when the Colonial Secretary imposed 'a virtual dictatorship', which George Wigg enlarged upon:

> . . . With confidence between black and white completely destroyed, and economic and political problems so interwoven, rapid action, except further repression, is impossible. If the situation is to be improved three steps are essential.
>
> First, Jomo Kenyatta and his associates must be brought to trial or released.
>
> Secondly, if they are released they should be given representation on the Royal Commission which is to inquire into Kenya's problems.
>
> And thirdly, MR LYTTELTON MUST GO. Not only has he demonstrably failed in his duty . . ., but his ignorance and incompetence have materially worsened the situation.
>
> Before he goes he should remind his successor of some words of Edmund Burke which were quoted a few days ago by a Member of the Kenya Legislative Council: – 'When peaceful methods fail, force remains, but when force fails nothing remains.'
>
> [7 November 1952]

By early 1953 white atrocities in Kenya gained as much attention as the Mau Mau terror. Fenner Brockway detailed them fiercely:

> . . . The collective punishments, which involved uprooting of Africans within a 25 mile radius of one murdered European, the destruction of their homes, the confiscation of their cattle, and deportation to the congested Kikuyu reserve.
>
> The 'scorched earth' destruction of crops on African land bordering the Aberdare Mountains.
>
> The rounding up of African villages and townships, the arrest of the whole African population, men and women, for screening and searching.

The destruction of all African hutments in the suburbs of Nairobi and the eviction of hundreds of African families.

The closing of over a hundred African schools.

Brutalities in the reserves, in detention camps, in prisons.

Most disquieting of all are the reports of how the 'shoot to kill' order – when Africans refuse to halt or attempt to escape or to resist arrest – is being applied . . .

[24 July 1953]

Even so, Britain was learning no lessons about independence movements, colonial politics or the failure of force, as a rising young African leader made clear in Tribune some years later:

DARKEST DAYS AHEAD FOR KENYA

With the easing of the emergency situation politics among the Europeans changed. The liberals of the dark emergency days cast off the coat of liberalism. They talked loosely and boastfully of European control and leadership, which to the African merely spelt European domination . . .

Last year politics took a fresh turn when European and Asian election campaigns brought forth the usual racial slogans.

Once more the country echoed with cries about 'the sanctity of the white highlands', 'separate schools', and 'continued European control of the Government', leading to the famous election pronouncement by one spokesman – 'the time would come when the Africans would be told so far and no further' . . .

Neither I nor my colleagues believe in or advocate violence. In our efforts to achieve justice we shall neither lose hope nor spare any efforts.

Force shall not and has never prevailed. It is in justice that must lie the foundation of stability and happiness for all communities in Kenya . . .

[*Tom Mboya*, 14 June 1957]

As Kenya went, so Africa seemed to be going. Bob Millar and Fenner Brockway saw hopes for the Gold Coast in the advent of Kwame Nkrumah (11 December 1953), and indeed Dingle Foot praised its achievement of independence, later, as Ghana: '. . . The visitors from South and Central Africa were confronted with a state of affairs in which the colour bar has completely disappeared . . . there were the representatives of the Iron Curtain countries who, if rumour be correct, were frankly baffled by everything they saw and heard . . . neither Marx nor Lenin foresaw the spectacle of Nkrumah dancing with the Duchess of Kent . . .' (15 March 1957).

But other writers saw dangerous ferments rising in Nigeria, Uganda, Nyasaland (as Malawi then was) – and, especially, Southern Rhodesia.

LOOKING AT SOUTHERN RHODESIA

. . . Coming home, I am besieged by people telling me how completely things have changed. The word Partnership lards every conversation, political speech, newspaper article.

The Federation of Southern Rhodesia, Northern Rhodesia and Nyasaland was bulldozed through against the wishes of the Africans in the three territories; in return they were promised Partnership. The word Partnership varies with the occasion of its use; but in essence it is the expression of the desperate wish of the intelligent whites not to be thought as reactionary as the Nationalists in the Union of South Africa.

Strydom and his men say that the African and the white man must forever remain apart, except insofar as the African is useful; that white supremacy must be maintained.

In the Federation, partnership means that the races are potentially equal, and that the African must remain under the tutelage of the white man until he qualifies as civilised. The period of time this process will take varies from about fifty years (a very advanced view) to three thousand years.

One is an openly racist formulation; one paternalistic.

And the difference in practice?

In a shop in Salisbury I was waiting my turn to be served behind a couple of African women, when they were shouted at to get out of the way of the white madam.

In post offices, banks and public buildings there are separate facilities for white and black people; Africans are not allowed into restaurants, hotels or bars – for that matter they are not allowed to drink 'European' liquor.

They have to live in areas especially set aside for them both in the country and in the towns. They carry 'passes' – permits for movement. The lives of white and black are totally separate on every level.

This is in Southern Rhodesia: the legal structure is, except in minor details, almost identical with that in the Union . . .

[*Doris Lessing*, 8 June 1956]

And in the Rhodesian colony's older counterpart to the south, the South African writer Ruth First saw the apartheid walls flung even higher as black African independence northwards spelled danger for white supremacists, countered by:

> ... the Population Registration Act, under which every person in South Africa must carry an identity card which states his race ...
>
> The marginal men, the Coloureds, have been the first to be classified in large numbers. They are living through a nightmare as Government officials try to unravel the racial admixture first started three centuries ago by the early settlers ...
>
> A man who has always been Coloured, when he is made an African, has to forfeit a job with trade union rates of pay and take unskilled work; to carry a pass book and observe the night curfew; to move into fenced African locations; to remove his children from Coloured schools; to suffer the many daily humiliations inflicted on the African ...
>
> Classification does not create anything like the furore it should. White South Africans are hardened to this sort of thing. They live in a society which has elevated theories of race difference to a gospel ...
>
> Yet even the Nationalists have been made aware that the African people are daily disproving the myth of their inferiority. So the laws are amended ... and race theories are elaborated and sanctified as the Divine Will.
>
> [21 September 1956]

Back within the Empire proper, or what remained of it, British guns were still marshalled to delay the inevitable surges towards freedom. One small island shed a disproportionate amount of blood with its drive to a special kind of independence. But 'BULLETS WON'T CURE THE CYPRIOTS', warned Tom Driberg:

> Will the Tories never learn?
>
> Must the long-drawn-out tragedies of Ireland and Egypt and Kenya be repeated in Cyprus? ...
>
> 'Self-determination' means the right of all peoples to determine their own status and to decide, if they wish, for a change of sovereignty. This is what, in the case of Cyprus, Mr Lennox Boyd and the British Government reject ...
>
> [24 December 1954]

Tribune followed that crisis closely – with Driberg again ('The Talks That Were *Bound* to Fail' – 16 September 1955), and Ian Mikardo's visit to Archbishop Makarios:

> The situation in Cyprus in 1955 bears a terrifying resemblance to the

situation in Palestine in 1946 and 1947 . . . A people being gradually driven to the view that the British will, in the end, yield to force what they refuse to moderation; the prestige of responsible leaders being ruined by our contemptuous treatment of them; violence followed by retribution, followed by more violence in protest against the retribution; collective punishments hitting the innocent as well as the guilty and acting as recruiting-sergeants for the underground organisations; friendships between British settlers and the local population breaking under the strain; our soldiers browned off at being unjustly hated, and themselves becoming unjust haters in turn . . .

[11 November 1955]

By then, though, an even more potentially explosive nationalist movement had crowded nearly every other – Asia, black Africa, Cyprus and all – out of the headlines, and had given extra point to the Driberg and Mikardo allusions, above, to the Middle East.

That region saw violent flare-ups, during this period, in Iraq, Iran, Morocco, Tunisia, the Sudan, Algeria and the Lebanon. Tribune analysed them all in their turn, notably in outraged articles from its correspondent in France, Guy Henriques, on French counter-revolutionary excesses in its North African possessions – where, as usual, the first casualty was democracy.

But Britain had no reason to feel superior. The 'Middle East Madness' (Ray Alan, 19 September 1952) of the Western Powers had spawned a strategically crucial nationalist movement in the Arab nations, its fury directed principally at a tiny new state which had itself been born out of the blood and terror of an anti-colonial conflict. Israel's very existence – which at that time Tribune, in the person of Jennie Lee, could see as 'A Socialist Dream Come True' (22 January 1954) - enflamed Egypt especially, under its new and nearly independent government. There was no room for reason: 'Over and over again Israel has offered to meet her Arab neighbours at the conference tables and each time the offer has been rejected,' wrote Anthony Greenwood on 8 January 1954. Profiteering arms dealing with Israel and/or the Arabs enflamed the situation more, until Tribune was headlining 'THE FEARFUL DANGER' (4 November 1955), while in the same issue the Jewish Socialist Labour Party, Poale Zion, was warning grimly, 'Israel May Be Compelled to Fight'.

And it was. And so, in nearly the last manifestation of the gunboat reflex, was Britain.

An Egyptian coup brought Nasser to power, and he nationalized the Suez Canal in the summer of 1956. Then, goaded into accepting the old precept about the best defence, Israel took the offensive – and British and French troops as well flooded into the Middle East in what Michael Foot called

A CRIME AGAINST THE WORLD

The British Government has embarked on an act of aggression in wicked defiance of the law of nations.

The fatal step has been taken in company with an utterly discredited French Government, whose main aim is to seek support in an evil, imperialist struggle against the Arab peoples . . .

The crisis is represented as one which suddenly flared up on Monday night, when the news of Israel's attack on Egypt was received in London and Paris. Yet we know that claim to be false.

Ever since President Nasser nationalised the Suez Canal at the end of July the British and French Prime Ministers have refused to give a pledge that they would never resort to force, except in conformity with their undertakings under the United Nations Charter.

Now their embarrassed equivocations are revealed as the single strand of candour in the record of deceit.

Military plans were prepared. Cyprus was made available for French troops. The assault force was poised, ready for the signal.

Perhaps the French Government knew much more than the world has yet been told about the possibility of action by the Israelis.

Differing views are certainly possible about the decision of the Israeli Government. Israel has been subjected to severe provocation. For years the Government of Egypt (with the connivance of the great powers) has refused to obey the Security Council's ruling about the rights of Israeli shipping in the Suez Canal.

During recent months tension has mounted. British policy has often contributed to it. Never did the great powers seem ready to embark on the positive policy required for ensuring a permanent settlement in the area . . .

Instead, the British and French Governments have seized the opportunity to take the law into their own hands. They have come near to disrupting the only machinery which can establish a real peace . . .

Indeed not since Neville Chamberlain presented Hitler's terms to the Czechs in 1938 has a powerful Western nation treated a small nation with such brutal contempt . . .

[2 November 1956]

When the firing had ceased and the UN had taken charge of the Israel – Egypt borders, news spread that the crime was worse even than Foot had surmised. 'Did They Plot This War?' Tribune asked (23

November 1956), and a few weeks later the answer came: 'THEY KNEW!' (14 December 1956). Naked aggression had been bad enough, even when it resulted in humiliation. But the facts about prior 'collusion' lent the whole episode an air of sordid villainy from which, in a different political atmosphere, the Tories should never have recovered.

Instead, the Conservatives clung to the power which they had retained in the 1955 election. They did discard Eden, as rightful scapegoat, and the traditional 'magic circle' of Tory kingmakers cast up Harold Macmillan in 'one of the shadiest political intrigues in the history of the Tory Party' (Michael Foot, 18 January 1957). Perhaps they also clung because some of Labour's oppositional effort was blunted by electoral defeat and by its own previous leadership change, when Attlee slid away to his earldom and left Hugh Gaitskell in his chair. The deep divisions in the party remained, needless to say: Tribune was asking 'What's Wrong with the Labour Party?' in 1957, and was snarling – '. . . The idea that the Labour Party can sneak back into office by representing itself merely as a respectable moderate, alternative administration never had much to be said for it' (Michael Foot, 22 November 1957).

Relentless opposition to the Tory Government, that was what Tribune demanded (and provided) – and not only in the international arenas already looked at. The economic crisis took equal precedence, as when Labour economist Thomas Balogh examined Tory thinking:

> . . . Its assumptions have been falsified because of a number of events, of which the recently announced cuts in Commonwealth – especially Australian – imports are the most important. These may reduce British exports by as much as £200 million. Also important is the fact that demand in the United States continues to be slack. Resistance to British goods may well spread from textiles to metal goods . . .
>
> Nevertheless, the Government continues to dream of re-adjusting our balance of payment by increasing production and exports as well as the invisible incomes from abroad. And this miracle is to be achieved exclusively by monetary policy . . .
>
> [16 May 1952]

But Tory *actions* drew even more outrage. George Strauss led the charge for Tribune over the government's hasty 'sell-out' of steel back to private ownership ('It's the People *versus* the Steel Barons',

31 October 1952). David Stark Murray and Renée Short among others expressed bitterness at squeezes on the National Health Service.

Similar cutbacks and starvations showed up in the social services, especially old-age pensions; in housing muddles ('Butler *versus* the Homeless', 4 November 1955); in education ('Our children are the first victims of the Tory economy axe' – Fred Peart, 22 February 1952). On that last subject, the 1950s saw an escalation in the battle over the 11-plus, while the first few comprehensives were being watched hopefully by educationalists and reported on by contributors like Margaret Cole:

> The controversy, it is true, has become a *little* less savage, a *little* less violent in expression than it was a couple of years ago; some few people, who are capable of using their own eyes, have stopped saying, since they looked at Kidbrooke and other schools in being, that a comprehensive school 'must be' a perpetual traffic-jam, a universal sausage machine of mediocrity in which the child is a lonely atom and all individuality and all initiative suppressed . . .
>
> [21 October 1955]

Such domestic subjects remained in prominent view after Michael Foot returned to Tribune in 1956 to take up the editorship relinquished by Robert Edwards.

Foot's return naturally meant changes, but broadly the character of the Tribune of the 1950s remained the same. In everything from the busy, demanding layout (with plentiful illustration) to the extended letters pages as a forum for heated argument, both editors beat drums and blew trumpets to awaken reader response and involvement, and to keep them awake. It was a time of splendid campaigns and crusades, among them the glory days of the fight against capital punishment, when Sydney Silverman was among the leaders battling 'to wipe out this dark and bloody stain on our civilisation once and for all' (2 December 1955).

And Tribune similarly plunged into the heat of controversy over vital new social issues like the Wolfenden Report concerning prostitution and homosexuality ('What Shall We Do with Prostitutes?' – Lena Jeger, 19 December 1958); or like the new problems surrounding Commonwealth immigration, which would come to an ugly head also in 1958.

Tribune, in short, whether under Edwards or Foot, concerned

itself more deeply than ever with 'the state of the nation'. And it seldom found that state healthy.

This coverage, and this stirring of adrenalin, was carried further by Edwards's use of weekly columnists, with whom he was almost as profligate as Hartshorn had been. Mikardo kept up his 'Straight Talk' and Mallalieu continued a 'Westminster Commentary' (though in 1954 he turned *sports* columnist briefly, and by 1956 Hugh Delargy was reporting from Parliament). In the early 1950s there were also Laurence Thompson columnizing for a while, Jennie Lee briefly maintaining the tradition of 'As I Please', and newcomer 'John Kerr' with an array of snippets and comments called 'Facts Behind the News'. By 1954 Aneurin Bevan was producing a weekly column answering readers' questions; Elizabeth Thomas had joined the paper with a column of parliamentary quotes, 'Pocket Hansard'; and Robert J. Edwards had begun his column, 'Speaking for Myself', later taken over by the pseudonymous John Marullus and eventually evolving through a string of other disguises into the present 'Diary'.

Also 1954 saw the first contribution from the only one of the 1950s columnists still writing for the paper in 1977 – the Rev. Donald Soper. His first article joined in a merry campaign against the far-Right absurdities of 'Moral Rearmament', and he continued to stir brews of controversy from then on – as with his thoughts on atheism:

GOD AND DR HUXLEY

Dr Julian Huxley was reported the other day to have announced that in a hundred years' time it will be impossible for an intelligent man to believe in God . . .

Were this periodical devoted first of all to the defence of Christian theology I should be at some pains to argue that there is a deal more arrogance than erudition in Huxley's atheism – the arrogance, for instance, of claiming that the 'public knowledge' of the laboratory is infallible whereas the 'private knowledge' of the oratory is illusory . . .

Yet I imagine that many readers who think of themselves as practical socialists will already have lost interest in what I have written. As they see it, this row between science and religion is a private fight, the only certain outcome of which is to distract those who take part in it from the public battle for social justice and world peace . . .

Now I agree wholeheartedly that it is the classless society that matters, but I am equally sure that unless the classless society is the Kingdom of God, intended by God and made possible by God, then it is a forlorn waste of time to look for it . . .

[*Donald Soper*, 28 October 1955]

Dr Huxley was never one to shirk a fight:

MAN AND HIS GODS

Dr Soper accuses me of arrogance, of disregarding the evidence from the moral and aesthetic realms, of taking an 'abstractly intellectual' view of the problem of the place of God or gods in religion, and of claiming that the 'public knowledge' of the laboratory is infallible.

I am not guilty of any of these things. Ever since I was a young man I have been searching – not for '*the* Truth', for there is no such thing – but for more and better truth, not arrogantly but always with a sense of wonder at the back of my mind . . .

Above all, I have insisted on the always limited (though steadily increasing) certitude of public knowledge gained by the scientific method, as against the infallibility claimed for certain religious dogmas . . .

Disbelief in God is not arrogance: on the contrary, it is born of that mixture of humility, reverence and confidence needed for any human advance – humility in accepting the facts of reality (*all* the known facts), reverence in face of the facts (including the facts of our own nature), and confidence in the capacity of human minds collectively to discover more of the truth that can set us free.

[*Julian Huxley*, 18 November 1955]

One more weekly column needs special mention, because it shows that, with all this material crammed into eight and then twelve bulging pages, something had to make way. In Edwards's Tribune it was the books and arts coverage. Book reviews shrank into only one principal feature – a column entitled 'Books and People' in which literary editor Bruce Bain mentioned and commented on as many books as was decently possible. Now and then Daniel George, Mervyn Jones or Raymond Fletcher might deputize for Bain (and Fletcher inherited the column entirely in mid-1957).

But sometimes a special book might warrant a separate review of its own: and though the literary coverage had been curtailed, the quality of the reviewers had not – with writers like A. J. P. Taylor, Julian Symons, Geoffrey Goodman, Christopher Hill, Wayland Young, Mervyn Stockwood, Keith Waterhouse, Sydney Tremayne,

Sid Chaplin, Mordecai Richler, Norman Nicholson, N. F. Simpson, Bernard Miles.

The other arts felt the axe as well, not from philistinism but from sheer lack of space. Poems vanished entirely. Films were somewhat neglected until Julian Symons revived film reviewing in 1955, which then went through several writers until in 1957 Derek Hill took over and remained. Broadcasting received only sporadic attention, from Peter de Francia and others, until the later 1950s; art, music and the rest rarely got a look-in until about the same time (when, for one, Edward Lockspeiser began a long and distinguished run as music reviewer).

Theatre reviewing did not suffer so much, undoubtedly because of the influence of Bruce Bain's *alter ego* Richard Findlater. His knowledgeable individuality welcomed Joan Littlewood's Theatre Royal in East London, in 1953 ('Stratford's Left-wing Stage', 6 March); it went out of step with most other critics by praising the convention-smashing arrival of *Waiting for Godot* ('I Go for These Tramps!', 12 August 1955); and in 1956 it recognized in another theatrical event just how much old orders were changing in that year of upheaval:

> THIS MONSTER REALLY LIVES
>
> I have already made it clear, in these columns, that I am a partisan of the English Stage Company. Its regime at the Royal Court is likely to make theatre history, if it gets the support it deserves. But its existence is already justified by one play alone – John Osborne's *Look Back in Anger*, which I saw belatedly last week.
>
> I watched it with surprise, anger, excitement and admiration. Surprise, because it puts on the stage – for the first time in my experience – a sector of English life hitherto beyond the West End pale: anger, because the central figure – a Wain-Amis un-hero with a giant chip on his shoulder – is a monster of juvenile egotism; excitement, because this same monster, by name Jimmy Porter, is turbulently and unprecedently alive; admiration, because of the wit, truth and dramatic intensity of John Osborne's writing, and the skill, integrity and emotional force of Kenneth Haigh's acting in the enormously taxing role of Jimmy . . .
>
> I am also influenced, no doubt, by the novelty of the setting – a one-roomed flat in a large Midland town seems quite exotic after the customary opulence of Shaftesbury-avenue interiors – and by the unwonted accuracy of social tone. England, as represented in the West End drama, is still tidily divided into the comic working-class (with accents and aspidistras) and the not-so-comic upper-middle-class (who

talk and live posh). *Look Back in Anger* does suggest, at least, that class apartheid is no longer as strict as our drama supposes, and that the old country has changed a bit since Pinero . . .

[*Richard Findlater*, 1 June 1956]

Some restoration of arts coverage (but not of poems) could be managed because of Tribune's growth to twelve pages in October 1955, when Edwards grandly claimed '90,000 readers' (but the noun was carefully chosen) although the price went up to 6d. in early 1956. That year also brought a larger page size; and further rises in sales allowed, in autumn 1957, a paper of sixteen pages a week. Throughout these years, even in the cramped days of the eight-pager, the *concern* for the arts did not diminish. Separate special articles on aspects of the arts world proliferated, and as provocatively as anything else in the paper. Take John Berger, for instance, fighting an old fight:

DEAR ENEMY . . .

You are the man who kills art in the welfare state. You are the pampered worker who cares for nothing but football pools and fish and chips. You are the brute whose indifference to the finer things of life keeps scores of painters and artists starving in garrets and corrupting in advertising agencies. That, at least, is how the story goes. As an art critic and a painter, I have been brought up to despair of you – you scoundrel.

I'm writing this letter to inform you that for the last two months I have been organising an exhibition of about 150 paintings and drawings which are now on show at the Whitechapel Art Gallery . . .

I planned this exhibition not for the critics and the Bond Street art-fanciers but for you, and all your friends who can't stand modern art.

For the fact of the matter is that I don't believe you're a Philistine at all. I think it's modern art, and not you, that's to blame. And so I hope that if you're in London you'll be able to see this exhibition . . .

You might not agree with all the pictures, but I think you *would* agree that all of them are trying to make a statement which really has something to do with the way the majority of people live and the issues they have to face; also, that they are trying to do this without being sentimental or patronising . . .

But the reason why I hope you'll go to this exhibition is not just that I think its subject matter will interest you. There's a more important reason – that you may see why painting matters, and help to direct its use. In all times of real imaginative achievement, the art of the period has served the faith and ideals of the vital, dominant class. The future

> power of this country is in the hands of the working class, and so obviously it is some form of living Socialist faith that the art of the future will serve . . .
>
> [26 September 1952]

At various other times Tribune made room for Paul Rotha to attack the Rank Organization's debilitating grip on British films, another old fight ('The Riddle of Mr Rank', 19 September 1952); for Wolf Mankowitz to bewail the state of writing in Britain ('How to survive in a free-lance middle-ditch capitalist society, competitive and yet destructive towards initiative . . .', 13 July 1956). The American poet Kenneth Rexroth wrote on literary developments in his country, on the threshold of the 'Beat' era (13 and 20 February 1953). George Woodcock reported unfavourably on new Canadian writing (1 May 1953). Sydney Tremayne prophetically advised poets to go out and read aloud to the people (20 November 1953). And Kenneth Tynan debated acidically with Henry Fairlie on the then fashionable topic of Angry Young Men:

> A great deal of contemporary youthful anger derives from people who suffered in childhood from the depression, reached adulthood during or after the post-war social revolution, and went out into the world to find that the old gang – what Mr Fairlie, in an earlier incarnation, called 'the Establishment' – was still disconcertingly in charge. This is the source of John Osborne's anger, and I find it perfectly justified. He is annoyed not because society has been 'levelled', but because it has not . . .
>
> [1 November 1957]

Because then, as now, Tribune erected no barrier between culture and politics, the two often came together in ringing outcries – for instance, against the sitting duck of commercial television and its licence to print money ('those who sell the goods will call the tune', warned an editorial of 20 November 1953). And, still on culture and politics, some big guns fired rounds in a debate on Labour's policy on the arts – or its lack of one, bemoaned by Compton Mackenzie on 26 December 1952. Herbert Read, conversely, wanted to 'Keep Whitehall Out!' – because 'A fermentation of the arts can only take place among the people . . . The business of the state in this matter (if it has any business at all) is to set up this process of fermentation . . .' (13 February 1953).

All this extension of concern with the 'state of the nation' also restored to prominence in Tribune an area that had never been neglected in the paper but that began under Edwards to receive a regular, extensive, newsy, in-depth coverage – the area of industrial matters, the state of the unions. Trade unionists themselves began to appear in Tribune's columns – Arthur Horner, Bryn Roberts, Clive Jenkins. And, given the penchant for columnists, it was natural that Tribune should again acquire a weekly 'industrial reporter', in the person of Ian Aitken for some time, succeeded in 1956 by Richard Clements.

There was much to report, especially the continuing disharmony between the Labour Left and the many Right-wing unions, dominated by Deakin's mighty TGWU. But even when Deakin's death and the accession of Frank Cousins moved that union Leftwards in – when else? – 1956, unions remained newsworthy, in part because of the frequent and bitter industrial disputes which Bevan saw as 'A DECLARATION OF CLASS WAR' (22 March 1957).

All the same, while the Tories may have declared war, not many unionists took up arms. A series by that dean of socialist thinkers, G. D. H. Cole, analysed 'What is Wrong with the Trade Unions?', and found many answers – among them, an overweening concern with 'discipline' in some unions, as part of a general fear of communism. But Cole also decried the 'APATHY IN THE UNIONS' (6 January 1956), brought about by enormous growth of some unions, creating a lack of homogeneity in the membership and also a rise in 'the proportion of apathetic members' who are in the union not because they are keen or activist but because they have to be in order to work. Out of this came a gap between the leadership plus hard-core activists and the rank and file with its tendency to apathy.

Cole had a point – but then, at the beginning of that remarkable year, 1956, unionists were not the only sufferers from apathy. In other contexts, though, there were more apt terms: disillusion, anxiety, impotent anger, a dispiriting sense of a world undergoing breakdown, hurtling towards an unknown future beyond all ordinary control or comprehension. In Britain, continuing economic decline, diplomatic impotence and internecine domestic political wrangling must have offered little to counteract an air of weariness and indifference. Even some of the circuses that traditionally went with the bread lost a little glamour: much of England went into shock when the Hungarian footballers came in 1954 and thrashed the England team at its own national game; and Tribune was not alone in its distaste, expressed by Canon John Collins, for the sycophantic vulgarity and 'cashing-in' visible during the accession of Queen Elizabeth ('CORONATION RACKETS', 22 May 1953).

Internationally, too, the world was bruised and reeling with tensions, crises and disruptions one after another. Many came to their calamitous heads, to rival Suez, in that year of turning-points, 1956. And most grew out of inexorable glacial extensions of the Cold War.

Briefly, when new leaders had emerged in the Kremlin, the world held its breath in hopes of a thaw – and still did so in spite of the unnerving defection of Burgess and Maclean. ('The things that Burgess saw as he looked at British life from Eton to Bevin to Eden were in themselves quite enough to produce the situation which finally sent him to Moscow . . .' remarked Claud Cockburn later, in a review of a book on the runaways by Tom Driberg – 30 November 1956). Then in no time the new Soviet rulers overturned a monolithic myth, or cult, and created one of the most momentous upheavals ever in international socialism.

SPEECHES THAT SHOOK THE WORLD

The world this week is still trying to work out the significance of three amazing speeches delivered at the congress of the Communist Party of the Soviet Union. Put together with all that has happened since the death of Stalin, they reveal a change whose importance cannot be exaggerated . . .

The Khrushchev message took six hours to deliver, but its essence can be summed up in three words: *Think for yourselves*! Two hundred million people, long imprisoned by dogma and mesmerised by the frown of a dictator, are encouraged to start working out for themselves the answers to the manifold problems of an expanding economy . . .

It would be absurd to see Khrushchev as a sudden convert to liberal ideas. It is equally absurd to discount the significance of the change and dismiss it as a trivial manoeuvre . . .

The new leaders seem determined to turn their backs on the throttling and ultimately inefficient system of one-man rule. For twenty years, said Mikoyan, 'the cult of personality flourished and this exerted an extremely negative influence on the party and its activity'. That's putting it mildly! . . .

[*Front-page editorial*, 24 February 1956]

Inevitably the Western communist parties went into convulsion, with shock and bitterness spreading like a contagion. Few spoke of their disillusion more strongly, in Britain, than Lawrence Daly:

WHY I QUIT

I have recently resigned from the Communist Party and from its Scottish District Committee, and would be grateful if you would give me space to explain briefly the reasons for my decision, which are as follows.

1. The recent revelations in the Soviet Union appear to confirm certain doubts about, and disagreements with, Soviet Policy which I had expressed (all too inadequately) inside the Communist Party over a number of years.

2. The Communist Party's unquestioning acceptance of the anti-Stalin criticisms, which is as reprehensible as was its previous unquestioning acceptance of every aspect of Soviet Policy while Stalin was in power.

3. This attitude of blind loyalty to the Soviet leaders instead of loyalty to Communist principles is the basic error which has led the Communist Party to support and defend (or deny and ignore) the most colossal mistakes and monstrous crimes . . .

I remain what I was when I joined the Communist Party sixteen years ago – a believer in Socialism as the only ultimate answer to the exploitation of man by man . . .

[29 June 1956]

Shortly, though, the double-think within Khrushchev's 'liberalization' manifested itself. Hungary and Poland seemed to take him at his word, began 'thinking for themselves', and were soon happily 'ON THE KNIFE EDGE OF FREEDOM!' (26 October 1956). But a week later, while Britain was in the throes of the 'criminal madness' of Suez, and France was staining the sands of Algeria with nationalist blood, the Soviet tanks rolled into Budapest where they were met by freedom fighters armed with little more than cobblestones and courage.

THOUSANDS MAY DIE – FREEDOM WILL LIVE

. . . We do not know, with any precision, the politics of the rebels. The Russian tanks are there to stop us from knowing.

We do know that the Communist regime was devoid of any support at all, and that the revolt would have been bloodlessly successful in a day if there had been no Russian troops in the country.

Since every man and woman in Hungary willing to load a rifle or wave a banner was behind the rising, are we to suppose that they all want capitalism?

Of course, if they did, the Russian army would still have no more right to impose its will on them than the British army has to stop British Guiana going Communist. But the facts speak otherwise and refute this imbecile logic.

In a demand for national independence, freedom from foreign occupation, and free elections diverse groups came together – patriotic Communists, Social-Democrats, and spokesmen of the peasantry.

It was their coming together, in the coalition formed last Saturday by Imre Nagy, that represented the real threat to Russia. This government did not 'disintegrate'. It was killed when it was gaining real strength . . .

The plain fact is that the Communists have so little faith in their ideas, so little hope that these will survive in open competition with those of democratic Socialism or even, it seems, of reaction, that they justify armed and alien force to prevent such a competition . . .

[*Mervyn Jones*, 9 November 1956]

Saving itself from a similar fate, 'Poland Tries to Walk the Tightrope' (16 November 1956): its new leader, Gomulka, was avoiding any precipitate 'de-Stalinizing'. Tito's Yugoslavia, rehabilitated by Khrushchev, also kept a low profile, which meant a heavy clamp on anyone who spoke out – like Milovan Djilas, about whom Jennie Lee protested:

. . . Marshal Tito can know very little about us if he thinks that by gaoling Djilas, who has paid us the compliment of saying he agrees with much of our Socialist faith, he is doing other than lengthening the distance between Belgrade and the West.

Tito likes to see himself as a bridge between the Kremlin and the West. But this is not how bridges are built. This is a one-sided surrender to Soviet prejudices and an alarming sign of the rigidity of the Marshal's own outlook.

But even for Marshal Tito the world will not stand still. 'Cry freedom' is in the air . . .

[21 December 1956]

So 1956 left the world deeper in the mire of its apathy and disillusion, its bitterness and anger. And 1957 showed little improvement. Less likelihood emerged of the East – West bridges Jennie Lee had mentioned when in October mankind crossed a frontier once relegated only to fantasy adventure, and entered the space age. But praise was muted, for the Russians had taken this giant step, and the world could see – as indeed it had seen with the news of a Soviet ICBM capability – that America's material and technological supremacy was not unchallengeable. The position worsened with the second 'Sputnik' that year, and America reacted with what Tribune called 'The Retreat to Madness' (15 November 1957).

Frenzied expenditure occurred to catch up in the space race and keep ahead in the arms race. Dulles went in search of new brinks, and found them in Asia – where Mao's China continued to impress those who resented the old and new Western imperialisms. There Dulles chose two little offshore islands, claimed by Chiang Kai-shek, as a place to make a stand. There, too, other confrontations were building. Ian Mikardo visited Ho Chi Minh in 1957, and found him to be 'the most recent example of the classic revolutionaries – those who defy an Empire's power and an Empire's prisons with a handful of stones and a sling' (24 May 1957).

But he was by no means the only such revolutionary, as Hugh Delargy, the following year, pointed out with regard to a faraway, oppressed island:

> For two years a civil war has been raging in the Caribbean island of Cuba.
>
> It began with eight men, led by Fidel Castro, a 34-year-old lawyer who had secretly returned from exile . . . and who now called upon his countrymen to rise against the corrupt and dictatorial government of General Batista.
>
> Soon he was joined by many civilians, who left their homes to live hard and desperately and to risk their lives every day.
>
> Their precise numbers are unknown, but there are at least 1,200 men under arms; and some reporters put the figure very much higher. Many raids and ambushes have taken place and pitched battles fought . . . But Batista's 30,000 soldiers are still unable to subdue them . . .
>
> [19 December 1958]

Needless to say, Dulles's policy over Quemoy and elsewhere altered the world's anxiety neurosis into psychosis, for behind every move in his paranoid crusade against communism rose the menace of a mushroom cloud. Western leaders, including British, fell willingly or resignedly into step with the principle of 'massive retaliation' (by H-bomb, after 1954) as the ultimate deterrent. The concept had become more fearful when the Soviet Union acquired its own hydrogen bomb; equally shattering, from Tribune's point of view, was Britain's struggle to find the wherewithal that would lead to some small seat at the H-bomb table. That government decision galvanized and concentrated the growing opposition in Britain to the arms race, nuclear testing and the whole inhuman idea of 'deterrence'.

Tribune became a natural forum for the mostly Leftist resistance to the bomb. On 16 April 1954, a letter to the paper outlined the early steps in that struggle – the organizing of a mighty petition, aiming at 15 million signatures. The letter was signed by five MPs – Anthony Greenwood, Anthony Wedgwood Benn, Fenner Brockway, Sydney Silverman, George Thomas – plus Canon John Collins. The campaign built, and slowly accelerated, while world leaders paid lip-service to the ideal of disarmament, yet tested and stockpiled as frenetically as ever. Tribune campaigned tirelessly: 'STOP THE TESTS – AND SAVE THE CHILDREN FROM THIS HORROR!' (22 March 1957); 'H-BOMB TESTS – WILL LABOUR LEAD THE NATION?' (29 March 1957); 'IS SELWYN LLOYD IMMUNE TO STRONTIUM?' (3 May 1957). Elsewhere, scientists of world importance – Bertrand Russell among them – conferred in Canada in 1957 on means of halting the madness. And public protests and demonstrations began sporadically, as when a women's march drew 5,000 to Trafalgar Square in September 1957 – a venue that would soon become as closely associated with the movement as the slogan that had then begun to appear on placards: 'Ban the Bomb'.

Even so, the campaign was still going up through its gears, lacking a measure of cohesion. Nor had it truly caught the imagination of the people – not even that of the disaffected young, whose mood in early 1958 Mervyn Jones examined:

A YOUNG NEW YEAR TO US ALL

. . . In the circles I move in, the charge most often brought against the young is their lack of interest in politics. It has some basis in fact, and more in loose thinking.

I was in Trafalgar Square the first evening of the Suez war. It was thronged with young people, mostly students but some young workers too. Talking to them, I couldn't find one who belonged to any political party or club, or who had come there in response to any appeal. 'We just felt we couldn't stay at home,' they said.

They had no plans and little idea of what one did in such a situation, but finally about a thousand of them marched up Charing Cross Road shouting slogans, held a rather confused meeting, marched back to Westminster, and were viciously batoned by the police. The girls as well as the men stood their ground and several were badly hurt . . .

The Labour Party had called a demonstration for the Sunday, but so ignorant about politics were these young people that they didn't know they ought to copy their elders and let the war go on for three days.

So don't tell me that young people don't care about politics. What I will admit is this: young people don't care about political organisation, or about most party controversy, or about charades kept up by professionals to simulate a political struggle . . .

[10 January 1958]

Jones was echoing John Osborne's cry in *Look Back in Anger* about the lack, for the young, of a cause. But not all the young people of Britain wanted a cause – at least, not an idealistic, demanding, radical one. Some were quite happy merely with an outlet – which they found in the new rock-'n'-roll music, the Teddy Boy craze and idle violence. Soon, though, the violence became less directionless when it found a new target.

The 1950s had seen an influx of black immigrants, nowhere as many as popular misconception thought, but of course extra-visible in areas unused to black faces. Tribune campaigned hotly against prejudice, but the Mosleyite ultra-Right capitalized on it, and found in it a new lease of life. Nottingham and Notting Hill exploded with racial hatred.

'THE HEADLINES CALL IT A RACE RIOT – BUT IT'S JUST HOOLIGANISM,' SAID THE JAMAICAN

I have seen fear – the fear of mob violence and race hatred – dominate a part of my native city.

Fear . . . I try to interview a Labour Councillor in North Kensington, and am told he won't be at home. He has moved his family to stay with friends elsewhere for the time being. 'You see,' the explanation goes, 'he lives right in the danger area.' . . .

Fear . . . I walk down Portobello Road with a Negro. Two young women of his colour stop him: 'Can you fight, man? Come round where we live tonight. We're all alone – the rest of the house is white folks. Just passed four Teddy Boys on the corner. They didn't say anything, just showed us their knives.' . . .

The 'fun' begins. Five black men, grimly silent, stand warily in the yard of their house. A white boy rushes from a side-street, yelling: 'They're all in the area – they can't get out!' . . .

All at once, Westbourne Park Road is full of running, screaming

> people. All white: age, sixteen to twenty; quite a few of them girls . . . The darkness is bright with small, sudden fires, which burn harmlessly in grimy front gardens or are stamped out in the street when the police arrive . . .
>
> We move down to Talbot Road, where the largest force of police I've yet seen – maybe twenty, with two Black Marias – rings a Negro club. Coloured men come out and yell: 'What have we done? Why don't you chase up the gangs?' . . .
>
> The conviction is growing that someone is behind it . . . Several white people told me: 'You see older men who sit in cars and give directions.' Nobody can identify them . . .
>
> 'I reckon it's the Mosleyites,' declared a young policeman.
>
> Their paper, *Action*, is sold vigorously in the riot area. And on Monday they held a meeting just where the clashes had been worst, in a place where meetings have never been held before. Nobody can understand why it was allowed . . .
>
> [*Mervyn Jones*, 5 September 1958]

Nonetheless, in that same year, other young people, and farsighted people of all ages, classes or whatever, began coming together in a healthier alliance. The battle against the bomb had expanded further, and came to provide exactly the good, brave cause that the radical young had seemed to lack. The Campaign for Nuclear Disarmament (CND) had been born, in February 1958, and Michael Foot's Tribune was midwife, godfather and standard bearer.

Coincidentally, and perhaps symbolically, Tribune had taken up the banners for this latest, and one of its greatest, crusades only a few weeks after reaching and celebrating its majority in the first issue of 1958. Throughout that year the twenty-one-year-old paper reported on the growth and spread of CND, its meetings and rallies, and its preparations for a unique demonstration – a mass march over a great many miles to an atomic research station at Aldermaston. During these months Tribune wore a new front-page banner – 'The paper that leads the anti-H-bomb campaign' – and people flocked to it. Letters poured in, mostly statements of support, but some in the form of campaign-furthering gems in their own right, like Kenneth Tynan's:

> The inaugural meeting in London of the Campaign for Nuclear Disarmament included some thought-provoking analyses, notably by Bertrand Russell and Sir Stephen King-Hall, of our defence position as outlined by Mr Sandys.

Nuclear weapons are the basis of our defence: our possession of them makes us an automatic target for nuclear attack: we have no defence against nuclear attack.

This seems to be the situation in which the Government has placed us. What nobody has yet pointed out is the unique moral splendour of it all.

We are committed, if war breaks out, to a gesture of self-sacrifice unparalleled in human history. We have volunteered for annihilation.

Some may scoff at us: some may even call us suicidal maniacs. But we British have been called names before. We shall go to our graves in quiet heart, secure in the knowledge that by our sacrifice we shall have made our island uninhabitable to the invading hordes, or for that matter anybody else.

I do not wish to be accused of mealy-mouthed sentimentality: but is there not one family that should be spared? I am sure I speak for every member of it when I say that they would vastly prefer to stay with their people in the event of war and be wiped out alongside them.

All the same, I feel it my humble duty to suggest that the royal family should be evacuated from these islands without a moment's delay.

We would all, I feel sure, rest easier in our graves if we knew that somewhere in the world a British family survived to carry on the British traditions of civilised decency and respect for human life. And not only survived, but survived intact.

To expose the royal family to radiation would be to risk the most fearful dynastic consequences. Both patriotism and commonsense lead inescapably to the conclusion I have respectfully suggested.

The royal family should take up residence, with all convenient speed, in some distant British dependency. Let cowards flinch and traitors glare: we'll keep the old flag flying there.

[7 March 1958]

For the time being, Labour's Executive had viewed all this activity with tolerance. Its own Opposition stance pledged it to a disarmament policy, and it had not yet begun to see as a new kind of 'heresy' the radical call for *unilateral* disarmament. Nye Bevan, however, opposed that call, and had done so since late 1957, when Michael Foot had taken issue with him after that year's party conference:

BEVAN AND THE H-BOMB

. . . It is not, of course an argument about whether anyone likes or dislikes the bomb. Aneurin Bevan loathes the hideous weapon as passionately as anyone else . . .

The age of discipline brought Red scares, among them Gaitskell's assertion that one in six of the Labour Left were communist-backed, which inspired cartoonist 'Cor' (17 October 1952) – as colonial struggles inspired 'Abu' (then drawing as 'Abraham', 16 March 1956) and the cold-war dangers inspired Lewis (23 April 1954).

No. The crux of Aneurin Bevan's argument turns on a quite different axis. In a sentence, he is concerned about our relations with our allies both inside and outside the Commonwealth.

He fears that an abrupt rupture of our associations with them would mean forfeiting the chance of exerting influence upon them towards genuine policies of peace . . .

To stop making the bomb must imply not only a simultaneous removal of American bases from these islands, but also a complete abandonment of all our existing alliances – action, apparently, to be taken without any consultation even with members of the Commonwealth . . .

The flat answer is that it doesn't settle the matter one way or the other. Why, Britain has only had a tested H-bomb for a matter of months . . . Were we not members of all these alliances before we had the bomb? And does not the same apply to many other nations who, fortunately for the world and wisely for themselves, have no intention of attempting to make one? . . .

Of course it would be hypocritical to surrender our own bomb and merely to be content to shelter behind somebody else's. But it would not be immoral to abandon our own bomb and seek the best diplomatic means we could to ensure that others did the same.

The power of example might be one of the best ways of securing that end . . .

[*Michael Foot*, 11 October 1957]

The argument over unilateral abandonment would rage on; a corollary had begun to develop, more rapidly in 1958 as the first Aldermaston march proved a success, betokening 'a new mood in the country', as Donald Soper saw it (11 April 1958). Soon afterwards, the Labour Party held an official rally in London, where Bevan and Gaitskell together spoke against nuclear testing, and where the CNDers – with their strange, effective, semaphore logo – attended in mass, still willing to be allied with the party in its opposition to Tory desires to explode bombs.

But later that year news emerged of a civil-disobedience Direct Action Committee, and the arguments grew more complex. Tribune especially had hoped that Labour would see the strength of this groundswell of public opinion propelling the anti-bomb movement, and that the party would, in Mervyn Jones's words, 'seize on the dramatic protest' (12 December 1958) to channel, direct and lead it. But that was not to happen: and as a result, the protests in the party and in the nation were to grow ever more dramatic.

5 'FLOURISHING AND INTRANSIGENT' (1958–64)

In 1959 Labour went into an election battle weak and weary from its distracting internal dissensions. Nor was there any temporary truce. Michael Foot saw that the party was seeking to substitute 'a mildly progressive Tweedledum for a mildly reactionary Tweedledee', to 'entice the floating voter by the moderation and so-called "statesmanship" of the leadership' (2 January 1959). He added, correctly as it turned out, that this approach 'played into the hands of Macmillan and his publicity agents'.

'Supermac' put on his fur hat and won headlines with a Moscow visit, then returned and told the electorate it had 'never had it so good'. Even so, he clung to power for a few months longer in a Parliament that Richard Crossman described as 'born dead and . . . decomposing for a long time' (19 June 1959). Finally, in October, the Conservatives won a further five years for 'the unjust society, the casino society, the "I'm all right Jack" society' (editorial, 16 October 1959). And Labour sagged back into its welter of recrimination and disunity.

Aside from the brief promotion of a 'Lib-Lab' alliance by some malcontents on the Labour Right, the party rows that opened the 1960s centred round defence policy and nuclear disarmament. CND was gaining further in numbers and stature, witnessed especially by the thousands walking on the 1959 'march of hope' (Mervyn

Jones, 27 March 1959) and the eruption of similar movements in Europe and even the United States. Out of all this grew a conviction that a new radical spirit was abroad, an outpouring of commitment and activism flushing away the disillusion and emptiness of the 1950s. Certainly this spirit inhabited the purposefulness of the 'New Left', visible in the *New Left Review*, launched in the winter of 1959–60, and in its 'nerve centre', the New Left Club ('Comrades Among the Coffee Cups' – Mervyn Jones, 18 December 1959), its membership overlapping with CND and other rising protest movements like Anti-Apartheid.

Within this ideal growing-ground, CND's fortunes prospered, and began also to take effect in the political sphere – especially when the unions made their move. While the TUC remained cautious, the General and Municipal Workers threw its weight behind unilateral disarmament, Frank Cousins's Transport and General Workers were openly sympathetic, and in 1960 NATSOPA marched to Aldermaston. Richard Briginshaw wrote: '. . . in looking at our efforts to improve the conditions of our members and make sure wages keep pace with living costs, we all seemed to think too little, say too little, and certainly do insufficient, about the rich prospect of us all, employers and employees alike, being blown to hell . . .' (1 April 1960).

Similarly, in Parliament, some forty MPs put down a rebellious motion against huge arms spending and nuclear testing in Britain, on the principle, as Judith Hart put it, 'that talking peace means nothing unless action gives some proof of the genuineness of intention' (26 February 1960). She returned to that subject on the eve of that year's Aldermaston march:

> THE CHALLENGE OF POLITICS
>
> Once in every generation it comes: the catalyst of savage discontent. A single issue; but it rises to an intensity of protest which, taken at the flood, can surge into revolutionary fervour.
>
> And the test of politicians is what they make of it. If they can successfully relate it to its wider context; if they can recognise its dynamism; if they can rise to the challenge it throws out to them – then they can capture the spirit of a whole generation and lead it forward to conquer new worlds . . .
>
> Indeed, because our march from Aldermaston to Trafalgar Square represents so much more than a cry of protest about the bomb itself, it is of supreme importance – if we are to be true to ourselves and to

> the idealism we share – that we should begin to understand the link between morals and politics . . .
>
> The fulfilment of social morality in the modern world can be achieved only through the exercise of political power. That is the reality of morals and politics. That is, of course, why I am a member of the Labour Party; because I possess that thing so usefully summarised as a social conscience and understand that a political party, with all its irritations and frustrations, is the only means I have of giving effective expression to my ethical beliefs . . .
>
> It is probably true that politicians may be judged by their response to the challenge of the Campaign. But it is quite certain that those who march from Aldermaston will be judged by their response to the challenge of politics. They have it in their power to create a new world. For so much can be done if they will recognise their own power to do it.
>
> [15 April 1960]

That march proved the mightiest of all, coinciding with the gift of the government's abandoning their Blue Streak missile programme, which meant discarding the principle of the 'independent' deterrent, one of the main props in the defence of the British bomb. Trafalgar Square bulged with 100,000 demonstrators that Easter; afterwards, USDAW, the AEU, the printers and other unions went unilateralist, joined by the Cooperative Movement. The Labour leadership went to conference that year with its backs to the wall.

And at that Scarborough conference, when the TGWU and other giants weighed in for unilateralism, the Labour rank and file overrode those bomb-defending leaders – and Gaitskell defiantly promised to 'fight, fight and fight again'. Michael Foot pointed out wryly that this was precisely the sort of 'persistent and public advocacy in opposition to the policy of the party' (14 October 1960), in Gaitskell's own phrasing, which would have brought the full disciplinary wrath of the leadership down on the Left in the 1950s. Yet, Foot added, Tribune would *defend* the right of Gaitskell, Brown and company to think and speak and argue freely, just as it had always claimed that right for Cripps, Bevan, Crossman, *et al.*, against the Gaitskellites.

But meanwhile, as they say in melodrama, clouds were gathering. Here was unilateralism victorious, official policy of the Labour Party and – in theory – awaiting only the next election to become official policy of a Labour Government. But perhaps it had peaked too soon. Out in the rest of the world the nuclear madness persisted. France tested its A-bomb ('DE GAULLE DROPS THE MASK', 21 August 1959) and Germany manoeuvred for a share of the NATO deterrent. The always shaky lull in nuclear tests ended when the Soviet Union and then the United States resumed the splashing about of fall-out in 1961, also resuming their bickering 'test-ban talks' which bore no fruit till 1963. The Polaris submarine arrived in late 1960 to make Britain an even more certain target. And an impatience, perhaps even a pessimism regarding CND's *political* progress, led to further outbursts of direct action that finally split the movement.

CIVIL DISOBEDIENCE

The Committee of 100 and its supporters propose to commit an act of civil disobedience on February 18 in connection with the arrival of the Polaris missiles in the Clyde which creates a special and deadly danger to the inhabitants of that region and to all Britain. The demonstration is to be non-violent, and any individual who allows himself to become violent will be disowned by the Committee.

We have been driven to a policy of civil disobedience by the lack of representation or the misrepresentation of the policy of unilateralists in the organs of public information. Broadcasting and television are practically closed to us. It is difficult, almost impossible, to get articles or even letters into the daily papers. Most of the press has gone over to Authority – possibly in fear of being, otherwise, gobbled up.

The Campaign for Nuclear Disarmament has been, and is, doing splendid work, but its doings are seldom thought by the press to have 'news value'. In consequence of the barrier put up by almost all organs of public information, the unilateralist point of view is given by the general public no serious hearing.

The public's attention must be called to the weight of reason and the strength of feeling which impel a large body of people in this country to support the policy of unilateralism – a far larger and more intelligent and informed body than it is recognised to be.

All sorts of legal methods are being employed and should continue to be employed to do this. But in order that these methods may carry their full weight, it is obvious that methods also should be adopted that are now considered to have 'news value' – methods of civil disobedience hitherto untried on a mass scale. Only by such means can the barrier of ignorance and indifference concerning the unilateralist point of view be broken down . . .

It must be made known to the public that Government and Authority are cajoling people by means of lies and concealment to

> join ignorantly in a march towards death. The civil disobedience demonstration of February 18 is a valiant attempt to break down the barrier against the fact becoming known . . .
>
> [*Letter from Bertrand Russell*, 3 February 1961]

Tribune objected:

> . . . the question arises as to whether this type of action is the beginning or the end of the protest against nuclear strategy . . .
>
> In a nutshell, the argument is as follows: having protested by sitting down outside the Ministry of Defence, all these demonstrators must now . . . realise that their action to succeed must be followed up by political action . . .
>
> It would be an immeasurable tragedy if the power which CND has built up by its long and methodical campaign were now to be dissipated in a fruitless discussion of method . . .
>
> [*Editorial*, 24 February 1961]

For a while it looked as if CND might survive the split, as James Cameron thought: '. . . the movement has its own logic, and no one has a right to say that there is but one way ahead, when the great objective will be achieved through a synthesis of methods, of people, of parties, all unequivocally united in their aim' (10 March 1961). Later that year it gained kudos with an international march to Moscow. But by then the Committee of 100 had begun dominating the protest scene and – given the self-righteous indignation of the media – uncommitted Britons were being alienated.

So they were all the more by 'OUR LUNATIC FRINGE': 'The group of demonstrators who broke away from the massive CND demonstration in Trafalgar Square to stage their own "direct action" protest outside the American Embassy and Savile Row police station could not, if they had been Empire Loyalists or Mosleyites, have done the nuclear disarmament movement greater disservice . . .' (Editorial, 7 April 1961).

Doubtless the 'disservice' of this and similar frenzied demonstrations aided Gaitskell in his fighting and fighting again, and some of the unions were stepping nervously back from the mêlée. The resumption of tests left many feeling hopeless about any British influence on international nuclear affairs; the drive of the Committee of 100 and the electrifying arrest of Bertrand Russell in September 1961 bled off from CND and the unilateralist Labour Left much of the fervour it had once gathered. At Blackpool in 1961 Labour conference voted against unilateralism – and though the fight would go on courageously for years, in Tribune as elsewhere, CND had begun its downhill slide.

The earlier post-election gloom and wrangling had also put Tribune and the Left at odds with the Gaitskellites over a far older and more traditional point of socialist principle – the integral fourth clause of the party constitution which calls for public ownership of the 'means of production'. As the Right menaced that principle, Tribune manned the barricades:

> Here are three things that have just happened:
>
> A country whose entire economy has been nationalised for over thirty years has brought off the astounding scientific and technical achievement represented by a picture of the far side of the moon.
>
> The privately owned British motor industry has slowed its assembly lines because it is unexpectedly short of deliveries from the privately owned British steel industry.
>
> Mr Douglas Jay, urging the Labour Party to 'modernise ourselves quickly into a vigorous, radical, expansionist open-minded party', suggests that the first step is to drop all proposals for further nationalisation, and steel nationalisation in particular.
>
> [*Editorial*, 23 October 1959]

At conference that year Gaitskell trod a careful line that did not precisely take him among the 'Jaywalkers', as Tribune called the anti-nationalizers. The leader borrowed formulae from Nye Bevan (including that famous phrase about controlling 'the commanding heights of the economy') to preserve a semblance of amity if not unity. Certainly the bulk of the Labour movement was united on behalf of Clause Four as it never was in the disarmament argument – and by mid-1960 the Jaywalkers had more or less been routed. Gaitskell did provide a few more flurries of 1950s-style 'discipline': Left-wingers in Parliament tried a motion of no confidence in his leadership, Anthony Greenwood resigned from the Shadow Cabinet, and in early 1961 five Left-wing MPs voted contrary to the leadership's dictates and had the whip withdrawn (Michael Foot, Sydney Silverman, Emrys Hughes, S. O. Davies and William Baxter). By 1962 the leadership was toying with the notion of expelling Bertrand Russell from the party, which Tribune condemned as 'GUILT BY

ASSOCIATION', when links with a 'proscribed' organization had been made a reason for expulsion (3 August 1962).

But conference that year put that sort of rigidity to death. And to a great extent the end of 1962 marked the end of the worst excesses of the age of discipline, for reasons due not so much to party democracy as to the sad fact of mortality.

Yet earlier mortality had struck at the greatest defender of that democracy, and the mightiest champion of Tribune and the Labour Left.

ANEURIN BEVAN

Aneurin Bevan was unique. There was no one else even remotely like him. As a man, a speaker and a political leader he always acted in a style completely individual to himself . . .

He was, I believe, the most *principled* great political leader of the century in the sense that to sustain and apply his principles in practice was the motive power of his life, the passion that absorbed him while others were engaged in the darker corners of the political workshop . . .

His eyes were fixed on the horizons of politics. He was obsessed by the broad tumultuous movements in society and the world at large. Ideas were his passion and he was interested in power as the vehicle for ideas . . .

He was indeed a rarity, for although born and bred in politics he had many other loves besides. He loved the soil with the heart of a peasant; hence his life-long desire, which he eventually fulfilled on his farm in Buckinghamshire, to escape from the smoke and rattle of the London he detested. He loved music and paintings. He could recite the poets and acclaimed them as the greatest of the species; do they not see further and deeper than the rest of mankind?

Most adept of all, perhaps, was his taste for argument – philosophical argument. In another incarnation he might have been the founder of a new school of logic and, whenever the opportunity occurred, he could confound the latest authority from the university with his nimble brilliance in disputation . . .

In short, Aneurin Bevan always thought for himself and usually preferred his own conclusions. Others did their homework with blue books and statistics; he chose to *think* or to think through argument.

This was his strength; some called it his weakness. Rarely was he content with the beaten path. Since the problems of Socialism, no less than those of world peace, are novel, he was convinced that new ways must be sought. The fertile brain was rarely inactive; the subtle tongue was always searching for new phrases and formulations to awaken the imagination . . .

The curiosity was, I suppose, not that such a man had to spend the bulk of his life in dispute with his own colleagues and in his own party but that he survived so successfully and influenced his times so powerfully. The reason for the achievement was the amazing combination of talents, talents of brain, charm and speech, which even his fiercest enemies never denied him – these plus the correct estimate of his political character always accepted in the Welsh home-town from which he came and so widely shared throughout the Labour movement as a whole in his stormiest trials . . .

Aneurin Bevan, I believe, did more than any other man of his time to keep alive democratic Socialism as the most adventurous, ambitious, intelligent, civilised and truly liberal of modern doctrines. This, the triumph of his whole life and personality, was the greatest of his achievements . . .

He wanted a Labour Party seriously determined to change society to its foundations and a Britain sufficiently independent and sceptical of all the clichés of the cold war to guide and lead the nations to a genuine peace.

These were the kind of causes which he served more eloquently, more subtly, more faithfully and, we must add, in view of the long hostility he encountered and surmounted, more courageously than any other British citizen of his time . . .

[*Michael Foot*, 8 July 1960]

It seemed again a decade full of Labour obituaries. Tribune mourned the losses of the great socialist thinkers G. D. H. Cole (January 1959) and R. H. Tawney (January 1962). It mourned, as old friends and contributors, Frank Horrabin (March 1962) and Bryn Roberts (September 1964); it paid homage to former friends who had become opponents, John Strachey (July 1963) and Morgan Phillips (January 1963). It paid respects to an opponent of long standing, Hugh Dalton (February 1962), and then, ultimately, to a more recent and most prominent foe:

THE LAST LEGACY OF HUGH GAITSKELL

. . . Hugh Gaitskell's death was surrounded with every conceivable circumstance of tragedy. He had won, for the time being at least, conclusive victories inside his own party. He had the leadership in his hands on his own terms. The likelihood that he would be the next Prime Minister of Britain was every week becoming more of a certainty . . .

In achieving what he did, he had revealed a rich combination of qualities, unsuspected by most of his early opponents. He commanded the respect, devotion and loyalty of those who knew him most intimately. He had, above all, as Anthony Crosland said, in the most perceptive tribute to him, 'a dogged bravery'. No one but a fool would doubt that strength of character as much as intellect was responsible for his growing reputation.

However, political leaders – particularly leaders of Socialist movements which aspire to *change* the world – must be judged by an even more severe test. And that final test must be: how much understanding, in word, demeanour and action, do they show of the age in which they live?

Precisely this single supreme quality of political imagination – combined imaginative sympathy, wisdom and power – was the one which Hugh Gaitskell, I believe, most lacked. And this was the profound reason why he often found himself in such deep hostility to the aspirations of many of those he hoped to lead. His idea of Socialism and theirs, his outlook on the world and theirs, jarred and clashed . . .

Ironically, the real challenge to Gaitskell, if he had become Prime Minister, would have been how much he was prepared to re-educate himself, to repudiate much of his past, to mobilise aspirations and acknowledge ideas which for so long he had bitterly fought. Who knows? This *might* have been within his compass. For this was the course which, no doubt unconsciously, he was starting to tread in the last months of his life . . .

[*Michael Foot*, 25 January 1963]

Gaitskell's death was to alter the Labour Party almost out of recognition. A not too bloody leadership battle brought Harold Wilson to that pinnacle, and Michael Foot expressed Tribune's pleasure at this elevation of a former contributor:

LABOUR'S NEW LEADER

This newspaper has many reasons for welcoming Harold Wilson's election as leader of the Labour Party. Like Stafford Cripps, Aneurin Bevan and (occasionally) Clem Attlee, he was in the past a frequent contributor to our columns.

A degree in this university is not an infallible guide to future greatness. But it's a good start . . .

It says much . . . for the qualities of Harold Wilson that he was at the top when his combination of attitudes was most needed.

Not merely qualities of acumen, political skill and survival-power which no one denies him. Other considerable qualities too for a Labour leader – a coherence of ideas, a readiness to follow unorthodox courses, a respect for democracy, a rooted opposition to Toryism and all its manifestations.

Above all, a deep and genuine love of the Labour movement. Anyone who doesn't know that Harold Wilson has *that*, knows nothing about him . . .

[22 February 1963]

A time had come by then for a new start for Tribune, too, and one that would reveal a considerably greater degree of continuity than the party's. In 1960 Michael Foot was adopted for Nye Bevan's constituency of Ebbw Vale, won it easily, and thereupon handed over the paper's editorship to the present incumbent, Richard Clements.

Of course, Clements brought changes. But he had been at Foot's right hand in running the paper for some time, and during that time too there had been changes, as always in a living and lively paper. More and more breadth and depth of news and behind-the-news coverage had emerged, in new features, like the round-up 'Newspoints', in an expanded industrial section, and more. In early 1959 the paper's front-page name was red-inked again, valuably symbolizing the qualities that were its basis and would never change. Malcolm Muggeridge said as much, reviewing Tribune in Tribune:

HERE'S TO THE GREAT FREEDOM FIGHTERS!

. . . What, of course, everyone likes (or dislikes) about *Tribune* is its liveliness. However misguided its opinions may seem to be, it has about it a flavour of authentic controversy . . .

I myself am profoundly in disagreement with some of *Tribune*'s basic assumptions. Yet I like and admire the vigorous straightforward way they are propounded. This is first-rate, hard-hitting journalism, and, alas, growing increasingly scarce.

Also, it is very good for the Labour Party leadership to be constantly harried and chivied, as they have been, and still are, by *Tribune*. Unfortunately, the Big Brass in Transport House and the Shadow Cabinet seem unappreciative of these attentions.

This is very foolish of them. Without such harrying and chivying the Labour Party would wither away. Its motor is on the Left even though its somewhat top-heavy body has a tendency to lurch Rightwards.

The Labour Party was brought into existence by angry, indignant men. If it ever ceased to have within it an element of anger and indignation it would become an empty shell, and disappear as rapidly as it grew into a national party . . .

My own pleasure in *Tribune* has been, like Orwell's, due rather to its larger Radicalism than to its espousal of Crippsism, Bevanism,

Mikardoism, or any other particular presentation of the Socialist cause.
It may justly be claimed that *Tribune*'s instinct has invariably been to uphold freedom. Its head may have been sometimes beguiled, but its heart has been staunch . . .
Thus, both as a journalist and as a citizen I hope that another twenty-one years will find *Tribune* more flourishing and intransigent than ever.

[*Malcolm Muggeridge*, 23 January 1959]

'Liveliness' and 'controversy' remained the hallmark after Clements took over; he also retained the paper's general appearance and approach, though he had reluctantly to raise its price to 7d. as costs spiralled up. Yet he still could claim a 40,000 readership in 1962, after the price rise – and doubtless he gained more with some unsought publicity when a Christmas joke backfired that year.

Within a handful of seasonal ruderies and mockeries (remember that this was the 'age of satire', displayed in the Saturday-night television programme 'That Was the Week That Was' and the still-fresh *Private Eye*), Tribune offered a not overwhelmingly funny joke letter from 'Chou En-lai', full of hard-line revolutionary sentiments:

Some cowards are afraid of being blown to bits by the nuclear bombs. This is an anti-Marxist-Leninist view of history. We prefer not to live at all if we cannot live under the leadership of the Communist Party and its revolutionary programme. So do not let the revisionists confuse you. Our slogan should be 'Better dead than not Red' . . .

[28 December 1962]

The Chinese were not amused, and Tribune found itself in the middle of an international incident. Peking held a press conference to denounce this 'forgery' and complained officially to the Foreign Office. The delighted and unrepentant Clements promptly fired off a cable to Chou En-lai offering him space in the paper to 'redress the balance', and mollified Chinese officials by publishing their formal statement, which 'hereby solemnly states that the above-said letter published in Tribune weekly is an out-and-out forgery aimed at smearing the policies of the People's Republic of China and defaming the leaders of the Chinese nation . . . ' (4 January 1963). Nothing more was heard from Chou, nor was Clements's enjoyment of a little healthy send-up dampened a jot.

It was all a good run up to the birth of a 'new Tribune' in late 1963. An advanced (offset litho) printing process made it possible; another price rise (to 1s.) financed it. The eighth of November was the launching date for the refurbished sixteen-page paper, glowing with clearer type, more photographs (from Euan Duff among others), further expansions of home affairs ('In Focus' round-up feature), industrial doings, the international scene ('Guide to a Changing World' feature). The letters pages gained even more prominence, too – but perhaps most striking of all was the liberating effect of the rebirth on the literary and arts pages.

Previously they had been crammed into two of the weekly twelve pages – still something of an advance on the 1950s constriction, when book reviewing had been almost entirely within the limits of the 'Books and People' column. That feature continued, mostly now as an extended one-book review, in the hands of Raymond Fletcher – a notable all-rounder for the paper then – until late 1961, when Anthony Arblaster joined Tribune and inherited it. By then Elizabeth Thomas had formally become the literary editor, making changes of her own that were given freer rein in the 1963 expansion.

As for other reviewing, Mervyn Jones retained theatre throughout the 1960s, and Derek Hill continued on films until mid-1961, succeeded then by the admirable Boleslaw Sulik. J. D. S. Haworth wrote on television and Edward Lockspeiser on music – though there were jazz columns (Edward Scobie, then Christopher Baillie), record reviews (Kennedy Brown, then John May) and eventually a column on the New Left's favourite listening, folk music (Fred Dallas, afterwards Stephen Sedley). And room was found for occasional reviews of ballet and radio, and a regular review of art exhibitions by Cicely Ben Tovim, who contributed many fine drawings of her own.

Within book reviewing, Elizabeth Thomas's pages displayed many familiar contributors from Labour's ranks and/or the Tribune tradition, and added numerous new ones like Caroline Wedgwood Benn, John Stonehouse, Norman Mackenzie, Illtyd Harrington, David Caute, Stuart Hall, Ray Gosling, Ellis Hillman, Paul Foot – many of whom contributed articles as well as book reviews to Tribune in those years. And more specifically 'literary' reviewers included Bernard Kops, Frank Norman, Jeremy Robson, Michael Kustow, Robert Nye (he began a monthly 'Pick of the Paperbacks'), Martin Seymour-Smith, Michael Horovitz, Philip Hobsbaum, Jim Burns – with occasional or one-time appearances by Spike Milligan, Bloke Modisane, Marghanita Laski.

At the same time, Elizabeth Thomas restored Tribune to its former role as a regular publisher of *poems*, and into her pages came Jon Silkin, Dannie Abse, Robert Nye, Jeremy Robson, Adrian Mitchell, Thomas Blackburn, Brian Jones, Jenny Joseph, Nathaniel Tarn and many more who do not deserve to be omitted from this list. The new literary editor also began an outspoken weekly column on books and art subjects, and put the paper in the forefront of the new craze for public poetry readings by organizing monthly Tribune readings, which lasted from 1963 to 1972.

As ever, the books and arts world was not relegated to a ghetto in the back pages of Tribune. Anything from that world might crop up anywhere in the paper – even poetry, as when a verse satirist took fine aim at the foundering Tory Party:

TORY FREEDOM WORKS
(or Don't Mind Us)

'The people will, I think, be wise to say: "thank you very much, let's carry on".' – HAROLD MACMILLAN, August 11, 1963.

While Uncle Mac was languishing in Anglo-Saxon attitudes,
Down fell the railways and up went the fares,
And bland Lord Home was polishing his pre-packed plastic platitudes,
Down came the fall-out and up went the shares.
Thank you very much, sir, please carry on, sir,
You've done a good job, sir, don't mind us.

'No parking!' mazy Marples cried and beamed all round in gratitude,
Crunch went the cars jam-packed in the squares,
And Heath received a belting in his longitudes and latitudes,
Scraped him off his knees and kicked him down the stairs.
Thank you very much, sir, please carry on, sir,
You've done a good job, sir, don't mind us.

While Selwyn and Maudling dozed and bore their bags with certitude,
Out came the dole queues and bang went the boom,
And Watkinson was doodling in a state of topsy turpitude,
Plop went the Blue Streak, straight in the tomb.
Thank you very much, sir, please carry on, sir,
You've done a good job, sir, don't mind us.

While bravely Brooke his duty did, aglow with moral rectitude,
Up went the death rate and out came the narks,
And Joseph set about his task with dazzling ineptitude,
Down fell the ceilings and in moved the sharks.

Thank you very much, sir, please carry on, sir,
You've done a good job, sir, don't mind us.

There was Butler the equivocal and Hailsham the ubiquitous.
Powell the pious who always said his prayers,
And others we've forgotten who were equally iniquitous,
And who *was* that Minister for extra-marital affairs?
God bless you all, sir, please carry on, sir,
You've done a great job, sir, – don't mind us.
[*Leon Rosselson*, 25 September 1964]

Earlier, a series of articles on the theme of 'Advance on the Left' had included some major statements on the cultural side of that advance, as when Raymond Williams decried the 'Angry Young Man' and 'Outsider' literary roles, 1950s fashions, as 'the fighting rearguard of an old conception, rather than the vanguard of a new' (27 March 1959). And the principle of Leftist cultural advance produced another view, and an activist contribution, from a leading young playwright:

YOU'RE ONLY LIVING HALF A LIFE

It is no longer, of course, strictly true that we have divided our society into classes of the privileged and the underprivileged. There have come about changes over the last century and a half brought about by organisations like the Labour Party and the trade unions, that have created a state of affairs where there is opportunity for everybody.

It is now possible, because of the economic advantages gained by the unions and the Socialist parties, for everyone to read books from the public libraries, listen to concerts on the radio, visit the theatres, and in general take part in the cultural life of the community.

But they forgot one thing – and this is to me the terrible crux of the problem and God knows how they missed it. The social and cultural habits of a group will continue for generations, unless something is done to break them, just as the economic habits will continue unless action is taken to weaken them.

The unions and the Labour Party had to take political action in order to convince the worker that the habit of taking ridiculously small wages for long hours was a useless habit. They had to make efforts to convince the stultified worker that he was as entitled to a fair share of the nation's economic life as anyone.

But what action was taken to convince the stultified worker that he was just as entitled to his share of the nation's cultural life? No one has suggested to him that it might be of interest, that it has a value for him.

The economic barriers of class may be less definable, but the cultural ones are still there. The worker is only enjoying half of life; he may be an engaged body but he's not an engaged soul in this process of living . . .

[*Arnold Wesker*, 12 February 1960]

Wesker soon launched his campaign for union involvement with the arts, and Tribune backed him unequivocally ('The Wesker campaign moves into the trade unions', 15 July 1960; 'Plans for Centre 42', 28 July 1961; 'Centre 42: What Did We Achieve?' – Michael Kustow, 11 January 1963). Elsewhere in the world of theatre, John Neville gave Tribune an interview on his pioneering venture of the Nottingham Playhouse (3 July 1964), and Joan Littlewood herself sent a dispatch from the front lines in Stratford East about her wildly successful and controversial Theatre Workshop production (highly praised in Tribune) *Oh, What a Lovely War*:

To be against war is one thing, to be against capitalism is one thing, but to be *for* life – that's something the theatre can do, can express and can incite in people. In this show the soldiers sing, as they did many years ago, 'I'd sooner stay in England and fornicate my bleeding life away'. It's not a bad line. It's better than war. And hate. Let us start presenting something positive as well as organising protest marches . . .

[19 April 1963]

Equally, as culture appeared anywhere in the paper, so direct political writing occurred in the 'cultural section', not just in reviews of political books but in special articles – like the concise and illuminating series on major figures in Labour history, 'Voices of Socialism', which appeared on the books pages from mid-1964. These, launched with Margaret Cole on Blatchford and then Ralph Miliband on Laski, were gathered into a highly popular pamphlet, and need no reproduction here.

Finally, it was a writer normally associated with arts matters who contributed a piece to the paper's ever wider and more outspoken coverage of the 'state of the nation' and thereby raised it to a level of provocation not seen even in Tribune since 'Thomas Rainsboro' of the 1940s.

A LETTER TO MY FELLOW COUNTRYMEN

This is a letter of hate. It is for you, my countrymen. I mean those men of my country who have defiled it. The men with manic fingers leading the sightless, feeble, betrayed body of my country to its death. You are its murderers, and there's little left in my own brain but the thoughts of murder for you.

I cannot even address you as I began as 'Dear', for that word alone would sin against my hatred. And this, my hatred for you, and those who tolerate you, is about all I have left and all the petty dignity my death may keep.

No, this is not the highly paid 'anger' or the 'rhetoric' you like to smile at (you've tried to mangle my language, too). You'll not pour pennies into my coffin for this; you are MY object. I am not yours. You are my vessel, you are MY hatred. That is my final identity. True, it will no doubt die with me in a short time and by your unceasing efforts.

But perhaps it could be preserved, somewhere, in the dead world that you have prepared for us, perhaps the tiny, unbared spark of my human hatred might kindle, just for the briefest moment in time, the life you lost for us.

I fear death. I dread it daily. I cling wretchedly to life, as I have always done. I fear death, but I cannot hate it as I hate you. It is only you I hate, and those who let you live, function and prosper.

My hatred for you is almost the only constant satisfaction you have left me. My favourite fantasy is four minutes or so non-commercial viewing as you fry in your democratically elected hot seats in Westminster, preferably with your condoning democratic constituents.

There is murder in my brain, and I carry a knife in my heart for every one of you. Macmillan, and you, Gaitskell, you particularly. I wish we could hang you all out, with your dirty washing, on your damned Oder-Neisse Line, and those seven out of ten Americans, too. I would willingly watch you all die for the West, if only I could keep my own miniscule portion of it, you could all go ahead and die for Berlin, for Democracy, to keep out the red hordes or whatever you like.

You have instructed me in my hatred for thirty years. You have perfected it, and made it the blunt, obsolete instrument it is now. I only hope it will keep me going. I think it will. I think it may sustain me in the last few months.

Till then, damn you, England. You're rotting now, and quite soon you'll disappear. My hate will outrun you yet, if only for a few seconds. I wish it could be eternal.

I write this from another country, with murder in my brain and a knife carried in my heart for every one of you. I am not alone. If WE had just the ultimate decency and courage, we would strike at you – now, before you blaspheme against the world in our name. There is nothing I should not give for your blood on my head.

But all I can offer you is my hatred. You will be untouched by that, for you are untouchable. Untouchable, unteachable, impregnable.

If you were offered the heart of Jesus Christ, your Lord and your Saviour – though not mine, alas – you'd sniff at it like sour offal. For that is the Kind of Men you are.

Believe me,

In sincere and utter hatred,
Your Fellow Countryman

[*John Osborne*, 18 August 1961]

These virulent sentiments – and perhaps Osborne's choice of Tribune as the medium for them – set off an 'incredible rumpus' in the national press, according to Tribune diarist 'Francis Flavius'. (The original Flavius, without the supererogatory forename, was one of the 'tribunes of the people' in republican Rome; another was Marullus, the pseudonym – with forename John – that had preceded Francis F. in the diary column.) More letters poured in about Osborne's outburst than could be printed – as letters usually did, and do, when the paper loosed its fury on aspects of the state of Britain.

Integral especially to this state-of-the-nation coverage was attention to the condition and aspirations of the working man and his unions. Much of the reportage came from staff writers, but also trade-unionist contributors: Jack Jones, Clive Jenkins, Jim Mortimer, Ernie Roberts, Eric Heffer, Will Paynter, Max Madden – built up the extensive picture of the happenings in those industrially disputatious years. (Jenkins also wrote a question-and-answers column on union matters until he began his much admired and long-standing column 'Trend' – before that word became trendy.)

Those were years of ballooning unemployment within Tory economic thinking, years of muddle and financial difficulty in private industry ('WHO CAUSED THE STEEL CRISIS? I SAY THE BOSSES ARE TO BLAME' – John Hughes, 13 March 1959). They were years of what Clements's book on the unions called, in its title, *Glory Without Power* – which, as Bryn Roberts of NUPE brought out in reviewing the book, grew in part out of union disunity and overlapping, but also out of deliberate government policy to freeze wages, create unemployment and 'provoke and prolong strikes' (17 April 1959).

It provoked plenty during the 1960s: railway workers when Dr Beeching's axe fell, seamen, postmen, teachers, television workers and *actors*, printers, engineers . . . Even beyond wage freezes and unemployment it is astonishing to think that a fight going on in the 1930s had not yet been won ('Now *Is* the Time for the 40-hour Week' – John Hughes, 3 May 1963). Nor, in spite of Tory protestations, had standards of living noticeably improved for ordinary people ('You've Never Had It So Good – if you earn over £1,500', said an article by Elizabeth Thomas, 2 October 1959). On that level, tax relief and profit booms paralleled wage pauses for the workers and clear underminings of the nation's education, its health ('HOW TO FIGHT FOR THE HEALTH SERVICE' – Jennie Lee, 10 February 1961) and its housing, regarding which racketeers and 'Rachmanism' happily exploited a 'Tory-freedom' Rent Act.

Another Tory Act both reflected and spawned social evil. In the wake of the 'race riots' of the late 1950s and other outbreaks of bigotry, the government proposed in 1961 to limit commonwealth immigration. 'Mr Butler's Bill pleases the Fascists', said an article by Tribune's David Boulton (10 November 1961) concerning the exploitation by Mosleyites and newly risen British Nazis of the nation's depth of colour prejudice.

Thus, while popular history tells us that Britain was on the threshold of its 'swinging 'sixties' – with the Beatles on early wing and Tribune's Anthony Nicholas glancing at the 'mods and rockers' rivalry (5 June 1964) – the subjects and targets of the paper then suggest a better name for the last gasps of the Macmillan era – the 'squalid 'sixties'. Blatant fascism in the streets again was bad enough, as were other glimpses of older evils revived like the cold horror of the trial of Adolf Eichmann ('It's all too fatally easy to forget . . . the gas chambers' – Ian Mikardo, 16 June 1961). Capital punishment still operated as the law's ultimate deterrent ('THE ROOTS OF VIOLENCE', Raymond Fletcher, 15 April 1960) and provided the ugly climax to the infamous trial of James Hanratty ('And They Call This British Justice!' – Sydney Silverman, 13 April 1962) while ferocious sentences were society's reply to the great train robbers in 1964.

Opinion will be divided as to whether the so-called 'sexual revolution' should be classified as swinging or squalid, but Tribune in any case was aware of its progress and its rationale – not only in supporting Leo Abse's campaigns for changing the laws on divorce, homosexuality and so forth ('A POLICY FOR SEX?' – editorial, 22 February 1963), but in an analysis by that controversial educationalist A. S. Neill, offering 'THE CURE FOR OUR ANTI-SEX SOCIETY':

Our system is a repressive one. From infancy we are taught to repress our sex and to sublimate it . . . in politics of all parties sex morality reigns. One evil thing about politics is that few politicians will dare to alter the sex laws, the divorce laws, those dealing with homosexuality; few will risk losing the Catholic or the Baptist or the what-not votes . . .

It is a frightening thought that our lives are in the hands of men who were forbidden to touch their genitals in their cradles, for all Cabinet Ministers and Presidents and totalitarian leaders were made anti-life in infancy, and it is unconscious emotion that makes war, not conscious reasoning . . .

[3 February 1961]

But sex in Britain meant squalor without question in one of the blackest stains on the declining Tory Government of those years, on which Anthony Arblaster was especially caustic:

WHERE EVERYTHING HAS A PRICE – AND NOTHING A VALUE

It is barely a week since Mr Profumo's sensational confession and resignation, yet already the really important issues involved are being lost sight of. Or perhaps it would be truer to say that they have hardly, as yet, been grasped at all.

What *has* been grasped well enough is the fact that the Profumo affair is a 'scandal' of the first order. It has all the right ingredients – sexual indiscretion, political repercussions, and the possibility of a security risk. So it was only to be expected that the popular press should give it exhaustive, and exhausting, coverage . . .

But the security issue may well prove to be a damp squib. Many more besides myself are, I suspect, heartily bored with the subject. We have heard too much of it lately. And it is not in any case so serious as the implications of Mr Profumo's deliberate lying. If this were an isolated act of deception, it could perhaps be passed over as the hasty act of a not very scrupulous man in a difficult position. But an isolated act of deception is precisely what it is not. It is the latest and perhaps the most blatant example of the dishonesty which has become almost a matter of habit with Tory Ministers . . .

Never before has the full truth about the society which the Tories have fostered and nourished stared us so clearly in the face . . .

It is that the world of Christine Keeler and Mr Profumo is all of a piece with the shoddy commercialisation of society which the Conservatives have so happily encouraged and celebrated. It is a world in which everything is for sale, even the bodies and souls of men and women. A world in which everything has a price and nothing a value . . .

Bingo halls, betting shops, and long drinking hours. Bread and circuses. Life is better with the Conservatives, but best of all is to be a member of the London upper classes and be able to call a prostitute on the phone when you want one. Must our ideas of pleasure really be so limited? Does this have to be our picture of the good society, our idea of success? . . .

[14 June 1963]

That was also the year of the security scandal that arose over a pathetic minor civil servant ('THE VASSALL CASE', 3 May 1963), and the further spies-under-the-bed nastiness in truths about Kim Philby's penetration of high official circles ('THE CASE OF MR PHILBY', 5 July 1963).

All in all, a lively time for newspapers – though what was happening to the nation's press itself formed part of the picture of the 'squalid sixties'. Roy Thomson came to London with all the money printed from Scottish ITV to buy up the *Sunday Times*, while the rest of Fleet Street trembled over assorted deaths and departures. No one on Tribune much mourned the demise of the *Star* or the *Empire News*, but bitterness rose when the *News Chronicle* – one of the few dailies at all palatable to radicals – was absorbed in 1960 by the Tory *Daily Mail*; and, again, when the last Labour daily, the *Herald*, metamorphosed into the swinging *Sun*. What chance had Labour and socialism now, to have its case put fairly to the newspaper-reading, media-watching millions? Jill Craigie examined that question, as crucial today for Labour as then:

. . . It is sinister enough when only a few men own between them most of the newspapers in the country. It is no less appalling when a tiny group of men own most of the cinemas, film production companies . . . , theatres, film, theatrical and writing agencies and many more subsidiary companies as well.

But when these two tiny groups of men are also given the control of television channels and when, instead of competing with each other, they gang up to grab for themselves an even larger slice of the mass media, then their power over what we may hear, read and see begins to reach Hitlerian proportions . . .

[7 August 1964]

The nation, then, was not in a very healthy state. And to that mosaic Tribune added handfuls of other pieces, some iceberg-tip hints of tortuous problems to come. There was advance warning of environmentalist doom-fears in, say, Maurice Goldsmith's review of a key tract on pollution, Rachel Carson's *Silent Spring* ('WE ARE POISONING THE EARTH AROUND US', 1 March 1963), linking with an earlier warning from Dick Joyce on the dangers of too many people ('THE BIRTHRATE EXPLOSION', 13 October 1961). There was a neatly ominous note in Clive Jenkins's column about the cost of prestige in the form of flying white elephants, when he wrote that the new plan for Concorde was being reassessed; 'indignant denials' poured out awhile, then the rest of the press caught up with the costly redesigning and possible cancellation that was indeed the fact (31 January 1964).

So too Ellis Hillman saw a chance of Britain recouping some prestige and perhaps profit in the North Sea ('THE HUNT FOR OIL OFF OUR COASTS') as early as 10 May 1963, while the same area had earlier staged a further act in a fishy tragicomedy concluded only in 1976 ('HOW BRITAIN WAGES HER SHAMEFUL COD WAR' – Richard Clements, 14 August 1959). And elsewhere one of Britain's oldest domestic sores was festering worse than ever: Martin Ennals of the NCCL, writing a regular 'Civil Liberties' corner in the paper, reminded readers of it:

> Our ignorance about Northern Ireland is astonishing. Some of us have been there and experienced this atmosphere of distrust, discrimination, plotting and hate. But the silence in England about conditions in Ulster almost amounts to criminal negligence . . .
>
> Few realise that in the UK there exists detention without trial, government on religious grounds, calculated discrmination against a large minority, and an armed police force . . .
>
> [7 February 1964]

There were sores like that, some indeed gangrenous, all over the world: the state of the planet was fairly shaky too as the 1960s advanced. Yet for a moment at the decade's beginning international observers felt a tentative hope. The West's leading nation elected a new leader, who spoke optimistically of new frontiers.

'That President Kennedy enters the White House determined to be no dummy,' wrote Raymond Fletcher, 'is one indication, therefore, that 1961 may be a good year for peace-making' (6 January 1961). Not for this brave young man, it seemed, the excesses of the Dulles Cold War, which had climaxed when America was caught with its spy-planes down during a summit talk with Soviet leaders in 1960. But before any time had elapsed, Kennedy proved more fiercely crisis-prone than anyone had dreamed.

'HANDS OFF CUBA!' Tribune shouted on 14 April 1961, as anti-Castro Cubans and the CIA charged ashore at the Bay of Pigs. The next week, when 'KENNEDY PLANS NAVAL BLOCKADE OF CUBA', Havana had cabled Tribune ('Cuba basely attacked by imperialism . . . Brothers of the world, we seek your help and solidarity' – 21 April 1961). The following week it was 'Kennedy Plunges Towards the Brink'. And when, about the same time, the Soviet Union began making menacing noises about Berlin, the president showed little caution about brinks there either. 'It is a simple matter to trace today's Berlin bravado directly to the humiliations of the Bay of Pigs,' wrote John Sutherland from Washington (14 July 1961). War threats became visible preparations, worsened when East Germany – newly 'sovereign' with Soviet blessings – closed its frontiers and erected that infamous wall. But negotiation and some Khrushchev moderation brought the world 'BACK FROM THE BRINK' (8 September 1961) – even though other powder-kegs remained, and Khrushchev had not run out of matches.

The Soviets were running into difficulties in many areas, especially in their deepening rift with Mao's China – which overshadowed even their space-race success with Yuri Gagarin in orbit in spring 1961, a year ahead of the first American astronaut. It was no time to expect 'revisionist' liberalism from Russia – regrettably, for talks without tension seemed humanity's only hope in those years. So indeed it had seemed to an important British novelist after a visit to the Soviet Union:

LETTER TO ALEXEI SURKOV

Every communication between East and West is of terrible importance; and I use the word *terrible* deliberately. Never very far from my mind is a recently published photograph of an American officer with two keys hanging round his neck. They are about the size of ordinary Yale Keys. He is smiling; though I don't see what he has to smile about.

For when he and his British colleague who has about his neck a similar pair of keys so decide it, the nuclear missiles will be released. I needn't explain the consequences; I don't want to think of them, since I have a wife and a three-year-old son.

My point is this: in America and in Russia, too, there exist men with the same power. Whether they are military men or civilians, whether they turn keys or press buttons or pick up telephones, is quite irrelevant. We all live on the brink of nuclear war; and if ever we plunge over the brink it will be because we didn't understand each other . . .

Please don't think that I imply that the tone of all communications between East and West must be one of fulsome praise for each other's way of life. For obvious reasons – the main ones on my side being that I believe both in Christianity and parliamentary democracy – that's impossible for both of us. What is not impossible is sincerity. What is not impossible is respect for each other as men and brothers. And what is imperative is that we should try to discover common ground. We can build up a worthwhile relationship on the basis of our likenesses, but not on our differences.

When keys only open doors, when buttons only summon waiters, when telephones are only painted red to match the curtains, then indeed there will be time to argue about our differences . . .

[*John Braine*, 6 December 1960]

But understanding was drowned in a renewed flood of posturings and rocket-rattling. Kennedy vengefully blockaded Cuba and became to Tribune one of 'THE WAR CRIMINALS' (26 October 1962). News emerged that Soviet missiles lurked on that island, ninety miles from fortress America, and Khrushchev was sending ships with more. Confrontation moved towards collision, and for a short time the world knew the ultimate terror and despair.

When the wiser counsels prevailed and doomsday was averted, 'Francis Flavius' felt '. . . we were about as fortunate as a man who feels the rope break when he is being hanged' (2 November 1962). But at least the trauma had shown mankind the true nature of a strategy based on nuclear deterrence, which Raymond Fletcher coldly called 'incineration without representation' (2 November 1962).

Even before the terror of 1962 Tribune had determined that the American President was 'THE FALLEN IDOL' (28 April 1961). The paper was less stringent ('that he grew in office is a fact that nobody can dispute' – Raymond Fletcher, 29 November 1963) when the idol fell in actuality, to bullets.

The new president from Texas inherited the problems and the errors, and to some extent enlarged both, in domestic areas like that of civil rights and the 'race question' and in foreign anti-communist adventurings. The Johnson era – another name for the 'squalid 'sixties' – might, however, have built on the New Frontier's civil rights progress, noted by Tribune's new American correspondent (and still in that position today), Roy Bennett:

. . . Every indication points to a successful closing of debate and final passage of the Civil Rights Bill in late June . . . This bill delivers to the Negro community the potentialities of a new level of Federal power on public accommodation, school desegregation, equal employment opportunities, non-discriminatory public housing and numerous other issues. Its basic strength is that it gives the Justice Department and the Federal Government new powers to act on the behalf of the rights of the individual . . .

No one denies the existence of 'white backlash' (a negative reaction by part of the white population to militant civil rights activities). But it is obvious that a social change as fundamental as desegregation cannot occur without serious disruption of established social patterns . . .

[12 June 1964]

The ominous references to 'backlash' and 'disruption' hinted at the strong smell of violence in the American air. Far away in South-East Asia, however, the smell since long before Kennedy's time had been of blood, cordite and napalm.

Laos, Cambodia, Thailand, above all Vietnam were theatres where the United States was staging its defence of 'freedom' by supporting purulent Right-wing régimes with arms, money and 'military advisers' – which last euphemism gave way to outright participation in LBJ's first presidential year. 'Vietnam: another Korea?' Tribune asked (6 March 1964). When the attacks began on the North later that year, by 'American forces in South Vietnam, literally crazy with anti-Communism' (7 August 1964), the answer had become self-evident.

Behind the spectral 'escalation' of what was to become one of the ugliest wars in history lay – as William Warbey said – an 'irrational fear and hatred of Chinese Communism' (29 May 1964). That fear had grown when Mao's forces overran the mountains of Tibet to poise themselves on India's frontiers. The Soviets, analysed by Dev Murarka on 11 May 1962, offered support to India as a gambit in its struggle against 'CHINA'S CAMPAIGN OF HATE' (2 November 1962). India, too, had other problems – religious violence and killings within its borders, and then the untimely departure of its first and greatest leader. Jennie Lee mused on ways 'we could begin to repay the immense debt we owe to Jawaharlal Nehru for the love he gave us, for his indestructible faith that in the end the better side of human nature would triumph – and to pay in the one way he would have welcomed, that is by continuing his fight against the crippling poverty and age-old superstitions that warp the lives of so many of his countrymen' (5 June 1964).

Beside these thunderous events in Asia, British troubles abroad may have seemed trivial – though perhaps not to those who had to deal with what William Warbey called the 'showdown in Malaysia' and 'THE MAD WAR IN BORNEO' (7 February 1964). Even these Asian embattlings were overshadowed by transformation and upheaval in the Middle East and Africa. Troops went into Kuwait, ostensibly at the invitation of its feudal leader but in reality to protect, as Ian Campbell put it, 'not that country's independence but our own entrenched financial position' (7 July 1961). Troops went into Aden three years later, this time to protect a South Arabian Federation foisted on the people of that region, 'created out of a hotchpotch of sheikhdoms, sultanates and emirates tacked on to the colony of Aden, in order to provide some sort of justification for the Aden base . . .' (15 May 1964).

In Africa, similarly, 1959 opened with crisis in Nyasaland and 1964 closed with crisis in Rhodesia. For some time the standard old British responses dominated: Michael Foot demonstrated that '. . . the main objective of the despots has been to force down the throats of the Africans the plan for Federation with Southern and Northern Rhodesia . . .' by what he called 'police-state' methods (31 July 1959). In the same issue, Barbara Castle led an outcry against police-state concentration camps in Kenya: 'ITEM: 11 MEN KILLED BY BEATING / PENALTY: ONE CAMP CHIEF RETIRED'.

The next year Macmillan spoke blandly about winds of change, a belated perception of the cold draughts that Tory colonial policy had been feeling for years. So had the (still die-hard today) white-supremacist spirit of settlerdom, fighting a desperate rearguard action against freedom for black Africans.

WELENSKY'S THREATS WON'T DETER US

The Northern Rhodesia Constitutional Conference has ended in a complete deadlock, and had it not been for the personality of Mr Iain Macleod, Africans would probably have walked out of the conference.

At the Conference, like one person, the African delegates demanded a clear African majority in both Legislative and Executive councils. All the territories to the north of Northern Rhodesia (the Congo, Tanganyika, etc.) have had advanced Constitutions, and Northern

Rhodesia's eastern neighbour, Nyasaland, was given a new Constitution in early 1960 . . .

Why was no agreement reached? . . . It is clear that it is the views of absent white settlers and the extreme Conservative elements which prevailed . . .

Settlers fully realise that Africans will soon rule Northern Rhodesia, but they regard this as the end – which is inevitable some day, but must be postponed as long as possible . . .

[*Kenneth Kaunda*, 24 February 1961]

Kaunda's country was soon reborn as independent Zambia, in the wake of other long-dreamed-of freedoms – Uganda, Kenya, Tanzania – and in the same year as Malawi. But Rhodesia, the 'Southern' dropped, went on its way, bringing Fenner Brockway to ask warningly 'WILL RHODESIA BECOME BRITAIN'S ALGERIA?' (23 February 1962). It seemed even more likely when Ian Smith took charge. His ilk had, of course, long been in charge southwards, in the worst example of master-race fascism in the post-war world.

Tribune and its South African correspondent, Myrna Blumberg, aided the anti-apartheid forces in the activist boycott that caught the radical imagination ('BOYCOTT SOUTH AFRICAN GOODS!' – 24 April 1959; 'BATTLE OF THE BOYCOTT' – 22 January 1960). The architects of apartheid chose those years to reveal themselves at their worst in the horror of Sharpeville – and the worldwide outrage that followed lent new strength to the Anti-Apartheid movement, and new ferocity to Tribune's attacks on the South African régime. (In 1960 Myrna Blumberg was arrested in her country and imprisoned for some months.) After South Africa made itself a republic in 1961, a great voice of its repressed black population spoke in Tribune about the Commonwealth's only possible response:

FOR DIGNITY OR GREED?

. . . No longer can the British people through their Government afford to continue in an attitude of lazy accommodation with the sin that is *apartheid*. The time has now come to dismiss the South African Government from the Commonwealth of Nations and to deny it the privileges that accrue from such membership.

The inauguration of the Republic in South Africa would most certainly not bring in its train any amelioration of the wretched plight of the non-whites of this country. If anything, the indications are that the non-whites would enter upon a phase of intensified repression in the name of *apartheid*, and a granite-like persistence in this policy has already been promised by the man who is to represent South Africa at the Commonwealth Premiers' Conference.

The African people are watching this drama with all the anxiety that is born of their anguish. They do not expect that denying South Africa membership of the Commonwealth will usher in their golden day. They know only too well the hard road ahead that must be traversed by them, before the darkness of race arrogance and prejudice is finally dispelled.

We are aware too that very strong forces – mainly financial and economic – are working in the opposite direction. The African people are watching to see whether Britain and other members of the Commonwealth are going to prefer economic and monetary considerations to human dignity and human happiness . . .

[*Albert Luthuli*, 10 March 1961]

Other imperial nations were similarly activated by the African winds. 'NATO ARMS BACK THE ANGOLA MASSACRES' (19 May 1961) and 'ANGOLA: THE FIGHT GOES ON' (4 May 1962) showed Portugal's notion of colonial progress. The black African's blood flowed also, earlier, when a wealthy and reaction-dominated province of the former Belgian Congo broke away from the newly independent nation and called itself Katanga. 'CONGO: who gains if Katanga breaks away?' asked David Boulton (15 July 1960), making it clear that the 'rebel' province was a pot into which many spoons reached – those of the mining interests predominantly, but also those of British and French imperialism, Rhodesian interests, and even Soviet involvement through the Congo's Leftist leader Patrice Lumumba. The United Nations hope of defusing the crisis dwindled with Lumumba's murder (when Tribune's outcry was aimed at 'BRITAIN'S SHARE IN THE CONGO CRIME' – 17 February 1961) and with the dubious air crash that killed Dag Hammarskjöld.

But in its display of the naked power of colonialism the Katanga crisis may have indirectly helped further to foster new and different alignments and motive forces in the world's power structure. At the beginning of the decade another great African leader had outlined for Tribune one of the most significant of these developments, in its overall form:

THE FUTURE OF AFRICAN NATIONALISM

. . . In Africa the anti-colonial struggle is essentially a struggle for human dignity.

The contending forces are not opposing ruling classes, one of which is tired of being ruled by the other. The anti-colonial forces in Africa are the people of Africa. They are struggling for the dignity of the common man and woman.

Independence for the country is an essential element in this because human equality is incompatible with the rule of one group by representatives of another. But once independence is attained, the nationalist organisations, composed of the common people, remain the dominant force in the society.

Because they draw their strength from the organisation of ordinary men and women they will have to go on to express the consciousness of human dignity and a quality in every aspect of the social, economic and political organisation of the country. The fullest development of the human spirit must be the motivating force in their future actions.

Theoretically, it is possible that the nationalist movements may degenerate into organisations controlled by a ruling clique, which uses the masses and ignores their real needs and desires. All the nationalist movements are led by privileged people – that is people who have had the privilege of education – for in Africa this is still a facility enjoyed by few, who are thus in a very advantageous position in relation to their fellow-countrymen.

But although uneducated, the African people are not sheep, nor are they likely to accept again any notion of their own inferiority. One inevitable element of the organisation of the African peoples in the struggle for independence has been the infusion of a consciousness of human dignity and the building up of individual as well as collective expectations.

This awakening of the human spirit has been accomplished, and it cannot be undone by anyone. Although there may be setbacks as a result of the prevailing ignorance of the forms of modern society, this fundamental success of the nationalist movement is the greatest possible safeguard against undemocratic tendencies within the nationalist organisations or outside them . . .

The nationalist movements must create an economic revolution, and this is a sphere which they enter for the first time when they have achieved political success. This is the twentieth century; every day Africans see evidence of the material wealth of the old nations. They now know it is not necessary for half their children to die in infancy, for people to be hungry, to exist in squalor . . .

This means that the new nationalist Governments will be essentially Socialist in outlook and actions. They will act deliberately to create and channel wealth, not stand aside holding the ring while individuals or groups compete for private profit . . .

[*Julius Nyerere*, 27 May 1960]

Elsewhere, a long way away from the third world, there was an economic partnership that dreamed – in theory – of becoming a power bloc in its own right. And Establishment Britain became further infected by that dream. It saw the enlarging Commonwealth full of uppity new nations shouting about things like neutralism and socialism. And then it saw the European Economic Community (EEC). For Macmillan and the Tories, it was no contest. Off went Edward Heath to knock at the EEC's opulent doors – and off went Tribune into a sustained and vituperative campaign.

Will Camp had fired early salvoes when the Tories were still dithering ('TWO FACES ON THE COMMON MARKET', 8 April 1960). Editorials in 1961 displayed the EEC as 'THE BAITED TRAP' (26 May) and 'GIVING UP ECONOMIC FREEDOM' (2 June). Yet there were dissenters:

> The one factor completely left out of *Tribune*'s analysis is the European working-class movement. Europe, like the United States, isn't only its Government, with the Kennedys, de Gaulles, and Adenauers. There are millions of organised workers, and it is to these organised workers that we must look . . .
>
> How are we ever to get a neutral Europe, if we cast ourselves off from the people of Europe? Surely joining the Common Market presents us with the opportunity of influencing the people of Europe in a way that is quite impossible at the present moment . . .
>
> Socialism is the opposite of insularity. European economic integration is inevitable. Surely our task as Socialists is to ensure that the direction it takes is affected by what action we take . . .
>
> [*Eric S. Heffer*, *letter*, 2 June 1961]

Then it was official Labour's turn to dither – by 'abstention' in a Commons vote – as 'Macmillan Goes Begging' (4 August 1961). Ultimately, Labour's Right fell in behind George Brown and Roy Jenkins, all for the Market. And British radicals, fearing the nation's subsumption in a bastion of uncontrolled capitalism, looked to Tribune for a lead and a platform.

THIS MONUMENTAL SWINDLE CALLED THE COMMON MARKET

The English conscience has been out for rent or hire for a long time. It is now up for outright purchase. Those who want to sell have called this historic transaction very simply – the Common Market. As drab a name for a monumental swindle has not been coined since a bright

German ad-man thought of putting wholesale murder on the market as National Socialism . . .

. . . this 'Europe' has never been anything more than an adroit piece of brand name dropping in a nightmare world of commercial jingle that has turned democracy into a hoax. For it is not a political idea at all. The Six – calling it a number already makes it sound like a Pretty Good Team – adds up to this: a squalid Chamber of Commerce with a large, impressive membership of political mercenaries. Napoleon's gibe about shopkeepers will explode in his tomb when Europe has at last become an explosive alliance of rich money-changers, a bizarre rabble of tradesmen . . .

A political idea must grow out of a man's need, and that need is not simply economic. Otherwise the point of his existence withers away, like the Liberal Party's *nouveau* marxist State, to a promised land of Common Market milk and honey, a desolate affair of obsessive shopping and guzzling. A nation has to do more than to keep counting its change. It has to count the cost of living without meaning, even if it means less money in the end . . .

[*John Osborne*, 12 October 1962]

As the campaign swelled, the paper reintroduced the Tribune public meeting, focused on its demand for a *referendum* on the issue of EEC membership. And it turned to Michael Barratt Brown for the positive side of the anti-Market case:

BRITAIN OUTSIDE THE MARKET

. . . the alternative is not 'some sort of tight Commonwealth', as Mr Gaitskell made clear. The alternative is a world-wide solution, which the Common Market either does not help forward or positively frustrates through its protectionist policies against imports of food, raw materials and conventional manufactures coming from outside Europe . . .

A great part of the economic argument of the Common Marketeers depends on the assumption that it is inevitable that the main growth in output and exports today shall be in consumer durables – motor cars, washing machines, refrigerators, vacuum cleaners. Such products, to be manufactured cheaply, do indeed require large markets or rich individual customers, such as are found in the rich West End of Europe.

But our sales of manufactures have always consisted of two kinds – finished consumption goods like textiles and pots and pans on the one hand and on the other capital equipment like railways, ships and machinery . . .

"Anti-H-bomb, anti-apartheid, anti . . . Don't you believe in anything, boy?"

"Indians are always welcome to Britain."
—THE QUEEN in a speech on her Indian tour.

Hirst's pocket cartoon from the early days of CND (20 January 1961); Cecily Ben-Tovim's drawing from the early days of immigration (10 March 1961); 'Graffito's' wry comment on the not-so-early days of the Vietnam war (26 June 1964).

"WATCH OUT! — HERE COMES OUR BIT NOW . . ."

What matters here is that the demand exists, if we can only help to organise it, for just the goods which we are in the best possible position to supply. The capital equipment for industrialisation that the developing lands so desperately need either is or could be the main stock-in-trade of an advanced industrial country like Britain.

And the crucial point is that sale of these goods does not depend on a rich market of individuals, as does the sale of consumer durables. It depends on Governments in the developing lands being able to mobilise their resources and to plan economic development on the basis of their available resources. Here is a far bigger market than Western Europe, but it needs our help to organise the potential into reality . . .

[9 November 1962]

But Heath's efforts and Macmillan's dream foundered on the reefs of de Gaulle's obduracy, and it was one more Tory disaster to add to the squalid list dominated by spies and scandals. Dominated, too, by the unsightly machinations that elevated an amateurish earl to the Tory leadership when Macmillan allowed himself to be prised out of it. All this plus increasingly evident economic shakiness gave Labour a strong chance in the approaching election, all the better as Wilson's leadership brought a pause to the rending party conflicts of a few years before. So in October 1964 Tribune's hopes were fulfilled when the end came to the thirteen Tory years. The paper's 'celebration issue' gleefully told the nation: 'TRIBUNE takes over from ETON in the Cabinet!' – with pictures of Wilson, R. H. S. Crossman, Barbara Castle, Frank Cousins, Anthony Greenwood and Fred Lee, all names well known in those columns, not to mention the unpictured new Minister for the Arts, Jennie Lee.

'To change the course of history with a majority of only four is not an easy assignment,' wrote Michael Foot in that same issue (23 October 1964). And he added, in the inimitable Tribune style: 'It is merely possible and necessary.'

6 'FRUSTRATION AND DISILLUSION' (1964–70)

'The first year of the Labour Government has sadly disillusioned many active Socialists. Indeed so deep is the frustration and despair that in some cases members of the Labour Party are unwilling any longer to take part in its activities . . .' (Richard Clements, 24 September 1965).

Disillusion, only a year after Harold Wilson's accession? Clearly the 'Tribune Cabinet's' post-election honeymoon had been, for the Left, brief and unsatisfactory. The government gave offence on nearly every major policy decision it made: over old-age pensions; over early foreign-affairs moves; above all, over what Tribune called 'the body blow' of honouring contracts to sell planes to South Africa (4 December 1964). With all this, too, came the Labour formulations – born out of an inherited economic crisis – of a stringent incomes policy and deflationary tactics.

The pressures were undeniable. Bankers and speculators and foreign financiers pressed for the usual deflationary package, especially after heavy British borrowing from the International Monetary Fund. When the Wilson government tried to introduce a few social-welfare increases and import surcharges, and murmured about new nationalizations, a crippling 'run' on sterling resulted. Hence the incomes policy, with a wage-rise ceiling of 3 to 3½ per cent, to which many sympathetic unions tried gallantly to adhere.

But discontent spread, all the more with news of an 18 per cent rise in dividends in 1965.

'. . . as Mr Brown and Mr Gunter apparently define it, "social priority" is to be the determining factor for wage increases and "the profit motive" is to govern increases in prices, dividends and profits . . .' wrote Richard Clements (28 May 1965). And Jack Jones rejected an incomes policy that was not integrally woven into an overall economic plan: 'The truth is that the Government will have to give evidence of its ability to control the private sector with some precision . . .' (21 May 1965).

Reaction at this placing of the burden of the crisis on the workers' backs led to a rash of industrial disputes, mostly unofficial, occasioning 'the usual middle-class cant about strikers "holding the nation to ransom" ' (Clements, 3 September 1965). Unrest spread through key areas – docks, mines, car workers – while the incomes policy argument hotted up. John Hughes and Ken Alexander voiced detailed economic criticisms and alternatives: '. . . orthodox deflationary measures in response to the balance-of-payments crisis have largely halted industrial growth . . . We would favour a tougher line on property income and its taxation . . . A clear commitment to redistribution is needed . . . a clear commitment to social priorities in incomes . . .' (10 December 1965). Michael Barratt Brown and Royden Harrison also offered prescriptions:

> Our position has always been that the trade unions could use the demand for an incomes policy to pressure the Government into taking more radical measures of interference on behalf of Labour in the market economy. There is no sign that the trade unions, least of all those on the Left, have seen this as an opportunity to be grasped. Purely defensive postures have been maintained . . .
>
> [17 December 1965]

So emerged once again 'THE DILEMMA OF THE LEFT' (Sydney Silverman, 24 September 1965): dared they fight for socialism so fiercely as to risk bringing down the government, with its tiny majority? Most readers' letters warned against rocking the boat ('Do you want the Tories back in power or what?' asked William Hormill of Maghull, in a letter of 24 September 1965). But Tribune demurred.

> OUR READERS AND 'TRIBUNE' POLICY
>
> . . . we have the job of putting the Government under constant pressure

to move towards the Left. Perhaps our readers do not fully appreciate how very heavy are the pressures in the opposite direction. They come, not only from the Tories, but from the massed ranks of financiers, businessmen and industrialists, who enjoy easy access to the Government's economic Ministers. They come from the City of London and the international bankers upon whose credit we now lean, and from the more subtle conservatism of the civil service. From all these quarters the Government is cajoled, threatened and entreated to water down or restrict any radical proposals it may make.

We have seen, in this first year of Labour Government, just how successful these pressures can be. We have seen old-fashioned restrictive economic policies adopted. We have seen cuts in public expenditure, and reforms in the social services postponed. We have had a plan which, because it is based upon the 'consensus and consent' of private enterprise, makes not a single proposal for the extension of public ownership. Steel nationalisation, despite its obvious priority, seems to have gone to the end of the queue.

It is our job to try and push or pull the Government in the opposite direction, and also to complain when it gives way to these reactionary interest groups. And because our power is less than theirs, because we have only a voice, it may be necessary to raise it. Otherwise our complaints may never be heard at all in those heavily insulated corridors . . .

[*Editorial*, 15 October 1965]

Once, pushing and pulling and complaining would have summoned the full wrath of the disciplinarians on the Labour Right. At least the Wilson era avoided a recurrence of those wretched times. But, for some, the age of discipline was not entirely past. That apostle of socialism and workers' control, Ken Coates, fell foul of what Tribune called 'witch-hunting' on the part of his local Labour Party in Nottingham. Tribune fought for him, and let him put his case against his expulsion – based, he asserted, on his opposition to some Labour government policies (including the incomes policy) and on his opposition to 'undemocratic persons who had concentrated considerable powers in their hands' (24 June 1966).

Coates stayed out in the cold until 1969. When he wrote the above words, however, Labour had in a general election assured itself of some years of warmth, with a solid majority. And then the boat began to be rocked with vigour – by none more than the National Union of Seamen, with a strike two months after the election. The government declared a state of emergency, 'ill-conceived' and threatening 'the most serious crisis the Government has yet to face', in

Eric Heffer's view (27 May 1966). After the 'SEVEN WEEKS THAT SHOOK THE LABOUR MOVEMENT' (8 July 1966), Jane McKerron asked for Tribune: 'What about the Government's future attitude? Has it learnt that it is impossible to use a small union with a genuine case as a scapegoat for a failing and wildly inconsistent incomes policy? . . .' (8 July).

By then Frank Cousins had resigned from the government, in time to miss a 'STRIKE STORM' (20 October 1967) that led Ray Gunter, Deakin-like, to find 'Communist-Trotskyite' agitators under every striker's bed (27 October 1967). But it was nearly thirty Labour MPs, not Communists, who had earlier abstained in a vote on the policy of 'deflation and wage freeze' (28 October 1966). And it was Tribune, not Trotskyites, who had shouted as the sterling crisis swelled: 'CALLAGHAN MUST GO!' – from the Exchequer, of course (6 January 1967) – while Anthony Arblaster defined the Harold Wilson style as 'GOVERNMENT BY DECEPTION' (17 March 1967).

Eventually matters reached 'LABOUR'S CRISIS OF CONFIDENCE' (28 October 1967), enhanced by nearly one million unemployed, the devaluation of the pound and swingeing cuts in the social services. Two years further on, the crisis deepened when the Wilson government gave birth to a White Paper containing proposals for legislation to control, limit and contain industrial action. Its title itself seemed almost designed to put up the backs of the formerly Bevanite Left: *In Place of Strife*. Tribune saw it as a 'A RECIPE FOR DISASTER' (10 January 1969). So did the new general secretary of the Transport and General Workers Union.

> The idea of legally enforced 'conciliation pauses', and official ballots on strikes, provides further opportunities for delay and frustration within a system of bureaucratic state intervention.
>
> In particular, the idea that fines may be enforced by allowing employers to deduct them from the pay packet . . . may well spark off further strikes even when the original dispute has been settled.
>
> We need faster settlement of disputes, not more Ministerial intervention, which can often be influenced by employer-backed alarmist press campaigns on a particular dispute . . .
>
> The sort of costly, time-consuming, harmful intervention by punitive measure and legal sanctions is certainly likely to cause many more strikes than they prevent . . .
>
> [*Jack Jones*, 24 January 1969]

Barbara Castle, principal author of *In Place of Strife*, made a reasoned reply:

> . . . Jack Jones has said: 'Strikes don't just happen. They have causes and it is these which have to be tackled.' I agree and this is the whole purpose of the White Paper's policy. It is a charter for tackling the causes of strikes . . .
>
> It seeks, too, to tackle these causes in ways which strengthen the trade union movement's authority . . .
>
> Far from wanting more Ministerial intervention in disputes, I want the unions themselves to face up to their responsibilities in preventing unnecessary disputes which can do wanton damage to other members of the community . . .
>
> The same approach lies behind my proposals for a 'conciliation pause'. This has one purpose only: to ensure that workers do not down tools before they have used the procedure for examining disputes which their own unions have negotiated . . .
>
> [7 February 1969]

But battle had commenced. The National Executive voted against the anti-strike proposals in the document ('. . . a symptom of what is happening to the Labour Government as it moves further and further from its moorings in the Labour movement . . .' – 4 April 1969); the Tribune Group carried the banner of the 'rising opposition' to the White Paper (11 April 1969); and Michael Foot depicted 'THE MADDEST SCENE IN MODERN HISTORY':

> . . . Harold Wilson and Co. have been persuaded that the way to establish themselves as big, brave men and women capable of *governing*; the way to prove they have hair on their chest; the way to show they don't give a damn for anybody, except of course the *New Mirror* or the *Daily Statesman* and, last, but by no means least, the public opinion polls, is to declare war on the trade unions . . .
>
> [18 April 1969]

As it happened, the anti-strike proposals did not reach the statute books: the government gave way, which, Clements wrote, 'can certainly be claimed as a victory' (27 June 1969). There were not so many of these about for Tribune – neither in the domestic sphere nor in the international.

Into Wilson's lap almost as soon as he assumed power had dropped the over-heated potato of southern Africa, and the blatant colonial rebellion of breakaway Rhodesia. Wilson and Ian Smith met and re-met, face to face and through intermediaries – but UDI was declared, and Smith's opponents (like Joshua Nkomo and Garfield Todd) were 'restricted'. Labour imposed sanctions that began to be flouted instantly, and Tribune bluntly advocated a short, sharp answer – sending in the army via a neighbouring and willing African nation ('SEND TROOPS TO ZAMBIA!' – 26 November 1965).

But no troops embarked, and Smith plus UDI remained intact as they still remained a decade later. Tribune espied 'Wilson's Rhodesian Munich' (25 October 1968) and among mutters of 'sell-out' Ben Whitaker took the front page to explain what granting independence before majority rule would mean:

> . . . The Commonwealth as a multi-racial ideal will be wrecked beyond repair . . . At the United Nations, all Britain's credit would vanish overnight . . .
>
> Most serious of all, future hopes for race relations in Britain as well as Africa would be given a fatal blow, and the chances of averting an ominous hardening of the racial divisions of the world – much the most dangerous source of future conflict – lost . . .
>
> [22 November 1968]

Africa remained in eruption continent-wide – a coup in Nigeria, a coup in Ghana, the death of Verwoerd – the first of which led to civil war and the secession of a new, ill-starred state, Biafra. That blood-bath brought at first only occasional keeping-in-touch references in Tribune ('NIGERIA: the questions war cannot settle' – 24 May 1968; 'THE TRAGEDY OF BIAFRA' – 19 July 1968) until reports of its true horrors aroused the radical humanitarian Left, as when Frank Allaun pointed out the role, in the shattered, starving country, of the oil interests ('By a rather odd coincidence easily the richest wells already in operation are in the Rivers State, the contested area, formerly part of Eastern Nigeria but now in Federal control . . .' – 28 March 1969).

A ceasefire finally ended the carnage, if not the famine. In another embattled area, earlier, another uneasy peace had exploded into war and back again to peace of sorts within a week: in 1967 Egypt's Nasser had closed the Gulf of Akaba, Israel's 'lifeline' to the Red Sea. Israel responded with force and achieved victory in a now-famous Six Days. Tribune had called for restraint on *both* sides, and earned a rebuke from Israel Herz of MAPAM: 'Didn't the authors of the editorial understand that to close the Straits of Tiran is to strangle the whole Israeli economy and that to accept this is to support our demise? . . .' (16 June 1967).

Tribune replied directly: 'We are apprehensive that the legacy of hatred and bitterness which [the war] will leave behind it in the Arab world will make it more, and not less, difficult to achieve a lasting settlement which will guarantee Israel's right to live' (16 June 1967).

Beyond the travails of Africa north and south, guns and blood and nationalisms wrote the continuing story of other ex-colonies. Antonio de Figueiredo, Tribune's expert on Portugal in particular, reported on the Cuban 'infection' spreading through Latin America, borne by powerful Marxist emissaries like Che Guevara, in 'A guide to the revolution on America's doorstep' (9 April 1965). In Europe, the opposite of a revolution brought fascism to power in Greece ('The recovery of Greek democracy is likely to be a long, bitter and quite possibly bloody business' – Anthony Arblaster, 28 April 1967). Also in Europe, a man called Dubček was quietly trying to create socialism with a human face in Czechoslovakia. 'The relaxation of censorship, the encouragement which the new leadership under Mr Dubček has given to critical discussion even of hitherto taboo subjects . . . have met with a quite extraordinarily eager response,' said an editorial on 15 March 1968. Another, later, was reassuring: 'Alarmist rumours about Soviet military pressure on Czechoslovakia can be discounted. The Russians have nothing to gain by repeating the Hungarian performance of 12 years ago . . .' (24 May 1968).

But then came 'The Czech crisis: NO SECOND HUNGARY' (19 July 1968), and finally 'A CRIME AGAINST SOCIALISM' (23 August 1968) – Michael Foot's words, precisely echoing the headline in 1956 when Soviet tanks had crushed another desperate striving for democracy.

Crushings were going on, it seemed, everywhere. India and Pakistan had begun 'THIS SENSELESS WAR' over Kashmir (10 September 1965), and four years later a 'revolutionary storm' (Abdul Kamir, 28 February 1969) threatened the always volatile mixture that was Pakistan itself. Before that, extremists had taken to the streets in Mao's China to call up the storm of the 'cultural revolution'. That leading Sinologist John Gittings asked:

> IS THERE SENSE IN THE SHAMBLES?
> . . . An enormous therapeutic shock has been administered, through the agency of the revolutionary 'masses', to the old self-satisfied

> bureaucracy, most of which has now been re-admitted to the fold. It has been another rectification campaign, similar (although larger in scope) to previous ones in the Communist Party's history. But unfortunately, the balance sheet is by no means as healthy as it initially appears.
>
> In the first place, the movement has shattered the previous unity of the top leadership, which had proved remarkably stable for decades. New rivalries have been created, and perhaps old latent antagonisms have been exacerbated . . .
>
> The erosion of party and government has in turn led to an erosion of social discipline, law and order, and to a slump in production. The extent of this may be exaggerated by some China Watchers, but the Chinese themselves admit to serious stoppages in industry and transport, outbreaks of hooliganism, theft and speculation in the towns, gambling and other lawlessness. The most optimistic estimate is that, if all goes well, production by the end of 1968 will be restored to the level of 1966 . . .
>
> [14 June 1968]

Throughout its reportage of all these different conflicts, Tribune returned wherever possible to the theme of Labour's failures: to intervene, to respond correctly, to respond at all. From Rhodesia to Anguilla, Tribune rejected the foreign policy of Wilson and George Brown, who left the economic-supremo hot seat to be Foreign Secretary, 1966–8. And outweighing his and Wilson's and Denis Healey's specific blunders, as Tribune saw them, was the overall insistence on a British presence 'East of Suez' – a 'delusion' to Wayland Young (17 September 1965), 'economic lunacy' to an editorial (10 June 1966) and to Frank Allaun 'an outlay of millions in the defence of an area which we can't defend' (3 February 1967).

What especially exercised Tribune's fury was the fact that out in the vaguely defined east-of-Suez area, prominent as an open wound, was the theatre for the ugliest and most indefensible of all the 1960s' wars. John Gittings, again, asked the question: 'What IS the Labour Government's Vietnam Policy?' (17 September 1965).

It seemed, in a nutshell, to be total acquiescence in America's evil war – when the bombs and napalm and defoliant rained down on North Vietnam perilously close to China; when, during hopeful feelers towards peace, 'AMERICA BOMBS OUT THE TALKS AGAIN' (17 February 1967). Angry, appalled visitors to Hanoi reported the truth about the bombing: Malcolm Caldwell announced that the Americans 'have virtual *carte blanche* to bomb wherever they care', which meant civilians (16 February 1967); Tariq Ali discovered that 'the Americans are using anti-personnel bombs the only purpose of which is to wound or maim civilians' (10 March 1967). But Britain's support of this near-genocide was never so virulently condemned as by the then greatest living voice of the anti-war movement, who bitingly labelled George Brown

LABOUR'S GOLDWATER

Perhaps George Brown should be given the benefit of the doubt, and we should treat seriously his outburst on Vietnam last week on the BBC. I know that many Labour Party members share the view of William Hamilton, one of the vice-chairmen of the Parliamentary Labour Party, that Mr Brown's utterances are no longer paid any attention, but so long as he is deputy leader of the party his enthusiasm for the American cause in Vietnam cannot be ignored so easily.

Mr Brown revealed all too clearly his attitude to the war:

(1) The United States should continue its war effort and finish the job. (With Goldwater Mr Brown asks: 'Why not victory?') Any interruption of this task is described as . . . 'weeping' and must be stopped.

(2) An American defeat in Vietnam would be a 'threat to freedom'. Mr Brown wants a 'free South Vietnam; free, I mean, to choose its own decisions'. How grotesque! The Saigon generals, ruling over a sea of napalm with CIA cash and dreading the day the people will be permitted 'to choose its own decisions' are the guardians of Mr Brown's freedom.

(3) The Labour Party should devote itself to contemplating the threat to freedom instead of 'just looking for the atrocities that may be committed by the Americans'.

(4) We should 'think about the atrocities that are committed by the other side and the terrible damage to freedom if the other side were to win'. (What does he think Fleet Street has been doing all these years?)

(5) Any American atrocities which may have been committed are justified by atrocities similarly committed in the past by other colonial powers such as Britain . . .

But the most dangerous aspect of Mr Brown's utterances is that they bore every sign of reflecting faithfully deeply ingrained ways of thought: America equals freedom. Nobody hearing him for the first time would guess that he is a prominent spokesman for a political party with a long anti-imperial tradition . . .

A long tradition of instinctive sympathy with oppressed peasants has been virtually wiped out by the present Government with its servility to bankers and Washington, its sale of weapons to barbarous regimes, its 'responsible' anti-communism and its NATO-dominated view of Britain's place in the world . . .

[*Bertrand Russell*, 28 November 1969]

The revulsion over Vietnam was of course international, as was the spirit it fed: of frustration, despair, rage, an outright rejection of failed or impotent or apparently irresponsible political leadership. Out of it, all-pervasively, sometimes frighteningly, there grew that enormous late-1960s movement of militant, radical, direct-action *protest* – and the equally direct and sometimes brutal authoritarian response to it. It was the age of protest, the time of confrontation, the day of the revolutionary. It was the era of Che Guevara, mythified all the more after his death in 1967; of 'red' Rudi Dutschke, Abbie Hoffman and Tariq Ali; of mass marches and student riots and battles with police all round the world.

In Britain it was the era of 'student power' (not to mention flower power) with marches and sit-ins and teach-ins and takeovers of art colleges and the London School of Economics, all of which reached its climacteric when blood reddened the pavements of Grosvenor Square in 'THE DEMO': '. . . it is precisely because many militant Leftists have come to agree . . . that non-violent demonstrations are "futile happenings" that they have in desperation looked for a solution in violence' (Editorial, 1 November 1968).

In that same year of confrontation France too felt the tremors, when the 'May revolution' produced 'the greatest pressure on the regime and a complete rejection of the society which that regime had fostered' (28 June 1968). But the anti-protest backlash introduced violences of its own, not only from police batons and tear gas. Rudi Dutschke was shot in Germany in 1968, while in America assassins cut short any good that might have been done by Martin Luther King and Robert Kennedy.

Both these American murders underlined the presence of strands other than the anti-war movement in the age of protest. Philip Altbach described in Tribune the evolution of the blazing civil rights struggle by America's black minority into 'BLACK POWER' (9 September 1966). Similarly Dilip Hiro, interviewing Stokely Carmichael in Tribune, was shown a future of 'more violent rebellions' and 'urban guerrilla warfare in America' (28 July 1967).

Black militancy had not then come to Britain, but there was no shortage of the racism that would impel it. The 1964 election had been tarnished by the Smethwick Tory candidate's 'notorious racialist campaign' ('Flavius', 27 November 1964). Soon Enoch Powell was making his bid for the headlines on that same bandwagon of bigotry, making him a primary object of loathing by the Left.

> . . . Mr Powell was not merely reporting on white racialism: he was encouraging it. He was endorsing the lies and exaggerations on which it feeds. He was helping to bring about the terrible conflict which he claims to fear . . . Mr Powell speaks for the white racialism which so far has not found a voice within the framework of conventional party politics . . .
>
> [*Editorial*, 26 April 1968]

But Labour itself had proved no true friend to racial harmony with its initial White Paper on immigration ('As white as leprosy . . .', 6 August 1965) on which Fenner Brockway issued a stinging rebuke entitled 'My head is bowed with shame' (13 August 1965). There was shame again three years later when Kenyan Asians with British passports occasioned further 'RACIALIST LAW FOR BRITAIN' from the very Labour government which had passed a lip-service Race Relations Act: 'Now that the Government is practising discrimination itself at the point of entry to this country, how can it ask employers, landlords and publicans not to do so? . . .' (1 March 1968).

Bigotry of a different sort, though, was producing in Great Britain a spirit of militant civil-rights protest akin to the American experience. In Northern Ireland, simmering religious hatred and political expediencies began coming to the boil, tirelessly reported by Tribune correspondent Andrew Boyd. 'FASCISM IN NORTHERN IRELAND' (24 June 1966) described the antics of Ian Paisley and his Protestant mobs. 'STAMP OUT THE VIOLENCE IN ULSTER,' Tribune demanded, as Boyd warned 'The gun comes back into Ulster politics' (1 July 1966). Out of riots, fear and death grew a tragic confrontation, as Catholics responded in kind to the Ulster Volunteer Force, Paisley and the Stormont government. The brief flowering of a civil rights activism stirred up their enemies even more, and made Belfast 'a city of naked terror' (Andrew Boyd, 8 August 1969).

Riots and counter-riots, already commonplace, drove Westminster to send in the army, which at least brought the disbanding of the vicious Royal Ulster Constabulary. But Catholic militants had enemies aplenty left, as when that prime mover of the civil-rights struggle, Bernadette Devlin, was imprisoned for her efforts. It seemed for Ulster that what was past was prelude – and new Tribune reporter Michael Walsh foresaw the monstrosities to come:

> There have been three bomb explosions in Dublin recently . . . This indicates that the security forces are unable to police the Eire – Ulster border. And if they cannot control the border, what chance have they if the whole province explodes?
>
> [2 January 1970]

As that explosion grew nearer, Tribune's Ulster coverage developed into one of the paper's finest campaigns, analysing and decrying the needs and failures of British society. So, too, it sought out other needs and failures within the state of the nation, concentrating as always on the whole range of social welfare, education and the ineradicable stain of poverty. Nowhere was it more evident than in the plight of the homeless, newly spotlighted by a variety of pressures – and a new pressure group called 'Shelter', speaking out in Tribune:

> The Pryde family live in a Manchester slum that is only fit for animals, and it is inhabited by rats. The house is so damp that two of their children suffer from tuberculosis, and another from bronchial asthma. There is no water supply to the bath, or to the lavatory, and both must be filled and emptied with a bucket.
>
> Half the windows are without glass, and there are holes in the ceilings, floors and walls. In fact, it looks so derelict that you would never believe anybody lived there if it was not for a little sign in the window saying: 'This house is occupied.'
>
> The Prydes are hopelessly overcrowded. They live in unbelievable squalor. Their rotten housing conditions are undermining their health, and their morale as a family is low . . .
>
> [*Des Wilson*, 19 September 1969]

Tribune also devoted space and concern to growing environmental worries, as in David Rubinstein's regular column on 'The Citizen and the Countryside' – on the *arts* pages! – from mid-1969. And it was a British environmental problem – or an inadequate official awareness of it – that led to one of the most cruel calamities of modern times, on which a front-page poem carried some of the outburst of rage and sorrow:

ABERFAN

Poor
Bloody
Wales.

Coal killed your
men.
Choked
lungs
Crushed
limbs

Entombed.

And now,
As pits close,
The
valley dies . . .

Coal plays its last bitter joke.

[*Llew Gardner*, 28 October 1966]

Other groupings of activists were emerging – like those of women, who for instance earned a two-page spread on their 'LONG HARD STRUGGLE FOR EQUAL RIGHTS . . .' (8 November 1968). Some of these groups, though, opted out of social struggle, when the age of the hippie arrived with all its concomitants. Caroline Coon, heading her new organization Release, described one of them:

ON THE DRUG SCENE

It is not true to say that only young people are suffering from the upheaval in our society, but the situation for us is more acute. There is no international crisis that we can adequately use to cover up our profound sense of dissatisfaction with the present domestic constitutional machinery, which has proved inadequate to our material needs and our spiritual aspirations alike.

Young people are increasingly outraged by the Government's position on Vietnam, South Africa, Rhodesia, Biafra, poverty, the homeless and civil rights. Institutions are seen to be irrevocably bound to the interests of capitalism . . .

The 'drug scene' is one way in which some young people are able to adapt to these social pressures. A great many people use socially acceptable drugs such as alcohol and nicotine, or drugs legally prescribed by doctors. And it may come as a surprise to some, but the largest group of people dependent on drugs are not young people but middle-aged and elderly people using barbiturates . . .

. . . the young drug user, as part of a minority group, is open to victimisation in a society mainly concerned with using legal measures to deal with a problem although medical and social solutions are likely to be more successful . . .

. . . we must ask ourselves whether indiscriminate raids on clubs, or searching anyone with long hair is really going to have any effect, apart from alienating a growing section of the public from the police force . . .

[16 May 1969]

Even for those still embedded in conventional society, upheavals of all sorts arrived in bewildering plenty. A man stepped on to the moon, fated it seems to be misquoted forever, fated also to be – like the whole space race – tainted, in Donald Soper's words, 'with national pride, national secrecy, and unhealthy national rivalry' (25 July 1969). The onslaught of the 'permissive' society – abortion and divorce reforms all part and parcel of nudity on stage and screen, and allied terrors – brought a censorship backlash to the media and the arts. It was savaged especially by Elizabeth Thomas, as when she joined in the fight over theatre censorship and over 'an attempt to tighten up the laws' (4 February 1965). That fight brought a famous victory when a Bill (piloted by George Strauss) meant that 'the Lord Chamberlain no longer has any control over what happens on the stage' (Elizabeth Thomas, 27 September 1968).

The 'cultural' side of Tribune remained ever thus outspoken and enterprising. It also remained over-crowded. The books coverage offered as always a kaleidoscope of socialist, radical, Labour movement reviewers rubbing shoulders with *literati* new or established. Jeremy Robson kept up his regular poetry reviews, Robert Nye continued his column on paperbacks until relinquishing it to poet-painter Alan Bold in 1970; in 1965 Jim Burns began a round-up of the 'little magazines' (almost unique in the press then), those hot-beds of tomorrow's literature.

And direct sampling of tomorrow's poetry continued, with so many of the weekly poems in Tribune still by newer, rising writers – Ted Walker, David Tipton, D. M. Thomas, D. M. Black, Martin Booth – joined of course by an encouraging admixture of more established names. Many of the poems quite rightly reflected an amazing national outburst of 'protest poetry', as crucial a part of the age of protest as any demo. Poems of that sort came from Christopher Logue, Bernard Kops, Karen Gershon, the South African Dennis Brutus and many more – but none of these poems gained more currency, had more public readings, expressed more accurately the bitter rage that led otherwise to Grosvenor Square, than one sent to Tribune by Adrian Mitchell:

TO WHOM IT MAY CONCERN
I was run over by the truth one day.
Ever since the accident I've walked this way
So stick my legs in plaster
Tell me lies about Vietnam.

Heard the alarm clock screaming with pain,
Couldn't find myself so I went back to sleep again
So fill my ears with silver
Stick my legs in plaster
Tell me lies about Vietnam.

Every time I shut my eyes all I see is flames.
Made a marble phone book, carved all the names
So coat my eyes with butter
Fill my ears with silver
Stick my legs in plaster
Tell me lies about Vietnam.

I smell something burning, hope it's just my brains.
They're only dropping peppermints and daisy-chains
So stuff my nose with garlic
Coat my eyes with butter
Fill my ears with silver
Stick my legs in plaster
Tell me lies about Vietnam.

Where were you at the time of the crime?
Down by the Cenotaph drinking slime
So chain my tongue with whisky
Stuff my nose with garlic
Coat my eyes with butter
Fill my ears with silver
Stick my legs in plaster
Tell me lies about Vietnam.

You put your bombers in, you put your conscience out,
You take the human being and you twist it all about

So scrub my skin with women
Chain my tongue with whisky
Stuff my nose with garlic
Coat my eyes with butter
Fill my ears with silver
Stick my legs in plaster
Tell me lies about Vietnam.

[16 April 1965]

On the arts side, Boleslaw Sulik remained film reviewer and Mervyn Jones theatre reviewer, until the latter gave way in 1966 to Simon Trussler (who had often deputized for him before, with wit and insight). Television reviewing fell, in succession, to J. D. S. Haworth, Clive Goodwin, Jason McColl and Marjorie Lampard. Margaret Richards reviewed art exhibitions, John May still dealt with records and Edward Lockspeiser with live classical music; Ronald Atkins began a jazz column in 1965.

Other areas of music reviewing showed special new departures. Stephen Sedley went on with folk music reviews, but this feature expanded in 1965 to a full examination of the folk scene by such contributors as Karl Dallas, Tony McCarthy, Norman Buchan, Bob Davenport and the renowned A. L. Lloyd. And the exploding world of 'pop' entered Tribune's columns – especially when Paul Jones, near-superstar singer with the Manfred Mann group, contributed feature reviews in the mid-1960s, and when progressive pop expert Dulan Barber began a 'Progressive Sounds' column in early 1969.

General arts features also contained surprises and feasts, many of them radiating outwards from the happy fact that Tribune's own Jennie Lee was conducting, as Minister for the Arts, a splendid battle against philistinism and cultural indifference. From the top of the communications world, the powerful head of the Granada Group entered Tribune to ally himself with most of Jennie Lee's vision:

LABOUR AND THE ARTS

Jennie Lee's White Paper suggests what can be done. In addition to what she says there, she has got to get the Government, in spite of all the economic problems of the present, to put up money to get things under way. This may take time. But there is something that can be done immediately.

She has pointed a finger at the local authorities: Do something now, she has told them. Under the 1948 Local Government Act the local authorities are entitled to raise up to a 6d. rate for encouragement of the arts. It was Nye Bevan himself who was responsible for introducing this enlightened clause into the Act. But how many local authorities are exercising this right? How many of them really care? There are far too many councils who think that when they have appointed an art master to the local secondary modern school they have made their gesture to the arts . . .

Perhaps this attitude arises from some trait in the British character which regards the arts with a certain moral suspicion. The attitude seems to be: 'artists aren't respectable, therefore they don't deserve support; concerts attract people with long hair; ballet is unhealthy; poets are incomprehensible.' The fact that there are a large number of extremely respectable artists who are pillars of propriety, that concerts attract the bald and bowler-hatted as well as the long-haired, that it is possible to have quite sensible conversation with poets, and that ballet dancing is very hard work – none of these unexciting truths can quite overcome that lurking suspicion. And that suspicion is given the backing of a virtue when it comes to money . . .

The history of the arts in this country would suggest that the most fruitful situation is when the strong centralising and standardising pressure of London is in conflict with a powerful individualism in the regions. The task of the present is to revitalise that individualism . . .

[*Sidney Bernstein*, 2 April 1965]

Without question, though, among all Jennie Lee's achievements in her Ministry, none can match her prolonged and successful struggle to create a remarkable educational experiment that has become a paradigm of socialist ideals in culture and social change. 'The Open University is launched,' wrote Elizabeth Thomas on 22 September 1967, reporting the establishment of an authoritative planning committee and Jennie Lee's own unswerving determination that 'there must be no compromise on standards'.

All this cultural coverage, in the later 1960s, came to be presented in less and less space: three to four pages was the rule in 1964 or 1965, rarely more than two pages after 1968. This squeeze was part of an overall compression of the paper, as rising costs and the economic climate eroded its financial position. Even in 1966, when sixteen pages a week could usually be managed, money troubles were accentuated by a move to a new office, Tribune's present address in the heart of Smithfield. As so often before, readers rallied to help –

with donations of every sort including office furniture. That hurdle safely crossed, the paper reached its thirtieth birthday in 1967 with a fanfare that was wholly in the context of those years' internecine quarrels. The birthday issue of 28 April 1967 gave space to what Michael Foot called 'nondescript ex-contributors' who had been invited to present their 'particular brand of deviationism' in that issue – for instance, Woodrow Wyatt:

> . . . I am sometimes puzzled by being regarded by *Tribune* as Right-wing. Take public ownership. I am just as much in favour of it as *Tribune*, but I don't want it done any more in a way which I regard as stultifying, old-fashioned wholesale nationalisation . . .
>
> [28 April 1967]

There were also nostalgic notes sounded by other former leading lights of the paper, neither nondescript nor deviationist.

> . . . I can even remember the days when I could read something in *Tribune*, disagree violently with it, and snort with derision at its author: 'Stupid old fogey: his generation is Stone Age: they just don't understand how young people feel these days.' Which, word for word, is the reaction of *Tribune*'s present Y.S. readers to every article I now contribute to the paper. *Sic transit* a Socialist reputation . . .
>
> [*Ian Mikardo*, 28 April]

Eventually, despite crisis and cost-counting, and with further appeals to readers, survival, if not safety, was assured: enough to allow a 'new-look' Tribune to appear in 1969. It introduced new printing techniques, livelier layout and other production improvements. It brought new features, like the 'People's Past' series of articles on socialist and Labour history, later collected into the anthology *People for the People*. And it brought new emphases, notably a further extension of the industrial coverage: a new 'Industrial Diary', for instance, along with even more contributions from major union leaders (Hugh Scanlon, Ernie Roberts, Tom Jackson, Lawrence Daly, Richard Briginshaw, Walter Anderson, Bob Wright, and, of course, Jack Jones) along with indefatigable and assiduous union news reporting by the paper's industrial reporter (from 1968), David Turner.

There had inevitably been changes before the 'new look' – in features, contributors, approaches. From 1965, new page-three editorials focused attention on world and home events of the week, while the concise notes of an 'In Focus' column searched out the state of the nation, and the back page surveyed the state of the world. Columnists came and went: Michael Foot began a sporadic column ('Soper writes political columns, I supply the sermons' – 19 March 1965) and Clive Jenkins ceased production on his (1969). David Tribe wrote weekly topical-satirical verses from 1966, and guest writers stirred up controversies in a 'Personally Speaking' slot from 1969. Also in 1969 George Gale became the resident cartoonist, as he still is.

Other changes, around if not in Tribune, brought sadness rather than celebration. The later 1960s seemed another time of loss, a gathering of obituary farewells to great names. In 1966 Tribune wrote on the deaths of two major but very different figures of the far Left, Wal Hannington and Sean O'Casey. In 1967 the paper mourned two men who had been integral to Tribune's existence at its beginnings, Victor Gollancz and Konni Zilliacus – and in the same year Ralph Miliband wrote the obituary of Isaac Deutscher and Geoffrey Bing wrote that of Clement Attlee.

Tribune lost many more doughty supporters from the Labour Party and movement – in 1968, Sydney Silverman and Arthur Horner; in 1969 – the year also that Ho Chi Minh died – Stephen Swingler, Emrys Hughes and Henry Collins. Then in 1970 a level of greatness, a breadth of mind and spirit, that is a rarity in any century went out of modern British life with the death of Bertrand Russell. Michael Foot lamented that loss.

> He became one of the chief glories of our nation and people, and I defy anyone who loves the English language and the English heritage to think of him without a glow of patriotism. The world-famous philosopher, the international publicist, the critic of all principalities and powers, the incorrigible dissenter, the foremost sceptic and exponent of free thought throughout the last half-dozen decades was English to the core, as uniquely English as the free-thinking Whig aristocracy in which he was reared and against whose complacencies and limitations he revolted . . .
>
> [6 February 1970]

Along with all these changes, there were invariably some old battles to be fought – or perhaps merely the one old battle, to create socialism. In a gathering of forces that must have reminded

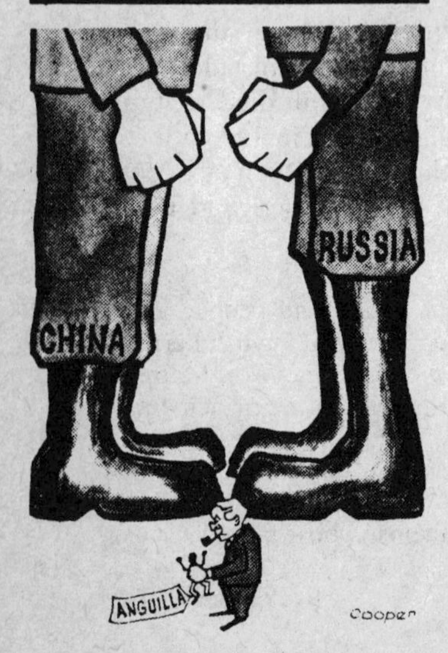

Settlement of island crises

"And then I made it clear to Rhodesia and all the other African states that I would never countenance a military solution to a political problem . . ."

'Graffito' again on some implications of Britain's support for America in Vietnam (5 November 1965); 'Abu's' view of American reaction to the growing peace movement (8 November 1968); Cooper's perspective on the quelling of the Anguilla 'revolt' (28 March 1969).

some a little of the dangerous days of Unity and the Socialist League, Tribune committed itself noisily to unequivocal support of a new Left-wing organization which took the title of 'The Socialist Charter'.

The Charter's aim was purely revivalist – to revive faith and confidence and activism, 'to reawaken a spirit of audacity within the Labour Party', to overcome the 'great gap . . . opening up between the hopes of ordinary people and the established processes of politics' (7 June 1968). For the next few years, Tribune carried each week a report on the Charter's progress, its meetings and rallies and conferences, from its registrar Brenda Brett. By October 1968 she was happily listing the considerable batch of local organizations who supported the Charter; by November a Charter logo had been designed (an arrow curiously bent round to the Right!). In June 1969, after a year of hectic activity, Tribune declared 'National Charter Week' – and so it went, on into 1970, to serve as rallying-point for the energies needed to fight the new as well as the old battles of the 1970s.

One of those battles had already had a good few opening skirmishes in the 1960s. It was seen in the previous section how Harold Macmillan had sought glory by taking Britain across the Channel into the Common Market. Harold Wilson had lost no time in seeking to follow the same course. When de Gaulle seemed less obdurate this time, Tribune irately issued 'A WARNING ON THE COMMON MARKET' (3 December 1965), followed by Basil Davidson being dubious about 'Going into Europe?' (21 January 1966) and Michael Barratt Brown analysing the 'COMMON MARKET: HOW THE GOVERNMENT SHOULD ACT' with some prophetic gloom:

> The one thing which entry to the Common Market cannot assure is the general advance in prosperity of the world's economy. I have warned frequently in the last few months that this advance is in grave danger. The effect on our trade even of a small reduction in the rate of growth of world trade could be acute . . . how will our exports fare then?
>
> [18 November 1966]

Editorials and other articles fuelled the Left-wing opposition to Wilson's EEC hopes – which were somewhat dashed when de

Gaulle threw cold water on the 'conditions' attached by Labour to Britain's approach. Tribune did not refrain from a gleeful 'WE TOLD YOU SO!' (19 May 1967). Yet the ardour of the Marketeers seemed undiminished, and they began instantly devising a further attempt ('BROWN GOES FLAT ON HIS BELLY', 14 June 1967).

For a moment, for them, things looked brighter after May 1969, when France wrested power from de Gaulle's hands. But by then time was running out, for Labour soon had to put its own continuance in power to the electoral test. The Labour movement gathered itself wearily, papered over the cracks and went into the fight, no less disillusioned and no more inspired by the leadership it was fighting for than it had been in 1965. Optimistic to the end, Tribune provided a before-the-event analysis of 'VICTORY FOR LABOUR: what it will mean' (12 June 1970). By 26 June, 'surprised and shocked', Tribune was sifting through the ashes of Labour's defeat, and bracing itself for the combat that would come with a Tory government led by Edward Heath.

7 LIFE BEGINS AT FORTY (1970–)

Tribune had predicted a 'rougher' political time when Edward Heath became Conservative leader. When he became Prime Minister, it could be seen that the prediction had been an underestimation of the fight to come. Richard Clements, soon after the election offering another of his 'STRATEGY . . .' editorials, pinned the right word on to the industrial approach of the Tories – 'intransigence' (17 July 1970). Some months later, Tribune warned against a new 'CHALLENGE TO THE LABOUR MOVEMENT' (9 October 1970), and in the same issue the industrial reporter David Turner described 'HOW THE TORIES WANT TO SHACKLE THE UNIONS'. He summed up the policies – anti-strike laws, 'cooling-off' periods, 'registration' of unions and an industrial relations court – all of which 'would tilt the balance of power between employers and workers even further in favour of the employers'. All of them, also, pumped up Tribune's adrenalin for the days of confrontation.

But then so did every other Tory proposal. Heath had taken power in a time of economic crisis, and the fear of a collapsing pound dominated his government's every move. As Chancellor, Anthony Barber hacked away at social services in public spending cuts ('ROBBING THE POOR TO PAY THE RICH' – 30 October 1970) while unemployment mounted within the orthodox anti-inflation 'squeeze' measures. Industrial unrest naturally erupted: dockers, council workers, postal workers, power workers, car workers went into the front lines of confrontation. And other Tory policies served as irritants in their meanness – the insistence on selling arms to South Africa, the decision of Margaret Thatcher, the Education Minister, to stop schoolchildren's milk, or the plan of Lord Eccles, Arts Minister, to charge fees for entering museums.

The Left laughed wryly when economic troubles undermined Rolls-Royce, of all symbolic firms, and drove the Tories into something very like public ownership. But no one laughed as the economy generally foundered in the squeeze, industry slowed and stumbled and more thousands were thrown out of work. The Industrial Relations Act and the National Industrial Relations Court placed their clammy grip on the unions in 1971 and 1972, called by Eric Heffer 'a vicious piece of class legislation' (28 April 1972).

In the midst of the industrial conflict Heath's government produced yet another bitter brew – the notorious Housing (Finance) Act 'with its attempt to end the principle of subsidised council housing' (Michael Walsh, 24 March 1972). Local councils girded themselves to oppose it in what Arthur Latham called 'THE GREAT HOUSING REVOLT' (24 March).

The working class as a whole seemed on the edge of revolt. The miners struck in 1972, and despite a state of emergency the Tories did not win that battle – nor did they win others with the AUEW, Upper Clyde shipworkers, gas workers – which led Richard Briginshaw to warn 'Beware of the Tory Revenge Seekers!' (3 March 1972). A group of picketing, and then imprisoned, dockers felt some of that vengefulness; so, later, did the nation, with the tightened 'Phase Two' of squeeze-and-freeze. Massive protests and demonstrations made May Day 1973 memorable, when nearly three million trade unionists staged a one-day stoppage that displayed their loathing of the Tory way with industrial relations: 'The Biggest May Day since 1926' (4 May 1973).

So confrontation had ended and war had begun. War went forward on the housing front as well, when eleven councillors of Clay Cross in Derbyshire led a glorious if costly resistance against the Tory rent Act, in the highest traditions of Labour history. In another theatre of war, when the winter of 1973 brought the full iciness of an energy crisis, the miners pressed a legitimate case for improved wages and conditions, and backed it with an overtime ban. Heath replied with the grim plan for a three-day week – 'HEATH'S BLACKOUT' (30 November 1973). It lent a certain Dickensian flavour (more *Bleak House* than *Pickwick*) to seasonal festivities, and Richard Clements came to ask: 'IF HEATH SURVIVES, CAN BRITAIN?' (21 December 1973).

To reinforce that view, Michael Meacher provided some dour statistics which asked '. . . whether a three-day working week, costing some £250 million per week in lost production, is really worth it when placed alongside the possibility of wage inflation which, on the most pessimistic assumptions, could not cost more than £1½ billion a year, or less than £30 million a week' (25 January 1974). But inevitably came ' "CUSTER" HEATH'S LAST STAND' (8 February 1974) with the threat of an election and the reality of a miners' strike. No one put the miners' case better than Will Paynter:

THE MINERS AND THE 'NATIONAL INTEREST'

. . . During post-war years, advice to miners as to what was the 'national interest' has been anything but consistent. In the decade following nationalisation, it required miners to work extended hours to get more coal. It required the industry to import coal at high world prices and sell inland at considerable loss.

It meant coal being sold to British industry at prices far below those applying in countries with which British industry competed. It required miners to exercise restraint in demands for improved wages and conditions . . .

But the doctrine of national interest changed in the next decade, the sixties, and the miners paid a heavy price for acting 'responsibly' during the earlier period. Now the 'national interest' required the rapid and drastic cut-back of coal production and both kinds of Governments operated accordingly.

Pits were closed, communities made derelict, men at 65, then 60, and later 55 years of age, retired from the industry. Unemployment in mining areas was far in excess of the national average; there was migration of young people and poverty and insecurity in the villages around the dead pits. The bargaining power of the union was weak and taken advantage of so that wage levels fell relative to others.

The union's preoccupation in this situation was aimed at stopping the destruction of the industry. We argued, demonstrated, pleaded, that it was against the long-term interests of Britain to base fuel policy on imported oil and nuclear energy, that both sources were unreliable and costly. We urged a fuel policy based on indigenous resources contending that a time would come when Britain would want more coal and would have insufficient pits or men to meet the demand.

That time has now arrived. The mess we are now in is the direct result of policies operated by successive Governments, and it is time that they acknowledged their blunders . . .

[8 February 1974]

Heath plunged on towards his Gadarene brink of an election, ostensibly intended to prove who was running the country. The press insisted that the choice of answers was either the Tory government or the unions; one might well have wondered what had happened to H.M. Loyal Opposition. Labour had, in fact, been opposing, though, to Tribunites, with a somewhat muted voice. Besides, the party had gone through some of the internal troubles that always seem to beset parties after electoral defeat. In 1970 Wayland Young had added a telling note to the post-mortems:

. . . We lost because we never took hold of the country . . . instead of . . . boldly doing that which had to be done, we acted blandly, as if we did not yet have the power . . . We lost because we started getting things right only halfway through our term, and if one has done most things wrong for three years, doing most things right for the next three years does not efface the memory . . .

We lost because we did not pay enough attention to little things which acquire great importance . . . We lost because we had already lost the active party workers . . . The party conference knew what words it wanted. The Government would not say them . . .

[17 July 1970]

By the time Eric Heffer came to write on Labour's 'period of renewal' and the movement to the Left resulting from 'learning the lessons' of defeat (10 August 1973), it had become plain that party unity left something to be desired. Perhaps it was because of this Leftwards shift, or perhaps it was the result, as Tribune thought, of challenges directed at the party constitution and democracy. In any case, two local parties grew weary of their sitting members' attitudes, and so Dick Taverne and Reg Prentice became new objects of antipathy for the Left. The latter remains so – and remains a media figurehead also for the 'moderate' stand against Red-stained Labour splits and revolutionary take-overs. In 1975 Tribune's editor showed a truer picture in terms of practical politics.

WHY PRENTICE'S 'MARTYR' ROLE LOOKS SO ABSURD IN NEWHAM

No one who saw Reg Prentice emerge from the Newham North East

Labour Party general management committee meeting on Wednesday last week could have misjudged his mood. He saw himself as the victim of a base conspiracy and one which had everything to do with national politics and little or nothing to do with Newham North East. Of course that suits his ego and the image which the national press has built up of this 'man of moderation' who is beset by sinister forces . . .

In fact, Mr Prentice's present predicament has *much* to do with Newham North East . . .

Until the last three or four years, the local Labour Party has shown hardly any life at all. Indeed, like Islington in the fifties and early sixties, it was about as difficult to join the Labour Party as it is to get into the Athenaeum. In the last decade, the area has changed as well as many younger, white-collar workers have been coming into it. For them it has been obvious that the only way to make any substantial changes in their surroundings was by joining the Labour Party and putting pressure on the Labour Council. When it became clear that Prentice was identified with the 'do-nothing' attitude, he came under pressure as well . . .

When the vote came at the GMC, it was very interesting to note that the 'moderates' within the Newham North East party, and by that I mean those who did not take a very sharp pro- or anti-Prentice line, came down against him: there is no other way to interpret the 29-19 vote . . .

So Mr Prentice and his followers are left crying 'conspiracy'. That certainly does not apply in Newham North East, nor for that matter does it apply on the basis of national politics. The 'fringe' Left groups associated with the 57 different varieties of Trotskyism who are hinted at as being the source of the 'conspiracy' are in favour of seeing the Labour Party break up. To them the Labour Party is reformism incarnate, the antithesis of the 'revolutionary' politics which they preach. What happened on July 23 was the opposite of what they wish to see occur; for it showed that democracy is not dead – indeed it has perked up enormously . . .

[*Richard Clements*, 1 August 1975]

Indeed, if any threat of a Labour split existed in the earlier 1970s, it came not from individually extreme cases of 'moderation' but from an overbearing issue that set brother against brother as well as any civil war: the Common Market.

Edward Heath, irrevocably set on erasing the memory of his previous European frustrations, rode as rough-shod over the country's uneasiness about the EEC as he did over industrial and economic hopes. But then every political party and allied groups seemed hopelessly split into pro- and anti-Marketeers, which helped to clear his path. Tribune was perhaps the most vociferous of the antis, watching Heath leap towards Europe 'at any cost' (21 May 1971) to perpetrate 'THE BIGGEST SELL-OUT SINCE MUNICH' (28 May 1971) when terms were finalized, which were also 'UNCONDITIONAL SURRENDER' (25 June 1971).

In desperation, Michael Barratt Brown and Royden Harrison once again outlined 'THE COMMON MARKET AND THE SOCIALIST ALTERNATIVE', hinging it on a dire vision of rising unemployment, higher taxes plus VAT, the flight of capital, overall inflation and the erosion of Labour's ideals and British sovereignty within European institutions – a not inaccurate piece of prophecy, as Peter Shore made clear a year after Heath had dragged us in with all those off-key fanfares.

ONE YEAR OF MISERY IN THE COMMON MARKET

In the two years since the Treaty of Accession was signed, Britain's trading position with the original Six has virtually collapsed . . . from a manageable deficit of £181 million in 1971 to £499 million in 1972 and to an insupportable £1,150 million deficit in 1973 . . .

The early prospect of complete freedom for capital to move to any part of Western Europe has been exactly as was predicted: a minor influx of European investment in Britain, a major efflux of British capital to Europe . . . Year One of the Common Market was also a year of record price rises, with food prices increasing by no less than 19 per cent . . .

It is not just food prices that are affected. Value added tax, our first Euro-tax, the one tax that no British Government can repeal unless it breaks the Treaty of Accession, was introduced only in April and its poison is still spreading through the economy . . .

None of this takes account of the indirect effects of membership on British prices. Already Britain, in the Common Market, has been forced, first, to float the pound and then to watch it sink steadily to a level some 20 per cent below where it was 18 months ago . . .

[*Peter Shore*, 4 January 1974]

But hope remained. Britain had not been allowed to have an election in 1972 on whether it wanted to be in Europe; the election came in 1974 when Heath sought that mandate for his final *putsch* against the unions. He failed to get it, Labour squeaked into power, and Richard Clements dryly editorialized 'As We Were Saying When We Were So Rudely Interrupted . . .' (8 March 1974). One of the things they had been saying was that – despite Heath's *fait accompli* – Britain might well remove itself from the EEC. The new Wilson government, maintaining a perilous overall majority even after a second election in 1974, not only went 'FULL SPEED AHEAD!' (18 October 1974) in the fields of improved industrial relations and the like, but went into renegotiations with the rest of the EEC and kept its promise of a referendum. Tribune exploded into a campaigning frenzy, with enormously successful public meetings round the country that harked back to the great days of socialist barnstorming.

No one was especially happy with the renegotiated terms, containing still those implicit threats to British employment, manufacturing, investment, currency and, of course, sovereignty. Certainly no one on the Left was anything but shatteringly disappointed when the high-cost overkill campaign of the pro-Market forces turned the 1975 referendum into a 'yes'. The poet Alan Brownjohn bluntly saw it as 'a derogation of the democratic process with the aid of money and polite blackmail' (13 June 1975). But Tribune bounced back with a cheeky slogan that still appears now and then as the EEC drains off investment, pumps up our prices and overburdens us with unsupportable imports: 'Don't blame us – we voted NO!' (13 June 1975).

Beyond the beef mountains and wine lakes of the European landscape, turmoil and violence and misery seemed, as ever, to dominate during the first half of the 1970s. Many of the old familiar trouble-spots were troubled once again – like the Middle East, where fighting broke out briefly in late 1973. And blood was also being shed in Cyprus, Ethiopia, the Lebanon, the tragically wounded Bangladesh, and, above all, the planet's most war-torn locale, Vietnam. Yet there, after some last-gasp assaults by Nixon's forces (Tribune bluntly called them 'atrocities' – Jean McMichael, 5 January 1973) something akin to peace finally, grudgingly, arrived. Two years later a regular Tribune contributor went to see what had happened in Vietnam since the guns had been silenced by the North's victory:

EYE-WITNESS IN VIETNAM

When the Thieu regime in South Vietnam was in a state of final disintegration earlier this year, the Western press was full of reports of refugees frantic with fear, of impending massacres and bloody purges to come. Columnists, who had justified the bombing of North Vietnam and accepted without protest the use of defoliants, anti-personnel bombs and napalm, wept bitter tears for the system that was coming to an end. When Saigon finally fell, the media announced that austerity had descended on the city . . .

What I saw in contrast to this was a city full of bustle and activity with very little apparent evidence of the traumatic experiences or the events of the spring. Everywhere shops were open, markets packed, and streets crowded with motor cycles, bicycles, rickshaw tricycles, buses and cars . . .

The Provisional Revolutionary Government was providing relief to prevent anyone from starving, but had not yet been able to deal with the frightful problem of homelessness, a legacy of the previous regime and the war . . .

Vietnam was formerly a rice-exporting country but one result of the last 30 years is that it cannot at present feed it own population. Before people can go back to the villages, however, investigations have to be made to ascertain whether land is available, wells frequently have to be dug, and temporary accommodation erected. Agricultural tools, seed and fertiliser must be provided and arrangements made to supply food for at least six months before the first crops can be harvested. Unexploded bombs and land polluted by defoliants present additional difficulties . . .

No socialist could fail to be deeply moved and impressed by this friendly, infinitely courageous and determined people who have won one of the most horrific wars of the twentieth century against the most incredible odds to secure control of their own affairs . . .

[*Stan Newens*, 19 September 1975]

America's traumatic defeat in South-East Asia had perhaps been foreseeable; its domestic traumas, as the crookery and tape-recording paranoia in the White House crept out into the light, came as a shock. Tribune's correspondent in the United States, Roy Bennett, charted the outflow from the Watergate sewers up to the last bow of the sick and tormented president ('No More Nixon', 4 August 1974). It was equally no more for several other objects of the Left's hatred: a few good guys could win, it seemed, here and there. The forces of democracy rose up at last, for instance, in Portugal, to the emotional delight of Antonio de Figueiredo, who had himself suffered direly at the hands of the long-lived fascist régime:

I RETURN TO FREE PORTUGAL

. . . As I recovered from the impact of arrival, I soon discovered that events had moved so fast in the previous days that suddenly there were no experts in Portuguese politics: we had all become historians. It is only now that one is beginning to understand that Portugal is living through a period which will confront political writers and sociologists with new lessons . . .

The junta, which proclaimed a few basic points meeting with the approval of the overwhelming majority of the population, confined itself to the overthrow of the President, the Government, and the repressive institutions, such as the secret police (DGS), the censorship board, the regime's single-party system, the para-military organisations and so on . . .

It is a genuine people's army, and when on May 1, revolution and the rights of labour were jointly hailed in the greatest street demonstrations Portugal has ever seen, the army was celebrated as a people's army, and not the mainstay of a repressive and obscurantist regime . . .

[10 May 1974]

Within only weeks the clutch of another fascist régime had been pulled loose from Greece ('The Army Split that Finally Unseated the Colonels' – 26 July 1974) – though, as Michael Walsh wrote, the government that took over in Greece was far from making a 'new Portugal' (26 July). Much the same could be said of the new government in Spain today, yet emotions ran even higher on the Left in late 1975 when the most notorious living exponent of everything it hated went finally to his grave.

Francisco Franco – the last of the fascist dictators – died, with some justification, the most hated man in Europe. In his last testament he claimed always to have acted out of love for his country, yet he expressed that love by keeping it in subjection, perpetuating injustice and denying his compatriots the right of their own judgment. He has left his country on the brink of another civil war. With lovers like that, Spain needs no enemies.

[*H. A. Jacobson*, 28 November 1975]

Meanwhile, a long and murderous conflict in Africa moved towards its conclusion, spurred by developments in Portugal, when Leftist forces in Angola found a colonial war had become a civil war. The world feared a new Vietnam in the making as Soviet aid and Cuban troops faced in 1975 a motley array of South African, West European and (some said) CIA opposition. A similar gathering of capitalist repressors had struck, years before, against the upthrust of socialism in South America, when the democratically elected Salvador Allende had in 1970 tried to end a history of corrupt government and foreign domination in Chile.

Anti-Allende forces – blatantly spearheaded by that defender of democracy, Richard Nixon – were not slow in aiding their Chilean counterparts to wreck Allende's hopes and plans, at whatever cost to the country. Those hopes finally died with Allende himself in a vicious Right-wing coup, and Judith Hart mourned the loss:

> The tragedy of Tuesday's military coup in Chile . . . is a tragedy of overwhelming proportions for Chile, for Latin America and for socialists everywhere . . .
>
> . . . the Popular Unity Government had carried out substantial land reform, brought major industries into Chilean public ownership, introduced worker participation, redistributed income, provided higher standards of living for the workers and peasants and recently announced an end of elitist systems of education . . .
>
> What is certain is that this is neither the final end of the Chilean experiment, nor of the powerful movement towards socialism in Latin America.
>
> [14 September 1973]

So defeats counterbalanced victories. Yet the latter in the 1970s have shown that patient and unremitting struggle can, sometimes, eventually, bring results – a fact that may be disturbing the sleep of the oppressors in Southern Africa today. The advocates of apartheid responded with guns and murder to rioting, stone-throwing Africans ('After Soweto massacre – EXPOSE VORSTER'S DECEIT' – 25 June 1976) while more organized black struggle in Rhodesia has meant guerrilla warfare, along with the return of the white mercenary as a force in Africa. Michael Walsh's reporting brought about a Tribune 'exclusive': 'Revealed: Undercover Recruiting for the Rhodesian Army' – in Britain itself (12 December 1975).

Hired-gun mercenaries seemed a peculiarly African answer to an old but more and more widespread form of conflict, guerrilla warfare – which itself more and more became an urban phenomenon. The 1970s so far have been the years of the terrorist: in the Middle East, in Africa, in South America, in Canada, in any place where a visitation of unexpected and callous violence might win some headlines for a 'cause'. The Palestinian Black September group proved among the most bloodthirsty of all with the killing of Israeli athletes at the Munich Olympics ('Cowardly, brutal and absolutely without any political justification' – 'Diary', 8 September 1972), and their letter bombs sent to Israeli embassies in many capitals including London. But terror from many sources led London – not to mention Birmingham – to fear the abandoned car, the unclaimed suitcase or carrier bag. The self-styled 'Angry Brigade' blasted the house of Tory Minister Robert Carr, but predominantly the 'insanity' (16 March 1973) of terror bombing was brought to England by the endless conflict in Northern Ireland.

Tribune had diligently recorded the escalating horrors of Ulster in the earlier 1970s when terrorist killing and bombing ran head-on into British Army retaliation, and many innocents were caught in the cross-fire. Michael Walsh visited Ulster for Tribune to produce a passionate series of reports and features, perhaps never excelled beyond a time in the furious days of 1971:

EYE-WITNESS IN ULSTER

On Sunday, as journalists stood at the back of a protest meeting off the Falls Road, there was an old man watching too. Nobody took much notice of him. His raincoat hid his broken arm. He was just part of the crowd. One morning last week David McGreevey was anything but that.

'For Jesus sake, he's only an old man,' a woman is said to have screamed as troops batoned McGreevey to the ground and dragged him up Theodore Street. 'The bastards' they say now as they remember it.

And when you talk to David McGreevey or Oscar Henderson, a man so wrecked that he can barely describe how he saw his son 'screaming under torture', you wonder whether there are still Catholics in Belfast who don't curse everything British.

You find that there are such people – despite internment, despite the stories of the four brutal days that followed it as the army smashed down barricades, and after that smashed down the people who got in the way, innocently or otherwise . . .

There were the Maguires, two families of them, Thomas and Joseph at number 60 and John and his son on the other side of the street.

Thomas and Joseph both work in the Harland and Wolff shipyard. 'These two lads wouldn't throw a stone if you asked them,' says Harry Donachie, who lives next door. 'Throughout my life I've been in no organisation of any kind and don't want to be,' says Joseph. 'But look at me.'

You look and see the fresh stitches in his forehead. 'I was going back to the door. I'd gone up the street to see what was going on. I walked back as they came down the street the other way. They had me at the door, split my forehead open.'

Then, it seems, the troops went for his brother, who hadn't stirred from inside the house. 'They hit me twice,' says Thomas . . .

Why did they arrest the Maguires? The guess round Lower Falls is that the army were working on information years out of date. When the troops failed to find the men they were looking for they simply 'lifted' every male over 14 in the house, say the theorists . . .

The O'Hagans were luckier. They weren't beaten up. But they might be childless now if they hadn't sent their three young children to relatives. Normally the children – they are aged three, four and five – sleep in the attic. On the night that the troops came through Earls Court Street, using covering fire as they advanced, two bullets thudded through that attic roof. The holes I saw were directly over two of the children's beds . . .

Further north, beyond the Crumlin Road, just near Bombay Street, there is a man who won't speak to me. I glimpse him as he takes my guide inside to talk. His face is gruesome; from what I can see of his head there is a grey gash across it, three inches wide. I'm not told why he won't be interviewed. Later I hear that he was beaten by the army somewhere in the Springfield Road area and his body shown to a mob of Protestants.

Rumour only. But 50 yards away there are the housewives of Bombay Street, the street which marks the northern 'peace line' between Catholic and Protestant. Bombay Street was destroyed in 1969, now there are new houses.

Mrs Hemsworth and the three of her friends who gather to talk have more than rumour. One is bruised. Mrs Hemsworth has a heavily bandaged knee. 'The soldiers came flying in at 4.30. I thought it must be them,' she says, gesturing towards the Protestant area ten yards away. 'I ran down the stairs right into them and got this from a baton.' . . .

And she didn't have to tell me the story about the dead dog. I'd heard it all the way down in the Eire refugee camp, of how soldiers had shot someone's pet, brandished the carcase before a Catholic crowd that hadn't been able to buy food for two days, and told the crowd, 'Here's your fresh meat.'

Another rumour? Perhaps. But a day in the Falls among the Hendersons and the Maguires is enough to convince anyone that it's not all rumour.

[20 August 1971]

Worse was to come, including the 'Bloody Sunday' massacre of the innocents in Derry, when Tribune had another eye-witness:

> . . . Suddenly from the other end of the long open space, at probably 300 yards, men, women and teenagers appeared. They were running for their lives . . .
>
> I have never seen such a thing as now happened. This packed crowd fell to the ground, and before I could see who was firing I was pulled to the floor of the lorry and held down while the shooting continued . . .
>
> [*Fenner Brockway*, 4 February 1972]

And beyond the capacity for violence of the IRA and British Army were the equally manic Protestant terrorisms and the continuing inability of British politicians to find a way out of the impasse.

Many were the impasses in those years from which Britain seemed unable to find egress. Seemingly, the pressure groups acted – when they could – and the government reacted. But at least within this process women achieved laws granting equal pay and banning sex discrimination, only half a century or so after the suffragists ('Backward Britain', 24 January 1975 – in which issue also Madeleine Simms viewed another piece of progress with pessimism: 'ABORTION LAWS: BEWARE THE WRECKERS'). Other forces of reaction and worse sparked off rioting in Red Lion Square, which led to the killing of one anti-fascist protester. Sydney Bidwell had watched the police violence that day, aimed as it was against the demonstrators who were standing against National Front racism, and he wondered angrily why authority could not have foreseen, and understood, that 'Our liberal and progressive youth will not stand idly by while racists are left free to push their poison' (21 June 1974).

Otherwise, liberal and progressive youth spent much energy forming extreme Left splinter groups and merrily slanging each other. The historian Walter Kendall noted:

> Revolution, not least in the university, has become something of a fashion nowadays. The children of the middle classes . . . are inclined somewhat to overreact to their discovery of social and economic original sin. They appear to imagine that if they rush headlong to the workers a magical transformation will take place . . .
>
> [25 April 1975]

On the other edge of the political spectrum, fascists and hooligans exacerbated the real problems of race relations in Britain, especially in the inner cities – out of which came also a headline-hunting irresponsibility in much of the media and a near-helplessness among our rulers. Brian Sedgemore, departing from his more frequent role as commentator on economic matters, was revolted by the government's failure to come to grips with the evil of racism: 'Parliament . . . revealed itself as a decadent chamber of cowardly men . . .' (28 May 1976).

That same 'decadent' chamber came nervously to consider other divisions, nationalist rather than racist, as political pressures from Scotland especially launched the 'devolution' debate, well into its stride as this is written. Behind it loomed, as genie or demon, the imminence of North Sea oil, which according to some of the faithful will soon save us all from grasping Arab sheikhs and foreign creditors alike. A new Tribune reporter, Stephen Kelly, sourly noted that 'THE OIL REVOLUTION' was in fact being carried forward by the mighty multinational oil companies, and it would be they who would soak up 'the sizeable and quick profits' if 'stringent Government controls are not enforced' (14 March 1975).

The government seemed unlikely to enforce much of anything – but, indeed, the abandonment of the forceful approach for the consultative produced at least one jewel in its crown, and a crucial one: in industrial relations. After the Heath years of squeeze, freeze and confrontation, the 1974 Wilson government joined with the unions and produced the 'social contract', as clear a statement of unity of purpose within the Labour movement as has been seen in post-war years. Jack Jones, at the outset, had perceived among unionists 'a determination . . . to have less strikes and more negotiations, with a special emphasis upon the need to build up voluntary conciliation and arbitration' (26 April 1974). And it worked: wages were held back, strikes were headed off.

Out of this union responsibility came clear proof that it was not and had never been the unions 'holding the country to ransom', undermining the economy and so on – because union self-restraint did not restore the economy to health. The recipe remained as before: worsening inflation and minimal growth, while national productivity was crippled on the one hand by the flight of investment capital abroad (now *there* is a 'holding to ransom'), and on the other by the inflow of burdensome imports. It all brought 'THE CRISIS' (31 January 1975), 'PANIC!' (4 July 1975), 'Public Expenditure Cuts' (20 February 1976) and the despairing question 'When will we ever learn?' (30 April 1976). Brian Sedgemore, surveying the government's desperate and often conflicting but uniformly useless measures, saw us at 'The point of no return': '. . . each crisis produces a package which sows the seeds of the next crisis simply because there is no way in which a Labour Government can quench the unquenchable thirst of the financial establishments, at home or abroad' (8 October 1976).

It had become a situation that might have bred an old-style party split. Indeed, Joan Lestor did resign from the government in February 1976, while others (not always on the Left) began reasserting principles of duty – to the movement, to the people, to the future – that went beyond duty merely to a visibly shaky Cabinet. It says much for individual determination to see a job through, in Labour ranks, that the party did not fall apart when the old master paperer-over of cracks finally had had enough of 10 Downing Street. While Donald Bruce wrote of 'Wilson's legacy to Labour' (19 March 1976), Tribune joyously entered into the battle for succession in which Michael Foot stood a clear chance of victory.

But the party opted for the Righter course, James Callaghan became Prime Minister to give Denis Healey his head, more paper went on over the policy divisions, and Tribune doggedly explained once again why argument and debate within the movement were necessary and healthy, as opposed to false semblances of unity, and therefore 'Why Callaghan must listen to the Labour movement' (9 April 1976).

Plus ça change, then, within Labour, within Britain and the world, within Tribune. As before, death as well as departures wrought many of the changes: in the 1970s the world bade mixed farewells to Nasser, de Gaulle, U Thant and Mao Tse-tung, aside from Franco and other notables already mentioned. For Tribune itself those years were a time of many personal sadnesses, with the passing of a mournfully large number of persons whose links with the paper went back many years: Raymond Postgate, Winifred Horrabin, Julius Braunthal, Richard Titmuss, Will Griffiths, Benn Levy, R. H. S. Crossman, Krishna Menon, Hugh Delargy, Vic Feather, Solly Sachs, Tom Driberg and Evelyn Anderson.

But at the same time those years brought forward-looking change and development to the paper. In 1972 a 'new Tribune' was unveiled, the newness derived from altered emphases (deeper industrial coverage, an extended concern with reportage and 'information' features) and some new names. Hugh Macpherson began his parliamentary column that year, 'a 'City Column' examined the financiers' dealings, Tony Heath and then Clive Griggs pored over the world of education, even Clive Jenkins returned for a while with a 'New Trend' column. But most of all the new Tribune wore a somewhat altered face – as lively a layout as ever, but with many shiftings of regular features to new positions, especially the transference of the books and arts pages out of their end-of-the-paper ghetto into the prominence of the centre spread.

At this point the present writer must emerge from the third person to tread the razor's edge between immodesty and reticence. Elizabeth Thomas left Tribune in 1971, and I became literary editor shortly thereafter. She had left a tremendous legacy of achievement and tradition on her pages; my intention was to carry on, as best I could, in my way, what she and others before her had established as the proper roles and obligations of the reviews section in a socialist paper.

So, as Elizabeth did, I have introduced many new reviewers to the paper – a good number of professionals in their field but also several new writers trying their wings in Tribune as new writers could always do. So, too, I have gone on publishing poets, many of them also young, unknown or upcoming. Special poetry features have sometimes greeted particular occasions, like the poetic 'Plain Fare' that mocked Heath's 'Fanfare for Europe' in January 1973, for which Alan Brownjohn borrowed the idiom of Scotland's beloved McGonagall:

> . . . And in conclusion, about this happy date I will say without a doubt
> That the EEC was something the bankers and employers could not do without,
> And the Queen and Mr Heath and the Government, and Mr Roy Jenkins, built a bridge across the Channel that day,
> Which I sincerely hope will never fall down, like the bridge over the River Tay.
>
> [5 January 1973]

On the book-reviewing side, many familiar writers still enlivened the paper's middle pages, and many new names have come to join them. Readers old and new can seek them out week by week, so they need no listing here – though special mention may be made of certain regulars who lend Tribune their expertise: Rodney Barker, elegant analyst of political writings; Colin Stoneman, knowledgeable advocate of ecological sense; Diana Leonard Barker, committed examiner of the women's movement; Martin Booth, perceptive surveyor of new poetry.

Arts reviewers, as always, came and went. Boleslaw Sulik gave up the film column in 1971 to 'Chuck Kusick', from behind which pseudonym Colin McArthur emerged in 1972. Margaret Richards still continues her coverage of art, long-serving music reviewer Edward Lockspeiser wrote unflaggingly until his death in 1973, his mantle then being taken up by David Simmons. Reviews of broadcasting passed through many hands – Paddy Kitchen, Judith Bull and Malcolm Levene in 1973, Terry Philpot in 1974, Audrey Williamson in 1975 and (as I write this) Kevin Cully in 1976. And Simon Trussler departed in 1972 from his theatre column, to be replaced by the lively enthusiasms of Catherine Itzin.

Also (very much in the Tribune tradition) the new review pages re-introduced a spot for comment and controversy in a new column 'Platform'. Usually it was editorially occupied by myself, as when it warmly greeted and interviewed the new Left-wing Arts Minister, Hugh Jenkins, on his accession in March 1974, and later paid tribute to his efforts and achievements when he returned, untimely, to the back benches ('A Change of Arts', 23 April 1976). In 'Platform', too, a trio of writers including Dulan Barber and the late B. S. Johnson depicted 'The author's plight – from inside' (1 June 1973) and put the case for a Public Lending Right, for which the column has hotly campaigned. Otherwise, that column has been the place where watch was kept generally on developments in the cultural world – Arts Council doings, the new National Theatre, the welcome upsurge of community arts and much more.

Novelty and nostalgia, in equal mixture, have thus been much of the recipe for the Tribune of the 1970s – when often unforeseen and startling changes mixed with evergreen, ever-rejuvenated traditions. Not the least of the evergreens was Tribune's often perilous financial position, still as always countered by the readership's loyalty and the editor's driving optimism. Recent years have seen the enlargement of the Tribune Group in Parliament – a notable development on which Neil Kinnock offered some facts to counter the media's scarifying attitude to the Group:

'RED TERROR' IN PARLIAMENT

The Group meets once (very occasionally twice) a week to discuss – or

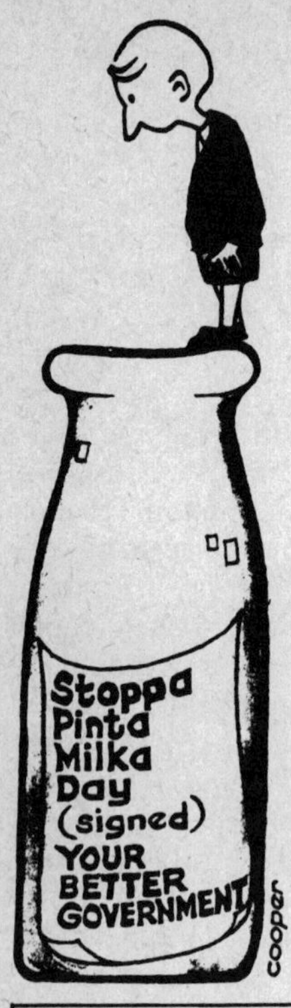

Cooper's comment on the Margaret Thatcher approach to school milk (30 October 1970); George Gale's view of some major issues in the election of 1974 (22 February 1974); and Gale again on the resignation of Harold Wilson (19 March 1976).

even more frequently debate – the issues before the movement, including the current business of the House of Commons, particularly campaigns demanding attention and action, and wider questions of party policy. The meeting is informal; the contributions brief (four minutes is a long speech) and the voices are collected to provide a consensus.

The character of the meeting varies with the matter under discussion from cool seminar to angry declamation and the action taken as a result of discussion relies for its effectiveness entirely on the commitment of individual members to the decision taken . . .

The Tribune Group depends for its strength and its membership on activity, not conspiracy. Plotting is part of politics but there are so many variables in any given Parliamentary situation that those who seek to influence policies or events by conspiring in back-bench huddles are born eunuchs.

Co-ordination is a different matter: ideals must, like any other motive force, be organised if they are to be effective and the Tribune Group's most frequent and telling activity is to give an organised lead to opinion in the PLP . . .

. . . we, like millions throughout the world, refuse to accept the permanence and desirability of the 'realities' of capitalism and totalitarianism or even concede the 'realism' of changing those systems and removing the stupidities and injustices which spawn by feeding and appeasing them . . .

Meanwhile, the dilemma of the Tribune Group is the same as the dilemma of democratic socialism – to preach and practise hot ideas with cool tongues and heads . . .

[*Neil Kinnock*, 29 November 1974]

Those years have also seen the restoration of the Tribune public meeting, at conference and other times, as an exciting and important arena for political debate. In these and many ways there has been a clear and steady enlargement of the paper's readership, potency and influence. It all created a natural setting – just as the advent of Tribune's fortieth year, in 1976, provided the natural timing – for some backward looking.

Hence the planning of this anthological account of Tribune's life and times, the hope and belief being that memories of the early years of the paper can bring home lessons for today – and tomorrow. For during all this time of remembering and weighing up the past there has been the overriding awareness that life *begins* at forty, and goes on. So recently Neil Kinnock led off a new series that reassesses, as it must always be reassessed in contemporary terms, 'SOCIALISM IN

OUR TIME' (1 October 1976). And in that issue, too, Richard Clements defiantly asked a question which must have been troublesome round that table in 1937 where Cripps, Wilkinson, *et al.*, decided to create a Tribune for the people: 'Does the Labour movement really want a socialist press?'

The answer will be emphatically yes, I have no doubt, nor do I doubt that munificent support from the movement will *not* instantly flow like rivers. Still, the existence of fighting socialist newspapers is inevitably a process of constant, simultaneous retrenchment and renewal: life begins also at forty-one, forty-two, 140. I can hope that some happy compiler will have the joys of mining through, as I have mined, that many years of Tribune's gloriously embattled achievement in the year 2076.

INDEX

Note: Page numbers in italics refer to Editorials or special articles that have been reproduced from *Tribune* at some length.